.

I give to you this Gift of
Kryah....

Kryah can be understood and
embraced.like a great bird in flight ... ad-
mired but never held... for the power of
Kryah is in the giving of the energy not the
taking of the energy... The source of all
things is a giving energy...not a taking energy, observe the flora around you and in
the silence of it all you may begin to understand the secrets of Source...

... don Lobos

SPECIAL MANUSCRIPT EDITION OF

Through the Eye of the Shaman
the Nagual Returns with the Gift of Kryah Volume 1

by Dr. Robert Ghost Wolf

Ascended Master Teachings

Wolf Lodge Cultural Foundation
Grail Publishing Ltd.
223 N Guadalupe St #178
Santa Fe, New Mexico 87501

Cover Art
by "my friend"
Frank Howell

Cover and interior design by Dr. Robert Ghost Wolf
Special *Literary* Contributions by The Indigenous Masters

Order this book online at www.trafford.com
or email orders@trafford.com

Most Trafford titles are also available at major online book retailers.

Print information available on the last page.

ISBN: 978-1-4120-0724-5 (sc)
ISBN: 978-1-4122-1433-9 (e)

Trafford rev. 10/26/2018

Trafford
PUBLISHING® www.trafford.com
North America & international
toll-free: 1 888 232 4444 (USA & Canada)
fax: 812 355 4082

Personal Message...

"...To you who holds this work in your hands... We can truly discover nothing in this reality...we can only remember...where we have been and who we really are ....

What you hold in your hands are teachings directly from the Ascended Masters...

" Masters that are of many races for there are of many kindoms that are born of the light. Therefore know that you have been guided here..

"Know also that you shall become all that you allow yourself to BE. For the only limitations of becoming are those that are self-imposed...Mother Father God the highest is un-limited and as the Creator is so were you created in divine perfection?

Magic Happens
only if we allow
the space...

" As long as there is one free voice in the wilderness,
the hope remains alive..."

OTIPEMSIWAK
"Those who own themselves"

The Nagual Returns   Manuscript Edition

FOREWORD

The book you are about to read is the compilation of information that took a lifetime to gather. There were as it turned out three volumes of notes taken in the recalling of the conversations and experiences of don Lobos. Who you might ask is don Lobos, he is the character that will bring you into this adventure, giving you his keys of wisdom and will be your guide in some future adventures as well. IS don lobos real…my friend can you catch the wind….yet is it not the wind real?

While you are reading this work, you may find that occasionally you are carried off to distant places of your own imagination. As you consciousness is triggered you just may remember that somewhere in your personal history, somewhere long, long ago……. Somewhere far, far away, you too were a part of a mystery school……and maybe you knew a Master who reminded you of don Lobos. Life is a mutable canvas nothing is written in stone no matter how ominous it may first appear, nothing in this universe is as unfathomable as the human consciousness. In reality you are eternal and without limitation. You are a child of Mother – Father God and as such no matter what your temporary situation may seem to be, nothing... absolutely nothing is impossible!

If the thought can be thought, and the vision seen then it can exist. All things come from the great void, which is a place of formless mystery where all things exist potentially, yet not materially…only human, has the ability through a trick of the heart to make all of that void and all of its potentials exist in manifested form…you are no less than the lilies of the field and yet the Father does provide for them…do you think you are any less?

Welcome to *the Awakening*, may your transition be one of joy and grace…and may you come to know how truly divine you are as you are lifted from the illusions of your past….

In the light Dr. Robert Ghost Wolf

Table of Contents

The Journey Begins

THE SECRETS OF KRYAH   CON'T.

Once there was a child who ran with the wolves...
and dared to dream ...

Owále piki'la, Wakan Tanka, ni'ci' un

Shunkmanitu Tanka Wanagi

and his friends in the South simply call him...

don Lobos

To those of us who greet the light of day...

This work is dedicated to many wonderful people that I have met along the path, and to the Masters who helped me along the way. Most of all I wish to dedicate this work to those who dare to LOVE in a world that would make it less than fashionable to believe in LOVE and living with grace and poise. Some times it cab appear that darkness has consumed all the goodness that we ever were. May you find as I did the sweetness in the waters of love and continue to renew your courage along our journey in this hall of mirrors. May you be renewed and know that romance and beauty are also a forever part of this reality....and that they go with us into forever with those dreamers who dared to cherish their gifts from Spirit.

I have learned much from the women I have been with, and much from being apart from them. For in my life I have been the warrior and the king and sometime the fool. In looking back upon the path of my own legacy I see clearly that there were times of sadness, and joy and there were also times of great and silent emptiness, times when I heard my own footsteps and had to face my own demons. In that aloneness, amidst the fear and self-doubt, as I would face my dark night sof the soul, I often felt a breeze upon my shoulder, reminding me of the dream we came to manifest. Giving me the courage to rise again and meet the day.

I remembered that once in another lifetime... I swore to a code by which mighty knights whose memory still lives with me to this day, created abetter way of being human. May I have the courage to live by that code to which I pledged so long ago...for these are the strangest of times indeed? Yet I heard a story once, which foretold that the world of goodness shall rise again, and that the **War of the Heavens** shall be made to rest..in the time of *the Awakening*. and by all indications this is that time.

This book is as well is intended for all the Ladies of Avalon and any woman who ever dreamed herself a princess once upon a fairy tale and had the courage to ride upon the Dragons wings. And to those brave lads who dared to become more then ordinary an believed in that magic. May your dreams of the Divine human unfold and be embraced in your lifetime, as we traverse the quatrains and meet our destinies ….as we awaken to one heart beating, one song, one people, one humanity………in a world free from fear always and a humanity living in the light…..

May you who read these pages never again forget that you are an eternal Being, a nd a votager of the light, who has set upon a journey for truth and to fulfill the Mother Father God's *Will*. For within each of us is a knight or a lady of the old code.

The flame of Love is eternal and lights our way as we pass through the darkness. Holding the Light close to our hearts, we realize that this world is much more mysterious than first meets the eye. For what we see is not always real, and what is real, we too often do not see — only the heart knows for certain what is the color of truth, and the true nature of a lie.

We are standing at the edge of time looking out upon new frontiers. We slowly place our foot upon New Earth as we step forth into the alchemical garden daring to call for change. We are the Children of the Sun and Moon and will always remain so in spirit. We have returned to finish what we have started so long ago………"Can I change things?" ……you wonder out loud as you view the broken dreams that lie behind you. yes you can, you have already abegun when you choose this book.

The transformation foreseem as 'the Awakening' has begun. We are becoming the new species a new Anu and it is our destiny to populate a new Universe, which has already been birthed. This silent transformation is occurring within. The purifier has already planted the seeds of change many, many lifetimes ago.

We are becoming that which we have dreamed, all of what we dreamed. And we are facing as well all that we have feared...for no one enters less they be initiated. We are letting go of the old shell of what We were, and entering the unknown region of what you will yet become in the potential of becoming all that we can be... for now is the time and we are being called to gather....as the architects of a greater reality.... We are growing up.

Welcome to *the Awakening*

Revelations in the Garden

Upon the top of the mountain, don Lobos gazes into the setting sun. Crimson and purple clouds merge with turquoise and phosphorescent pinks. As he looks into the distance, the Spirit of the Wolf merges with his own, his eyes transform from their normal emerald green to amber yellow. The voice of his Grandmother drifts into his consciousness ..... a voice from so long ago, from childhood, now carries him into a dream.

He sees the vision of this night as if it were only yesterday. A much younger don Lobos arrives back in his Grandmother's yard. Turning from the wooded path there is a distinct look of panic on the young boy's face. He looks around the garden panting and out of breath, then turns and scurries once again towards the house in the woods. An owl swoops down out of a nearby tree and startles the young boy causing him to trip over some tools in the garden that all crash about in a great clatter.

"OUCH!" he screams, stumbling to the ground in a heap.

There is a silence where for a moment the world seems to freeze. Staring out at the evening sky the boy's eyes catch the waxing Moon that lays down a velvet carpet of phosphorescence. Nearby the sound of the neighbor's hybrid Wolf sends a tingle down his spine and leaves us wondering is or is this not a true call from the wild. Within an instant there is an echo coming from the woods. He quickly sizes up his situation as he plots the stealth reentry into the house, so his evening escapade can remain his sovereign secret.

He finds an old pail lying in the nearby bushes where he stumbled. It seems sturdy enough and it would be a perfect height to lift him close enough to where he can manage to pull himself up over the windowsill. He reaches to the window and slides it open without a sound. Swinging his leg up he gets a fair hold on the sill and gathering his body, he is up and over the hurdle.

He touches his feet to the floor inside without making a sound. Turning from the window he is surprised to find his Grandmother sitting upon his bed awaiting his return. This startles him and he lets out a shout that sends Grandmother into a belly laugh.

Looking at the sight of him is even more reason to laugh. He is absolutely the worse for wear, with leaves stuck in his hair, and his shirt torn, looking much more like a bush or a part of the forest itself than a young man. He was exhausted from his jaunt in the woods, which turned out to be much more of an adventure than he could have ever hoped for.

In a moment her glance changes and she gets a glow in her eyes that the boy knows only too well. Almost as if she were a part of his own soul, Grandmother always seemed to know what he was thinking…. sometimes even before he did. It seemed sometimes that she could see through the very walls of that old house. This night proved to be no exception.

She holds him and looks intently into his eyes. "So what have we been up to in the middle of the night, what has happened to you?"

The boy struggles to gain his composure, but like a cat burglar caught in the act, he remains frozen in his emotion.

"Oooh I see. Do you want to talk about it?"

Lobos looks at her sheepishly, "I ……. I …" His words getting stuck in his throat.

" Well just come out with it, or do you want me to pull it out of you?" She takes hold of him once again this time a little tighter, and turns him around to get a full look at the boy.

" Grandma, I saw the Wolf!" he blurts out almost surprising himself. "The Spirit Wolf. You know the one you are always telling us about." He stammers and gets so excited that he seems to once again trip over his own words.

Realizing that little Lobos is quite shaken and somewhat altered, she draws him close to her and rocks him in her arms. As Lobos calms down, she remarks, " Well, a real adventure this time. Tell me what happened, and exactly how it happened."

The boy sits on the edge of his bed and Grandmother sits down beside him.

As little Lobos tells his tale, Grandmother begins to drift off to the place beyond his words. The place where she sees the vision of what has really occurred. The boy's tale wanders and Grandmother sits silently and listens intently to the story the youngster has to share. There is no light except for the moonlight, which streams in through the still opened window, as the pair sit in silhouette against the blue light of Sister Moon.

Grandmother was not a large woman by any means, actually she was quite petite. She was still a very pretty woman and despite her small stature, she possessed a power in her mannerisms that could still the stormiest night, if she chose. Rather than take steps when she walked, she almost floated over the ground, like a wind spirit. Her long gray hair cascaded well past her hips. The slightest breeze sent her hair flowing, often giving her the appearance of being a Spirit rather than mere flesh and blood.

She could be a stern woman, and her stare could make a mountain lion still in its tracks. Looking into her eyes one could go into the foreverness of her essence. She was a traveler through consciousness as well as time, and knew well the world of Spirit. Grandmother had many children, and even more grandchildren as is the custom with native people. In the true way there were never any orphans. Some of the children were her own, but most were placed in her care. She was everyone's Grandma.

She raised the children to be self sufficient and aware of Sacred. There was a power in understanding the role that Sacred played in the dance of life. One could call upon that sacredness and miracles would occur. They were taught the sacredness of life and all things in Earth Mother's creations and their relationship to all things in the web of life. Grandmother had seen much in her years, and her wisdom touched everyone who knew her. She had a sense of compassion in her for life, such a love for living that her radiance could fill a room.

She rarely ever raised her voice, just a stare of her steel blue green eyes was enough to drive the message home. When Grandmother was annoyed or would get into the Spirit of telling her tales, her eyes would sometimes turn a midnight blue, almost black. It was like looking into the stars in a midnight summer sky.

Occasionally she would lose her temper and everyone would go running, even the raccoons and squirrels would take off for the highest branches. Lobos would notice while watching from a safe distance that there would be strange sparks of yellow light that would flash from her eyes and if those eyes turned in your direction, you may as well have been hit by lightning. It was usually little Lobos who caught those glances.

It was too often realized by young Lobos that Grandmother always expected more from him than the others. It would take many years before he himself would come to understand that this was because she had seen the signs in him at a very early age. It was clear the gift of her lineage flowed through him. Therefore it was entirely possible that one day these powers might fully awaken within the child.

Grandmother would observe young Lobos closely, for one never knew what form the gift of power would take or how it would develop. What incident would draw it to one's life experience? The gift of power develops in its own way, within the essence of the individual soul carrying it. The unfolding of the gift was unique to each individual, and developed from the personal choices one made in their life experience. The gift and the form it will take within each individual is as unique as a fingerprint.

Sometimes it was slated that an individual would be the deliverer of great miracles. Other times they would develop great healing abilities. Still at other times one might become a prophet, a seer, the Divine messenger. Then there was that rare occurrence where the individual became the Master.

She taught him that often the difference between good and evil was merely *a trick of the light*. There was no clear difference in the higher reality. Life was a very impressionistic experience perceived by each of us differently, and its interpretation was usually colored by what people had been conditioned to as they grew up.

Never really understanding what life was, or what they were about, people are too easily caught up in always justifying their own separate realities. That, Grandmother would point out, was a reality of judgment. Grandmother emphasized always that to understand life, we had to look for the Divine cause in all things. There were no accidents and children were like empty canvases for an artist to paint upon. She knew inwardly that unless the principles of Divine Law were emphasized with the passing of each event in our life experience, one's pathway could too easily be long and arduous and needlessly painful.

There is a balance of the energies, which flow through us that must be learned early on by one possessing the gift. This strange power of empathic realizations and access to the higher octaves of thought can be very difficult to the aspiring initiate. The balance of realities between worlds must be managed to the extent that the young initiate can move back and forth between the octaves and lead a normal existence as well as the extraordinary existence.

If this is not developed, life will often be like riding an emotional roller coaster without a seat belt. For this power which grows within us, creates a hyper sensing of reality which intensifies all our experiences, reactionary as well as causal. We must develop our ability to open our sensatory capabilities without burning out our inner cellular communication system. If an imbalance occurs then the outcome is madness, whether manifested in temporal disorders such as epileptic seizures, or permanent insanity.

The merging of realities that an empathic experiences is not easily understood by the untrained and insensitive mind. Their mundane experience is living on a day to day basis dealing with heightened awareness that never ceases to flow.

Little Lobos relates his experience to his Grandmother and tries his best to explain the unexplainable:

How he was drawn as if by some unseen force to climb out his bedroom window and walk into the darkness of the forest.

How the animal just appeared seemingly out of nowhere.

How he was caught in the spell of the occurrence, and the communication that transpired between himself and the Wolf.

Grandmother listens intently feeling every word that comes from his lips, knowing full well what has occurred here. For this is not a world unfamiliar to her own experiences. He is wide eyed as he wrestles with the mixed emotions running through him, and with the innocence of a child, he wonders about this miraculous occurrence that will leave him changed forever. She reaches over and draws him near and again proceeds to rock him back into balance.

Grandmother's heart is filled with a mixture of happiness, concern, and humor, for little Lobos was her favorite after all. After wiping the dirt from his face, she removes some leaves from his hair. She kisses Lobos on the forehead and at the same time smacks his little bottom affectionately. She looks into his eyes and quiets the fear and bewilderment he is feeling from his recent experience with the Spirit World.

She realizes the child could not help himself. Even though Grandmother motions young Lobos to bed with a stern look, inside she is relieved in her own heart to be able to tuck him safely into his bed. Tonight he has taken his first steps upon the path which is his destiny. No longer will he see the world in an ordinary sense. From now on he will begin to see the world *through the eye of the Shaman.*

The power, which was growing inside young Lobos, was an intense force driving him constantly ever deeper within the inner core of his Being. The ways of Great Mystery know not age, nor gender nor race or culture. Grandmother would often see into her own past whenever young Lobos would venture off into the Spirit World. He was in so many ways very much as she herself was as a child. But then we are never without that connection to our lineage that goes back to the beginning of the dream.

Looking into his eyes she laughs softly to herself, her long hair cascading across her shoulders picking up the glow of the moonlight. "It is time," says a voice to her as she lifts her head towards the window to catch the shimmering of the evening stars. "It is time..." the voice repeats itself. She sighs realizing to herself that her grandson's time of innocence has come to an end. It is time that she begins his learning. Turning towards him with one of her most loving smiles, choosing her words carefully, she begins to address the issue.

"So you had yourself quite an adventure this evening didn't you? Well you were a very brave young warrior this night, a very brave warrior indeed." She pats him on the chest, as if acknowledging his little fast beating heart. "You are a very brave young man and I am very proud of you... Tonight you have seen *through the eye of the Shaman*.

"Grandson, when one meets a Spirit animal one must always look deep into the eyes of that Being. There are those who would believe that the creatures of the forest are soulless, but this is not a truth. We find many more two-legged creatures out of the forest that have lost their souls. But people always get things turned around.

"When that Spirit animal looks deeply into your heart or you into the Spirit of the animal before you, in that moment we touch their Spirit, and they touch ours. In that moment if we are without fear or anger, then our kindredness of Spirit can communicate. And we return to the oneness that we all are.

"We are the Masters here....and....this is true but only if we learn to honor each other's beingness. To become a Master in the Web of Life is an arduous journey. It is the unfolding of a fairy tale. It is constantly asking yourself why you are doing what you are doing. It is always acting from command central, the heart of the inner Being that you are, never allowing yourself just an arbitrary outbreak of random energy. For a Master qualifies their actions, therefore they have command in their every experience.

"The Universal Law governs the *IS*-ness of All That Is, from the tiniest molecule to the largest of Beings. From the rock to Grandfather Sun himself, all of these elements are there for us to employ their power, and they will if we know the key is to allow this to occur freely and without reservation.

"So becoming the Master is learning *the art of being* a Master...Not *just thinking* that we are the Master. Being a true Master does not mean that we rule through tyranny and imposing our *Will* upon everything. It is much more a matter of getting everyone and everything to cooperate. It has never been a matter of dominance, it has always been a matter of compassion. We must learn to call the energy to us, so that it responds to our wishes willingly.

"We can learn to cooperate with the dream and the dream will cooperate with us, it is a matter of mutual recognition and all are players in this great drama. Even the Wolf that you met tonight, is part of the great dance of life. There are many things about the Sacred Mother's reality that we will learn if we are open and willing to learn. The world is far more mysterious than most people realize.

"To most, their lives are a chain of mysterious circumstances and not very memorable events. The Master walks a very different path than most. For the Master's path has purpose. The Master always knows where their path is leading, and pays attention to even the smallest of details:

"The color of the lizard that crosses his path.
Remembering the sound of the wind in the trees.
Understanding how to detect the changes in the attitude of the Deer.
Paying attention to the habits of birds in flight.
Noticing the look in everyone's face.

"One never knows how energy will twist and turn, and the outcome of an event can be altered in a moment. Life remains a mystery and always will.

"Today you came face to face with the Alpha Wolf. You were scared weren't you? He made no sound yet you could feel his power. He was the Master today. He spared your miserable life, because he saw deep into you and touched your Spirit. He left his mark on you. Now all the creatures of the forest will know that you walk with the Wolf Spirit. It is now a part of you. It is your path.

"You will never forget this day Grandson, nor will you forget his yellow eyes staring deep into your soul …… stirring your hidden emotions and thoughts. You will always remember the power of those eyes as they looked deep into your soul. They have touched your spirit, and they made you remember every lifetime you have ever had in that one moment. You are so young for this to happen, but there are reasons for things that are not clear to us in the moment. In time you and I will know why, that is certain, but only Spirit dictates the when of something.

"Those yellow eyes, like little drops of moon glow....... One does not always see the yellow eyes for that is only to be seen when those Beings are showing you their power, their true essence. You have the power to see. This is not a new thing in our family, although it remains a mystery to most of them. For those that have the power, are too clever to let it be noticed by accident or by those who would give them away. Spirit and magic are not well accepted in this world anymore.   No, not any more.

"It was a good thing for you those eyes were not red. For that is the mark of those who are of the dark side. Remember that lesson well, for it will save your life more than once while on the path you are to walk for the people. It is your destiny to work with the Spirit world. It is your contract from the above world, the world you came from. That is the `real world' in so many ways.

"Remember when you were very little and you would tell me stories of what that world was like? Yes, you were much closer to it then. But now you are growing into a big warrior, and those memories can begin to fade. You must never lose them. That is part of the magic, part of the key to using the power. It is the key to the doorway home.

"I will share this little bit of the secret with you my Grandson, for today the Alpha Wolf has touched your soul and recognized your power. He knows your Spirit, and left his watermark there. You are water brothers now, and I have seen the signs I have been hoping for. For now you are truly the little Wolf. If you are courageous and do not lose yourself along the path of sorrows, one day you might just become the Alpha. I have seen it happen to some. But the path of the Wolf is not an easy one, not an easy one indeed.

"It is very difficult you see. The young Alpha Wolf has to leave the pack. He leaves the pack or else he will be eliminated by the dominant alpha who sees him as a threat. So the mother drives him off as soon as he is old enough to hunt for himself. To us humans this often seems cruel. That is because we are always trying to make everything like us. They must think Creator did not know what he was doing when the world was manifested. People can be so foolish. Always trying to change what is, instead of just understanding it.

"It is lonely at first for the young Wolf, then he learns to make the aloneness his ally. My dear young man, you are very impatient. You have gone and jumped the fence before you learned how to climb. But I understand, for once the fire burned in me like that. Once I too chased the wind. Now you will have to deal with things sooner then I would have planned. So listen carefully.

"When you speak to people always look into their eyes. Look for the blue corona that surrounds their color. If you do not see this blue corona, then know that they are just ordinary people, mischievous children who play in their games of destruction and confusion. They will always find ways to be lost in a forever game of conflict with their Spirit self and each other. For them balance is not possible, for they drift like leaves before the wind. And they do not hear the voice that speaks within. They, because of this flaw in behavior, are at best good imitators, and have no thoughts of their own.

"They are the Spirit Riders, and you have no need to drag them along your pathway. They can only slow you down along your journey and only distract you from your true purpose, and in the end they will leave you. They always leave you. Once they realize that they can no longer take any of your energy for their own use, the dissension begins in a relationship. Once there is nothing for them to learn from you to imitate for their own pathetic little monkey games, they will look for new blood.

"Some of these ordinary people may be only part Spirit, or worse, soulless ones. If you see the blue corona in their eyes, then you will know they are of Great Spirit, if the blue corona is not there, they very well might not be. Now these soulless ones are very clever. They are great distracters, however they too have their role in the game of life. Once we can remove good or evil from things then we can see it for what it truly is. This life is a grand school where we learn to master ourselves, and to know ourselves through the reality we create around us.

"You possess, as do I that blue corona, The Alpha saw that in your eyes this evening. He was able to enter through it to touch your soul so you would remember. He knew you would be worth waking up. Now you and he are kin. That is forever. But, I warn you Grandson, walk always in your integrity and honor, walk in `the Sacred,' or you will come to know the other side of that power very quickly, for the Wolf can be a harsh teacher.  If your intent should waver from `the Sacred' ....even I could not help you.

"You will always be different than most people Grandson. Yet, you are just the same as other children. You have the same needs to be liked, to play, and to interact and exchange energy with other humans. You have the need to be held and you have to give your love to someone and know that it is received. This, after all, is what we humans are about, loving, playing and interacting. We need each other to feel each other. We are also for that purpose the eyes, ears, feet, voice and heart of Creator. Always."

She paused for a moment and stared off seeming almost for the moment as if she were listening to someone else in the room. Then her eyes returned to little Lobos from the great void.

"Grandson, know that you will not walk the same path as many of your friends, and oftentimes what works for them, will not work for you. But that is OK. The Eagle is a solitary bird and is not afraid of its loneliness, nor does it think itself less because it seldom seeks the company of others. You will always feel things more intensely, and you will always be slightly out of sync with the crowd. I am not certain if it will be easier than normal or harder for you, we will have to wait and see, for now you have the mark of Spirit upon you.

"You must learn many things now, and you must learn them quickly. The Wolf has touched your soul, and you have the mark of the Wolf upon you. All creatures in the forest will know that you are under his protection, and guidance. And they will see in your eyes what they see in his. For now you too have the yellow eyes.   But I have rambled on far too long for your little mind. Come......you are tired and should get some sleep, it is very late."

She slaps him softly on his leg realizing that he was at times half asleep..."I do not have all night to waste taking care of foolish boys who go wandering out into the forest late at night thinking they can fool their Grandma."

She reassures him by softly meeting his intentful, bigger than usual eyes, which although half closed never lose sight of her every movement. She notices for an instant that his emerald eyes flash with the golden yellow. She strokes his forehead, and gives him a warm smile and a kiss. He knows she hears his thoughts and sees right into his heart.

A QUESTION OF BALANCE

The visions of Grandmother slowly fade into the spaces between worlds again. The symphony of songbirds begins to penetrate the landscape bringing don Lobos back to this reality. They continue performing their morning ballet amongst the branches of fruit trees. The scent of Jasmine and Woodrose mixed with the smell of the forest after a spring rain slowly drifts from the garden and touches his nostrils and he is acutely aware of the presence of Grandmother's Spirit.

The vision is suddenly broken by the rapid rustling of grouse being startled in the field. Someone is coming, he thinks to himself. Strange I did not sense them.

Through the trees he watches as a figure moves like a breeze across the earth and he almost recognizes the long hair flowing like liquid light. For a moment he thinks this a vision of Grandmother in her youth. Then the reality of this world catches up with him again. "No, it is Angelina. I must learn to recognize my own apprentices," he laughs to himself.

Angelina walks as if on air, and has the grace about her movement much the same as Grandmother's. She also has the aloof attitude of a Wolf. In the subdued light of the Moon, her long blonde hair shimmers with a phosphorescence....like liquid light.

He thinks silently to himself...."She chooses to be alone for much of her experience, yet she seems to already realize that she is never alone. She is strong willed but not of cold heart, perhaps the power will fill her one day. She is so excited by every new moment. She has not yet been crushed by the fears of those in the world around her. This is good. This is very good."

Angelina instinctively knows where don Lobos is sitting. He finds comfort in her awareness, and the grace of her movement. He recognizes her being sure of herself. As she draws closer, her gait shifts. As if something is disturbing her, she draws just close enough to make eye contact and acknowledge him.

"Don Lobos, good evening! May I join you?"

"Good evening Angelina! Please do.......come, sit with me, it is going to be a fine evening by the look of the sky."

Angelina joins him. Watching the horizon don Lobos notices that the sun has already set and will be completely gone in a few minutes. Excusing himself he reaches in front of her to the table, and lights two blue candles that are sitting there. Settling himself back in his large willow chair he could not help but notice how complementary the candlelight was to her features. The view of her against the azure blue and orange pink of the clouds could be a Maxfield Parrish painting set against the deepening blues and violet of the evening sky.

Somehow though, the uneasiness keeps bleeding through her serenity, and he elects to address the matter straight away.

"Angelina, something is troubling you? Do you want to talk about it?"

" Yes I am troubled, you are correct in seeing that in me. You always see into everyone don't you?"

"Well, not always. Even I can be fooled occasionally you know."

"Yes, but it is occasionally, it is not all the time." She laughs and seems to relax a little more.

Angelina continues. "I see the world of Spirit, I know that, you know that. I see it very clearly most of the time, but there is something from the past. It is like I have a memory about the past in a world that is not of this world and yet it is this world.

"When I think of how things are, I wonder why we try incessantly to bring them back to order, to this ideal. Well, where does this ideal come from? It is not expressed in the condition of the world *around* us that I see. The world we are *in* is spiritual and compassionate. It is a feeling world, filled with dreams that seem at times to be only a hopeless attempt on our part to achieve our idea of Utopia. It seems that we are trying to create a reality that can never be accepted in its beautiful simplicity.

"Don't get me wrong, the ideal is alive with me to the very core of my Being. But I do not see others accepting it truly. I do not see others grasping the essence of the pureness of which we speak.   Conditions always turn around and the dream between two people too quickly can become a nightmare. One is always trying to dominate the other, always trying to change the other. We become more sophisticated as we learn more, and we also become more devious, if you will. Are we totally corrupted within? I wonder sometimes.

"And then I get confused with this vision that keeps entering my reality. This feeling that seems to come from the past. What past? I can't even remember it, except in fragments. I know it is real, but I cannot touch it. I can't seem to hold it. If I am Divine, if I am a part of Creator, then why can't I resurrect that reality within my life? It can happen in the spiritual work we do. In small groups under certain conditions I have seen that.

"I guess what I mean is, why can't I experience that in the everyday world. Why can't I manifest that perfection? Am I God, or am I the fool thinking I am God?

"Am I just as corrupt as the others only coming from a different perception? Is everything I do just a justification of my own self created reality?

"I want to touch God. I want to know the truth. Yet sometimes the truth seems ambiguous, as if truth were just a concept and not a tangible reality at all. Are we responsible for truth or is truth the cause of our dilemma? Are we just swimming through a sea of casual circumstance where we have nothing to do with anything at all? Sometime I can see the result of my thoughts manifesting. Then there are times I lose the vision. I start to wonder if I am as mad as the rest of them out there.

"And then other times I have to say I had nothing to do with the occurrence. Sometimes I think events just spontaneously arise before us at random. Like the lottery. Sometimes your number hits and sometimes it doesn't. Sometimes I wonder if I can manifest at all. Yet I know that I have done certain things.

"Am I making any sense, or have I just lost it completely? I am sorry don Lobos. Forgive me, I just need to understand. No matter how much I learn, I seem to see only the separation that we have created between everything and ourselves. We are all so out of touch."

Don Lobos sits back in silence for a long still moment. He reaches into his jacket pocket and pulls out a silver case, which holds his American Spirit cigarettes. He pulls one out and lights it, still in silence. Blowing the smoke in four directions, he says a prayer for clarity. The prayer is barely audible and is a language that Angelina cannot understand. The smoke makes thirteen little spirals, creating a serpentine form before them.

Looking deeply into her blue eyes, don Lobos begins speaking in a deep whispered voice.

" Angelina, Angelina." Looking up at the stars that are beginning to appear above him he continues.

"This is a very serious thing you ask. And your question is very layered. It is after all many questions, is it not? I will try to answer you as simply as I can. For what you ask is about God and the deepest intimacy between the two of you. I must answer you so that you come to realize that you are worth loving, and in a manner that you come to recognize who and what you truly are. For this answer I must look through the eye of the Shaman and speak through the heart of the Shaman. I must go back to the beginning, to the *Kryah.*"

He stares into her eyes as if he were looking through them into some unforeseen place beyond her. She feels an energy with which she is unfamiliar. As his eyes turn the golden yellow of the sun, sparks seemed to fly out and touch the deepest recesses of her soul. She is startled for a moment, as he seems to be searching for some mysterious place beyond her. She is slightly uncomfortable, yet she remains receptive to his probing. After another period of silence, lessening his gaze, don Lobos begins speaking. His eyes glow yellow as if a fire were burning within them.

" Who are you Angelina?   Do you know who you are, can you remember any of it? You, my child, are so much more than mortal flesh. You are so much more than an entity lost in the mass confusion of consciousness. You, yourself are a part of the God-Force. The same Force that is igniting the thoughts you think. The same Force which allows you, your immortality. For thoughts are forever, God is forever, and you are the thought of God. That is what it is to be Hu-man. We are part of the whole and yet we are the whole in relation to our reality. We think, therefore we are.

"You are so much more than the temporal embodiment you know as your human form. You are so much more, that there are no words to describe what you are in the eyes of God. You are not some bastard child of an unforgiving Universe, abandoned to live a hellish life in pain and suffering, given no clue as to your existence or a guide to the rules of life, and then told that if you make a mistake you will be sentenced to an eternity of hell fire and brimstone.

"You are neither helpless, nor forgotten. You are neither happiness nor unhappiness. You are Divine; you are part of a collective consciousness that never ceases. You are a creator. And you have the same powers as that which created you, for you are part of that which created *You.* I am talking about *You*, not your body. Again I am talking about *You*, not your mortal existence. *You*, the real you. The one who is experiencing this dream. The one listening behind your ears to what we are saying here. Actually feeling what we are saying would be a more correct statement.

"You, my beloved sister, are God manifest in human form. You always have been. You never not were, you, always were. The mystery of yourself, is hidden from you in this condition however. Because how your mind thinks and how your mind thinks your body feels, is the result of a collection of lies you have lived with for thousands of lifetimes.

"Who are you? You are God-Woman, you are the Christos. The Christos is God-Man, God-Woman experiencing its own creation in the living embodiment you possess upon this plane. Living in a reality of limitation that you participated in the creation of. This is hard for you to realize because the 'mind' that you think with has been altered. You are blocked from contact with the real you due to circumstance of conditioning.

"The social conditions and cultural programming of your world have made it near impossible to believe in your own individual beingness, never mind your Divine Beingness. What you know of the Divine human is but an icon that has been set up before you....icons possessing strange and mystical powers greater than you could ever hope to possess. `The Real Story' has been lost to antiquity. You only have been allowed to know what others have told you. In essence what they wanted you to know. Unless you became a criminal and stole into their libraries and read forbidden texts, you wouldn't know that most of what we read has been altered, edited, and re-edited hundreds of times.

"Because you have no real experience you are blind to your true nature. You have accepted that you are incapable of possessing the ability to be absolute perfection, all-knowingness, and that you have Godly beauty. You focus upon your imperfections and your lack to such an extent that you can no longer see your perfection in God's eye.

"You have sought to find yourself in temples, in books and other Earthly experiences. You have tried to find yourself in ceremony, and sought the truth in Sacred objects, or in the magic of the sunset, or the creatures of this Earth. You have looked to Shamans, and prophets alike. Everywhere you have searched. Now you must come to search within to find the answers.

"The external things will no longer assist you in your pilgrimage. There is one place however you have not looked. You have not looked within the temple of the living God for your answers. That is within you. For you are the source of all questions, and all answers are in the questions you ask. The kingdom of Heaven is within. You have been looking without for resolution.

"Within you, you shall find the heroine, as well as the God you seek. You shall find the perfection in the dream that you are seeking to become. The unknown God you seek is waiting for you within your own goodness and purity. For all you seek is a state of mind, a state of being. It does not, nor can it exist outside of you. For you are the keeper of the flame.

"I am only one Being. There have been many Beings far greater than myself, who have sought to teach these truths. Most were crucified and tortured. It is human nature to first love and embrace those who walk in the Light, then they ridicule and ostracize them for being different, for daring to be more than the flock.....to be doing God's work. Then they turn around and worship them once again after they are no more. They even build their religions around such individuals. It is a fool's folly, but it is the condition here.

"These priests of orthodox religions are for the most part carriers of dogma and false truths. The truth within their teachings is so twisted they would not know a burning bush if it jumped out in front of them and spoke. They are victims of their own stupidity and ignorance, and ruled by their own fears. Unfortunately the truth is that their teachings have been handed down from one person's truth to another person and they turn it around so it could be that person's truth. Each one then having to justify why their truth was different than the other's truth. So reason it out what is left of their truth?

"And the one truth theory, what an absurd concept! They are asking us to believe that there is only one truth that covers everybody, and everything, on every dimension. It is like trying to create a blanket insurance policy for all experiences.

There are Divine Laws, which apply to the process of the whole. Yet each specific circumstance is unique. The law is a living law and it applies itself specifically to each condition. That is how magnificently the mind of God works. It can, because God does not have relative truth. God is not that limited."

"So then one persons truth may not be the same as another's?" Angelina queried.

"Truth is by its own nature as diversified as the mind of God. It is as endless as the Universe. Truth if anything, could only be an affirmation of the circumstance of the Divine Law of LOVE. And that law effects the whole of the Universe, not just one man's house or village or people. LOVE allows for everything to have its own truth. It is the way the Universe was designed. It is why there are so many different Beings on so many different planets, expressing on so many different planes of reality.

"Truth is a mutable reality that can only exist in the consciousness of God. For truth to you, and to me will always be different things. They may be similar but they are relative to your consciousness and mind, and by Divine Law they remain uniquely individual. For all that we are while on this plane, we can only experience relative truth....truth, as it concerns you or me individually.

"It is the nature of Divine Truth to be elastic and change as we change, to change as the situation transforms. As we grow it grows, so your truth today will not be your truth after the experiences of twenty years. Your truth in this moment will change with your next experience. Relative truth is all one can perceive. Which brings up the conversation of Truth vs. Divine Law and the differences between the terms. But we will leave that to your own consideration for the moment.

"It has taken many lifetimes and many, many experiences through the human drama to come back to what you are experiencing while with me; which are the original teachings, given to us eons ago. You should not condemn those experiences either, they were all part of the same journey to now. You are the culmination of all your experiences, every lifetime, every drama, all of them. It took all those experiences to bring you to this very moment. And how do you know that in the next moment you will not ascend? Then you would have another realization of what truth is, would you not?

"The original instructions given to all mankind long ago are alive in our memory. They are encoded in our DNA. They react with the molecular structure of All That Is. What I speak of to you now is already the past, only a fraction of a moment ago in thought it happened. So when we think, we are in a sense reviewing what has already been. You see now why truth is relative. These teachings were given to you so that you might be glorified, and uplifted to the Spirit of the Father - Mother Creator.......The Source of all that *IS*.

You are in a war entity, make no mistake about that. Even this hour you are battling that within you which is called Spirit, and that which is called intelligence, and that which is called body. And within those factions you are struggling to come to terms with the nature of reality. Even this moment you are battling with the concept of mortality that imprisons the flesh, and limits the mind. I tell you now that the forces of Light have already gathered to lift you and your brethren and sisteren. Whosoever shall know themselves, shall own themselves, only then shall they be uplifted into a realized reality of glorified Christos....the Godhead.

"We are advancing very rapidly into the foreverness of our destinies. We are advancing also into an accelerated understanding of our realities. There are many Spirits who are the lovers of man-kind, and woman-kind. There are many Gods and Goddesses who have been with you through the ages. You, I, and everything around us, are speeding towards a change in octaves, which will lead us to one common destiny. This is truth to those above as well as those here.

"One hand assists the other and it takes both hands to do the job. We are no less or more than those who are beyond the light of this plane. For we are much closer than most would acknowledge. The difference between worlds is like the difference between two sides of a doorway. One moment you are here and in the next you are there. Yes, relative truth once again.

"There are those like yourself that have the opportunity to become beacons in the storm, living channels of the Divine for the masses to follow into the Light. For there is a time coming when a great mass of our humanity will be divided one against another, not in 'war,' but in belief acceptance. 'My way is better than your way.' 'My way is righteous yours is not.' It is all conflict…. it is all polarity. Good, evil, higher, lower, richer and poorer. The madness of *IT*. *IT* isn't. There is only *IS*. And that *IS*, is forever. *IS,* is all there ever was or will be. *IS*, is in the *NOW,* the PAST the FUTURE!

"Remember always …IT isn't there, only *IS!"*

Angelina leans forward, curiously. "Tell me more about what is to happen, don Lobos."

"There is a new consciousness being birthed. Birth, as well as conception, occurs through chaos. For chaos, as you call it, is the opening of the doorway to manifestation. In order to have a thought that can change the circumstance, the thought changing the circumstance must be greater than the thought that created the circumstance.

"Therefore the new thought, possessing greater energy will begin the process of becoming; first an idea, then a thought in contemplation, then an emotion, then a dream of potential, then the energy builds and builds and POP we have an action. Then we have a manifestation of behavior, radical behavior. As a result of the action, we have a reaction. Change is activated, and reality must readjust itself to new thought, thus something new is born.

"This new consciousness that is being birthed is without restriction. It will take a generation to root itself into the present consciousness. Mankind will make a gigantic leap in their evolutionary process. This new consciousness is without dogmas, for dogma has no place to get a hold. The vibration is far too high for the lesser vibration to continue to exist. In a way the old corrupted consciousness would burn away.

"There are already thousands, yes, even millions who have come into alignment with this new consciousness. Every time our Sun reacts, it is birthing new substance for that consciousness to take hold, to imprint. Something new is being born and the entire Universe is in a state of excitement over this. The Heavens are filled with those observing what is happening here…..from their relative truths of course." He laughs to himself. " There are so many expressions of Man in this Universe, all of them beautiful, and all are sublime. All have the essence of the Father-Mother Creator.

"You are learning how to unite the consciousness of God-Creator with all peoples. Not just in this plane but simultaneously in all planes, and dimensions. For you are so much more than you allow yourself to feel, and realize. So which truth are you? Are you possibly all of them? Can you see the big picture yet? I hope so, because you are one of those who will be instrumental in bringing *them*, all of *them* together.

"Also you are experiencing a deliberate and Divinely directed change in your perception of time. Time will continue to change its nature from one instant to the next during the transition as we approach the moment of great shifting. You will experience many lifetimes in this lifetime, many realities, and many relationships, as this new consciousness is realized and manifests.

"Those who are caught up in the past will not make it through the veil between realities. That is not judgment, it is a matter of self worth, self-evaluation. Yet those who at first might appear lost, learning to hold onto the now, stretching and twisting against the dogma of the old and dying paradigm, will find hope in all things as the great awakening draws closer.

"When the great shifting occurs it will happen in your Heavens as well as within your Being, and to the Earth. No stone will go unturned. You are already feeling this pulling, like a tension, a sense that something is about to happen this moment. You are experiencing the shifting already within the core of your Being. For you are the one creating the nature of this reality. You are dreaming it. You are thinking it and thought dictates the nature of your reality. When the shifting occurs it will usher forth the *IS*; what has been termed the day of God the day of *Ishmael,* (IS-AM-REAL). And the nature of reality for the whole of mankind shall be transformed in a moment.

"This shifting, this emergence of the fifth world will cause all our inequities, our imbalances, pestilence, disease, all our disharmony to surface and be seen before our eyes. This is what is meant as the purification. In that experience much chaos shall be endured, for all the madness that ever was will be, until we decree *IT* as illusion and dispel *IT* to the void from which *IT* came. All that is not a part of valued life shall be cast off. It is *a war of valued life*. It is the coming into the Age of Light......The Emergence of the Fifth World.

"

All those who would seek to enslave their brothers and sisters; all who would deny our personal liberties to express our spirituality freely, shall be no more. All who would despise the creatures upon this Earth and her natural order, shall not see the manifestation of the age of enlightenment. Neither will they, at its culmination, be able to manifest again upon this plane until they come into alignment with the Source of all that *IS*.

"Only when they realize the universality of all that IS, in all Its magnificence, will there never again be an extermination of life. Rather, after the purification, we shall see upon this Earth, a celebration of life.... for life shall and will continue. For mortality is a part of the illusion of limitation, that which is of the Father-Mother Creator is forever as they are, as we are one in the same.

"There will be no need or place for greed or fear in the coming world. For all shall have what we now call Divine capabilities, and all shall possess clairvoyant abilities. We must all now learn to become the ever-flowing essence of Source. For the present conditions are due to our perceptions of limitation, and that which is birthing, is forever and unlimited.

"There will be no despots in the coming consciousness, for all shall be Lords of Light. No avatars, no gurus, only your brethren and sisteren. For the need for competition, and domination shall no longer exist. All shall be equal, yet all shall be unique, for the gift we give each other is in the allowing of each other's uniqueness.

"The gift we give ourselves is in the allowing of Self to be. This is accomplished by allowing and recognizing the Sacred that is within all things, in all actions. All this shall we come to know when we accept responsibility for our manifestations and our connected-ness to Creator. Then in the accepting of the responsibility of the creation and releasing of our thought forms upon this plane, we will re-quantify them, and declare the kingdom of Heaven upon the Earth. When we do this, in a glorious moment, the Heavens shall be opened to us.

"You my Angelina, are more beautiful than you know, and you are greatly loved by the Source of All That Is. More so, you are cherished. You will see many things in the coming days of change, but I tell you here, do not get caught up in the illusion of the transforming of time and space.   Do not let your eyes fool you. Feel what is going on all around you, and you will know the hearts of men. Feel deeply and knowingly, for the heart knows the pathway home. It always has. Know that you are greatly protected, that the Light which holds you, shall not abandon you in flight. Trust in your knowingness, listen to the gentle voice within.

"You are a beacon that will call forth to you, other Lights. You shall all rejoice in your sovereignty. Together you shall reverse the prophecies, for you, yourself have dreamed All That Is, and all who are, and they are but a part of Self. From the good-ness that is inside of you shall come forth great civilizations, the likes of which have not been seen even by the visionaries. A new wind is blowing across this plane. You will come to know the Lord of the Wind, for all are being called. And the Winds of Change, which you are witnessing, are for the glory of the *ISNESS*. The glory of Creator, the God of All That *IS*.

"There will be those who will call your knowing a madness, and unto them that judge, by their declaration, shall themselves be judged. They will hurl words at you like weapons, testing your reason. Hold fast to your heart, for your heart shall be your compass. They will ridicule you and blaspheme you with libelous tongue. For you are the sign, the messenger that brings the Light of Truth. When they attack you, show them their truth, and it will be your shield.

"They will say that what is occurring around them is not 'sanity.' It is not logical, they will curse the Heavens and the Earth, for their plight. And through your wondrous eyes you will see them drowning in the sea of madness. You will see the life essence leaving them. And in their eyes where there was once light, you will see only shadows.

"This you will see in whole areas, whole villages, and whole peoples. This is the *SAMPACU:* All those who have surrendered their life connection to Source; all places that no longer can sustain the Joy of life in its Divine creation; all who have surrendered their right to Divine sovereignty. All these shall be absorbed into the illusion and be replaced with the newness of what is being birthed.

"The power of the blue ray, the power of the Goddess Shiva, will be felt heavily upon this plane. For the old will be removed that the new may be allowed to seek its own destiny. For that which is no longer useful to the great plan of the living God/ Creator, shall no longer have position in this plane. It is again a matter of *a War of Valued Life.*

"All this and more you shall see in your lifetime, for this time is the shifting of a great Solar clock. Many who possess the cosmic knowledge of the Universe foresaw that this time would come, when the great cycles would experience a change in the rhythm of what has been for so long, and humanity would arrive at the gateway to forever.

"Live your dream, be the ideal of yourself. That is God at work within. You have the right and the power to seize the moment. It is simply a matter of taking *right action* that changes the course of events. How do I do that you might ask? Follow your intuition. Place the dream in front of you and follow your intuition. Follow the path of least resistance, the pathway with heart.   The road out of the labyrinth has always been in front of you, in plain sight.

"All of us are like birds that fly in and out of the clouds, knowing the destination point in our hearts, not questioning our ability to fly. We possess within us a secret code. This code was placed within us when we were still a formless essence in the Spirit world. It is the gift of *Kryah.*"

The Gift of Kryah

As he looks for a moment into the stillness, don Lobos notices that the evening has begun to take on a phosphorescence, as the light of the moon comes through the tree tops above them. The light seems to create a veil that lays upon the branches of the trees, like the white Mantilla lays across Angelina's shoulders. There is a moment when the scent of the flowers from the garden mixes intoxicatingly with the essence that Angelina is wearing this evening. His awareness of this blending of fragrances surprises don Lobos, so as to make him notice the subtle magic of the moment.

Angelina catches a flower petal that ripples down from the trees that surround them. She strokes the soft petal and brings it to her own delicate nose. It is as if she, in a different way, also is touched by the enchantment. She stares again into the depths of his soft eyes making a gesture with her hands indicating that she is waiting for him to continue, but for the moment time itself has stopped. She breaks the silence with her words.....

" I would really like to know all you can share with me about this gift of the *Kryah...*"

With a look of solemnity, don Lobos begins to speak from a part of him that Angelina is no stranger to. It is the energy that emanates from *the Nagual* that he has become.

"The gift of *Kryah* is all around us, and constantly accessible. We are immersed in it. *Kryah* is within everything. *Kryah* is the map back home, it has always been there. It is in the leaf, and the petal of the flower. *Kryah* is in the rock as well as the butterfly, and in the air we breathe. Mostly it is within us. You will never see red in the rainbow if you are the color red. You will see everything else. Look at how long you have come back and forth from this plane. What is it that always takes you the longest to see and understand? Yourself, we are the last to realize ourselves.

"*Kryah* is in the heart of you, it can be found in your inner most dreams and reflected in the songs of the birds in flight. *Kryah* is the feeling rebounding off the laughing water in the river that plays and splashes across the boulder that has fallen into its path. It is spontaneous, and free willed. Yet it is immutable, and forever.

"How does everything know what it is in the fabric of the dream? Did you ever wonder? How is it that the rose does not bleed into the tree? What makes the same Life Force express as a horse, or a dove?   What takes the Soul energy and allows it to express as male or female? Is it not amazing that the same substance that makes you up, also makes up the beggar upon the street. The very same physical composition, yet the two expressions are so different.   What enables one to be the poet and the other the leper? Have you ever wondered?

"You ask me what will it be like in the future? Why do we play the game? What will reality be like? You say to me…as if truth were just a concept and not a tangible reality, 'Are we responsible for truth or is truth actually the cause of our dilemma?'

"You are tearing yourself apart with self doubt, my dear……tearing yourself apart.

"Think of all your thoughts and feelings during the course of a day, or even an hour. All are different, each thought unique and possessing a purpose all its own. Each thought is born within the innocence of itself, for the sake of being. Can you see what those thoughts are truly about, can you reason out what they are actually creating for you?

"Can you see the whole fabric of humanity from the Shaman's eye? Can you imagine how many billions, trillions of thoughts there must be about the nature of reality? They are all truth, and they all are reality. Thoughts are forever. So which ones do you choose to breathe life into? Which ones will you choose to embrace, and hold dear to you. Know always that your most dominant thoughts will dictate the nature of your reality.

"Can you see the foreverness of it all? Can you see the ingenious process behind the game to create the ultimate freedom for your Spirit? Can you see your uniqueness in it all? What a Master Plan! *Kryah* is the cosmic map created when God drew up the Master Plan for the whole of the Universe. The understanding of *Kryah*, is understanding the process.   It is the Mystery, the secret key that unlocks the door to the alchemist. With the understanding of *Kryah*, we can transform reality by following the natural pathway conceived in the original creation, the original process of consciousness.

"This process, this game of life, is God, Angelina. The process, the plan, the great experiment, it is the mind of God realizing itself and coming to conclusions, and letting other ideas go. It is the nature of the void. In some ways we are like fish swimming in the ocean of forever. We wonder where that ocean is at times, because we cannot see it. Yet always it is all around us. We are in it and we are part of it and it is a part of us.

"We are but thoughts in the mind of God. Each one of us an idea, each one of us a potential reality. A dream developing a potential outcome. Each one of us having the ability to make our own choices on whether to participate in the game or not. *Freedom of choice*! It's all about freedom of choice and then standing out of the way...... let *Kryah* do the rest. It does all the time, anyway. Do you understand?"

Angelina twists a lock of her beautiful hair around her finger, contemplatively. "I think so.....So what you're saying is, I really don't have to worry about anything, I just put my intentions out..... and then allow *Kryah* to work its magic."

Don Lobos gives her a nod of approval, validating her response. "Angelina, you are a student who is wise beyond her years, and yet still as innocent as a child."

THE AGE OF INNOCENSE

"Let us talk about the pain and the suffering you see; the corruption, and the twisting of truths; the hopelessness that is manifesting in everyone around you; the decay that is expressing in everything around you. Yes that exists. *IT* all exists. *IT* is everywhere. *IT* always has existed as long as there were Beings who think *IT* is part of the condition. If you choose to wake up, then your eyes will be open. You can also make the conscious choice to remain asleep, and your **eye** will remain shut. Then you will not see the results of maligned thoughts, and what they can and do manifest.

"In your seeing you must struggle to go beyond the first impulse of what your Mind first grasps as truth. Use your second and third attention. In the first stage the Mind is only capable of comprehending the signal that it is receiving. The Mind is unique to you personally. God does not speak to your Mind. God speaks to your awareness through emotion. You do not know what God says, because God says nothing, God feels. God feels everything, and thus is in the perfect state of knowing.

"No one's Mind is the same as the next. That is because what goes into the Mind is filtered by you. And your conditioning programs you. The manipulated DNA programs you, in your blood. So we must stop allowing your conditioning to dictate the nature of your reality.

"How?..... How, you may ask? Do what God does! Let it go. *Kryah* will take over. God created *Kryah* so God could dream, so God could create. Let go, and *go* into the wonderment of it all. See how one paradigm exists along side the other, each being its own thought manifestation independent of the other.

"The creation game is all about *Choice*...Real freedom of choice is almost impossible for the Mind to conceive, let alone embrace and understand the realm of possibilities. Realize your developed EGO will panic when faced with the responsibilities for the maintaining of that reality. As you become liberated from the web of social consciousness and learn to have your own thoughts, it will resist. To have freedom is to take the responsibility for that freedom. *Kryah* is the river, but you must navigate the river.

"The age of innocence was/is never over. It exists all around you. Look at the world around you from a distance. Is life not a fairytale? Is life not filled with endless possibilities? Once the vision is capable of being seen you can be, and have anything you desire.

"The tampering and manipulation, which once occurred upon our plane, was limited by its own nature. This manufactured plan for genetic manipulation of the species does not have the ability to adjust to the new consciousness that is emerging. It never could, because in *IT,* there is no true Life Force.

"Our present circumstance is the result of a synthesized condition created to prevent us from realizing our total potential. It is not natural. It is not part of *Kryah*, and not God's idea. What is falling away at this time are the false images, the icons, and the illusion of the image, the programming that held the old picture together.

"It is the age of judgment and tyranny that is passing from this plane, not the innocence. Existence on this plane has been for lifetimes now, an experience of ignorance, domination, pain, power and the misuse of *Will*. The whole has been manipulated by the few, who hide themselves behind secret cartels, to create the illusion of power. Even those tyrants are living in the effects of the hell they created.

"This experience of fear and living in limitation is coming to a rather quick ending.....simply because it serves no useful function in the scheme of things any longer. The plan no longer works in *the war of valued life*.

"Now if you find yourself losing your sense of forever, if you can't feel yourself any longer, ask yourself these questions. Where did you accumulate all this knowingness that you possess? Where did you develop all your feelings, likes and dislikes? Where did you develop your uniqueness, your personality? Do you really think you could have developed all that you are to this point of glorious realization in but one lifetime? You are much too beautiful, and sophisticated a Being to have accomplished this in only a moment's expression upon the eternalness of life's drama.

"Your life is an accumulation from the vastness of your experiences, realized through your expressing lifetime after lifetime in the drama until you learned it, memorized it and could hear the music of it in your own ears. In each of those experiences you gathered values, and wisdom which has helped you formulate your character and unique and beautiful personality..... the every essence of what you are....the `you,' that is having this experience."

THE MYTH OF REALITY

An almost full Moon, lights the evening. The stillness that accompanies sunset begins to quicken as the sounds of silence become filled with the chattering of night birds. A giant nebulous shadow seems to move in and around Angelina and don Lobos. There is a fluttering sound like wings and then stillness. Suddenly the shadow twists and turns in and around them. After a timeless moment the mystery makes itself known, as a giant moth lands on a nearby limb.

The patterns appear psychedelic and a little too brilliant for this reality. With the moonlight shining down upon It, the moth seems bigger than life, and the patterns on the fragile wings appear as a face staring back at them. The moth is aware of their presence, and almost seems to move its wings in a slow motion dance trying to communicate a message to them.

Watching Angelina mesmerized with her attention fixed upon the giant moth, don Lobos finds the moment to bring the experience into clarity. " The Moth of Knowledge! Do you know the difference between the Moth and you….. and why the Moth has the advantage?"

She looks at him quizzically……" …the advantage? I don't understand."

"The Moth knows it is forever, it doesn't wonder, it knows. The Moth lives totally in the moment. It does not question or judge its own existence, therefore it knows not of inner conflict. It loves itself and it allows itself, expressing freely the *Tonal* or Spiritual Energy, which comes through its form. So when it enters our energy fields it is capable of stopping the show and commanding our attention. Thus commanding all of reality for the moment to become aware of its presence. In that way it is forever.

"Next time you are in the market place, look into the crowd. Look without any kind of judgment. Do not stop at the external show that promenades before you. See through the actors playing their parts. As the simple observer in the dream you will see the twisting of the *Tonal's* before you. In some areas of this world the *Tonal* is gone from the People, it is non-existent.

"As you look into the dream you will see those individuals who have become broken, and cannot even hold the light of a moth. You see Angelina, when that which is Spirit can no longer express through the embodiment, the dream of a people collapses and they lose the ability to project their own energy field, which is part of the *Tonal*. Their consciousness implodes and their reality can no longer express upon this plane.

"The *Tonal* is very strong in our Moth, as it is in you and I. We are the ones commanding the dream. With the others I speak of, it is like the light was being squeezed out of them. They are gray, and appear as people hidden within costumes acting like puppets. The *Tonal* can be in a single individual, it can be in a group, or at rare times in an entire People, as it was when the Mayan, and Egyptians were in their zenith of their dream upon this plane. Now they are ghosts of their former continence. Their power and brilliance and illuminessence withers like a tree that can no longer bear fruit.

"Death is a temporal state. It is a chosen reality. It has nothing to do with the Spirit of a thing. It has nothing to do with the *Kryah*. It had nothing to do with creation. If anything it is actually dis-creation. The state of Death is the ultimate result of denying the Life Force. It was simply an experiment, the ultimate limitation."

Angelina's turns away from the Moth and returns her glance to don Lobos, reacting to his statement.

" An experiment, with the ultimate limitation? What does that mean? Everything dies…we all die…"

"You are eternal. Death is your myth. If you believe a myth long enough it becomes your reality. Originally we chose to explore this temporal reality. It was a concept of limitation that we have explored, and now the time for that experience is coming to a close. We are forever Beings. This knowledge is imprinted in our holographic and genetic coding, it is part of the *Kryah*. We long for our immortality as a natural state of being. It is part of the frustration of being here upon this plane of expression. We are always filled with this terrible longing. There is somehow a missing piece, a fullness that is lacking from our experience here. In our desperation to fill this emptiness within us, we have even tried to make death forever through many of our contemporary religions.

"When we speak of the original teachings, we are speaking of the original teachings of life which have been stolen from us. This has been an apocalyptic tragedy that has happened upon every continent to all peoples on a global level for over 2000 years. When something is stolen from the Mayan, or the Tibetans, or any People, it is a crime against the whole of humanity. The whole of humanity suffers.

"We have suffered the loss of our manuscripts, our codexes, and our temples of learning have been leveled and burned. All the codes to our beginnings and cosmic calculations about the Universe that present science has yet to even dream the potentials of, have been lost to humanity. They have even succeeded to a great degree in eliminating our ceremony, our rituals, which are Divine tools created to keep us awake and aware of our Spiritual realities. In many areas the people have suffered such severe oppression and genocide to their cultures that they have never recovered from the shock and terror they've experienced.

"We have gone through almost a total devastation of humanity's true Spirituality. The criminals who did these diabolical and insane acts eliminated the competitors that had different beliefs, through tyrannical conquest, murder, biological warfare and campaigns of genocide. There is however much of the ancient knowledge that has survived these holocausts. Most have either been carried off to some hidden chambers in the basement of some museum or church in Rome, or recently collected and put in depositories by the Japanese.

"Occasionally one is able to gain access to these depositories. There, one finds an amazing amount of these artifacts that hold the keys to humanity's origins, collected from lifetimes of conquests and looting. They are still being held by the same pirates who pillaged our sacred temples and sacred places. All being claimed by politically sanctioned cults that were dubbed orthodox religions by the ruling classes that created them.

"Reason it out! What great Master, male or female that ever appeared to us, ever started their own religion? Which one of them if any, did anything but realign us to the great truths of universal knowing? Were not the religions always started by the followers? Were not the wars fought over the differences of opinions between the different factions amongst those followers?

"This situation is still going on in this world. It is more a reality than those defending the charade would care for the media to show. So many discoveries go untold. People are killed if they find pieces of these ancient truths and try to bring attention to them. Why do you think we do not just lead open tours to these hidden places?

"Most people in our contemporary societies live in insulated bubbles. They are kept so busy running round the gerbil wheel that they care little to understand what is going on around them.   They are only focused on their reaction to the exterior environment, and not the cause of the conditions. Their lives are unconscious and robotic.

"They know nothing from their own personal experience. Most of their experiences they buy on video. It is always someone else's experience they accept as their own; always someone else's reporting on the state of reality to them; living through someone else's vision; evaluating, and creating their perceptions of realty with someone else's thoughts, through someone else's eyes. They are spoon fed synthetic facts about manufactured happenings through the television, to steer their thought processes. Thus they never even have a hope of truly knowing what the truth actually is.

"For the most part they are trapped in synthetic urban and sub-urban environments cut off totally from reality and the people outside.   They live in people farms, little more than fuel for a system that in the end devours them and their energy, casting them aside like toys that children get tired of. They are manipulated constantly through a program of financial tyranny and kept in the spin of chasing elusive dreams and images that have nothing to do with them in reality. It is as if they were on drugs and needed to get their fix at anyone's expense….. even their own life.

"Most people are caught in the consciousness based upon retail materialism. When the truth begins to surface about an issue, the media immediately unleashes their campaigns of misinformation through a vehicle that is totally controlled, and effects billions in a matter of hours.

"People in our advanced societies have become little more than puppets, hardly possessing enough energy to think. They come here to these places where we live to find something they lost. They come to these places where the last vestiges of the past glory of humanity's efforts to become more than mere food for the worms still remains. They are hoping to be saved from the inevitable conclusion to the game they are caught up in. The best they can hope for otherwise is to eventually retire in some convalescent home, only to die of boredom and cancer, because they do not possess the ability to have original thoughts. Without that they can no longer dream. Without dreams there is no life.

"Even that is coming to an ending. Everything is changing with this purification that has come. The purification is like a fever that is building slowly for the moment but in a few years it will encompass the whole of humanity. This world will soon find itself in the throws of a Spiritual fever, a Divine fever that will purge the corruption of consciousness forever from this plane."

Emergence of the Christos

"As the energy of the Christos, the Super-Consciousness that is our heritage, is flooding back into this plane, we are seeing our limitations and flaws in the synthetic world we have created. These religions that were created in a period of darkness and ignorance, out of fear by petty tyrants, are at best filtered views of a part of the whole. Their foundation is mostly built upon limited opinions. Their dogmas are built upon superstitions and interpretations of the Masters' original teachings, with personal opinions that lack the slightest degree of veracity.

"Humanity has been here for millions of years. We have a true knowledge here that has been proven and tested for thousands upon thousands of lifetimes. When you stray from the original teachings, and build organizations around the concept of hiding those eternal truths, it is like building castles in the sand. They will not stand the test of time.

"For their theories and concepts are unconscionable, unrealistic and lack any tangible substance to sustain them through the transition. As we speak these false temples that would worship death, and keep the knowledge of life from the people are crumbling at an alarming speed before the Creator's immortal eyes.

"Many of the concepts that these philosophies are built upon can be likened to a goldfish looking outside through its little world of glass, struggling to see through the distortion of its crystal prison, and philosophizing on conditions that exist beyond its constrained reality.....then declaring those theories to be uncontestable truths, for all reality.

"To know the truth of reality beyond its limited experience, the fish must learn to get out of the bowl and walk around and touch reality for itself. How can it? It has become Body-Mind Consciousness, instead of God-Consciousness. If you leave it in there long enough, even if you freed it to swim in the ocean, it would still live its entire existence within an area no bigger than the confines of it bowl.

"All truth can be tested. Truth should be tested. How else is one to take a hypothesis and declare it a constant? Truth does not need to hide, nor be defended. Only untruth need be protected. Truth is what truth IS, for no reason but to sustain the nature of itself. 'Do not question,' they would tell you. For one not to question is lunacy! That is such an unnatural state of Being that it is humorous to even consider. Yet tyrants would and have dictated just such a state of existence for thousands of years.

"They have stolen the truths of life and twisted the message of Spirit beyond recognition. In the fear induced madness of *Churchianity* they have taken ancient treasures and placed them in cages. They have collected our artifacts and ancient texts as if these things represented their own knowledge, and wisdom. But you know that is why they cannot understand them. They have the physical evidence that some-thing once existed, but not the cosmic knowledge of those who created them. They might as well have books without words.

"I used to think when I went to the Vatican, and the great museums in Europe, where so many of these things were held ...that it is so ironical they keep everything locked up in vaults, and behind cages. Just as they keep the truth out of reach from the human Spirit that seeks to gain the knowledge thereof, the works of Masters and Sages then become little more than ornamentation, with no living function in the fabric of reality. As if in a trance they walk around these ancient secrets of eternal life, while they themselves are dying from lack of knowledge.

"If you question anything these so called *Lords of Truth* lay before you, no matter how ridiculous their stories, or dare to ask why, or how, or who... you are shunned away, and outcast. You are fairly warned that someone or something will come and punish you. You will spend eternity in Hell for your act of daring to ask, that's if they themselves do not throw you in prison. That is not the *Will* of God. That is the tyrant speaking out of fear of discovery.

"Now who is practicing demonology, and witchcraft? Who is declaring spells, and conjuring condemnation and judgment? What would the *IS* behind everything in the Universe have to fear from you or I? What possible threat could we present to such a Force, such a Being?

"Everything that we do, every act that we do is for some afterlife that is promised to you if you follow the rules you are never given. And yet in the paradox of the next moment you are instructed to be afraid of that outcome. You are told that death is a monstrous horrible thing. There will be the wailing and the gnashing of teeth. Judgment will fall upon you and the darkness shall consume you. There is only one life, this life, then there is repentance ahead in some forever place. This will be a place of forever, where you will pay restitution for eternity for a crime you never committed, and for breaking rules that never existed.

"Only Life is forever, Angelina, never forget that. The body can be mutilated, you can hack it to pieces but you can never destroy the Life Force that is within it. That is an immutable, and immanent truth, and it is Universal Law. One can never destroy another person, ever, for their essence is immortal and forever. Death is like having a cold. It is a temporary stage of Beingness, a small doorway of experience on our journey to the whole of life that we pass through if we choose upon a very long journey. Death is an illusion but man's inhumanity to man, the induced suffering that humanity endures, well that is an entirely different matter."

Seeing Death as the Myth is is

" I understand what you are talking about." replies Angelina in a thoughtful manner. " Our reality is created by our reactions to the circumstances in our life……..and death is an illusion made to appear real to us. So if I know that my essence will never die, then I will not fear death, and therefore I will embrace life always."

" Yes, that is well said. Death….. the concept of death, has been perhaps the greatest of illusions we have suffered, for it has caught most of humanity in an iron grasp. Most people live to die, they do not live for living. They do not live for the Glory of God. They do not live for Joy. They live to fulfill the desires and dictates of the death cults they have come to call religions. Everyone has died in wars, everyone has been betrayed. Everyone has been broken hearted and has had their dreams thrashed…….everyone without exception. Yet still, they are alive in all of IT. *IT* is all a game…..a drama of the highest order. It is a game of virtual reality, and even we can get caught in the spider's web from time to time.

"The moment your life ebbs from your physical embodiment, you become pure essence of the God Force. Death is an unnatural state of Being. Death is *IT.* And as we discussed, *IT* does not exist. Yet, we all have the power to decree a state of mind for the purpose of experience. The realization must come from within. It must be born of the living Spirit itself. This reality is a place where we must make our own choices.

"The body itself is created by attitude, which is the possessor of the body. The *you* that thinks and feels in the silence behind your eyes, always lives. All the experiences of each lifetime are for the learning, for your mastery over the emotional reality. For once mastered, the emotions are part of the key to manifesting the realities of experience. Emotion is the language of Creator. Emotion and the passion of desire, are the keys to manifesting empowered thought into living expression upon the physical plane, as well as beyond the physical plane.

"Life is a dream, a grand dream. *IT* is a façade, a veil of perception laid upon the true reality. Life is simply our thoughts playing with matter. The manifestations are due to the laws of *Kryah.* Through that original knowledge we created a virtual reality game, but something went wrong with the program. If the present condition persists, *IT* can create emotional ties to this plane that can and will keep the Spirit, the eternal you, caught as if in a spider's web.

"Most get caught in that web and believe that the illusion is the reality. They are looking for answers in the illusion, which is the *IT*. Only by understanding what is the cause of the condition can we hope to change the condition."

Angelina's eyes light up, as she nervously delivers a string of poignant questions to don Lobos. "Why then is it so hard for us to live as God intended upon this plane? Why is it if we are part of God, do we hunger for human experience, which is so limited? Why, don Lobos, is it so hard to hold to the ideal? Despite what I believe within, I see such a hard time coming for everyone and myself because I am part of the drama. Are the fundamentalists correct, when they tell us that we are here to suffer?"

Don Lobos smiles and looks again to the heavens, "The stars are brilliant this evening and there is a luminescence of blue to all the heavenly light touches," he comments, taking time to sort his response to Angelina's question. He returns his gaze into her eyes, and speaks.

"My child, this is a dilemma, is it not? I have asked myself this same question so many times. I still wonder if it is all worth it, I have a human side, after all. Yet, I see the beauty in that as well. You see that side is so innocent in its perceptions, so child-like in its desires. Yet again, when I allow myself to see *through the eye of the Shaman*, when I remove myself from this circumstance of my body-mind existence, I can see it clearly.

"Everyone that is here upon this plane at this time has chosen perhaps the most arduous of human experiences for themselves. There are seven heavens, seven stars in the Pleiades, seven levels to the light spectrum, seven sacred fires, and this is the seventh generation, at least mine is. There are seven perceptions of consciousness upon this plane. At this moment we are experiencing the plane of demonstration….. learning from experience."

THE DIVINE CRIMINAL ... A REBEL WITH A CAUSE

"There are five types of Beings that manifest as humans on this planet. The Light Keepers consist of Light Conductors, with their Alpha and Beta Assistors. The Light Resistors have Light Destroyers, with their Alpha and Beta Distracters. Then there are Earth Bounders.

"We also have Doubles, and Counter Souls, those living in direct conflict with us, yet they are in every way the same as us, parallel existences some would call it. My dear it is a grand, grand fairytale.

"There are the many levels that comprise the individual players in the human drama! But that is a conversation for a later time. We shall concern ourselves with the matter of Spirit. It is difficult for our Spirit, which is formless, to exist within the confines of the density of our bodies and the physicality of this plane. It would be, even if conditions were in balance, never mind that they are so out of balance.

"As Spiritual Beings, we constantly struggle with the memory of being formless, and that becomes a desire that can overwhelm us and drive us homeward bound, or to insanity. At times, our experiences bring us discomfort and even a feeling of sadness. We come from *IS*. *IS*, is an unconditional reality. Here we are subject to a very dense consciousness filled with judgment. The nature of the people is one of condemning each other for differences, rather than praising for originality, and sovereignty of thought and perception. For the most part, society sadly bases its perceptions on *the appearance of*, rather than *the essence of*.

"If society considers it fashionable to look a certain way, believe a certain way and even to speak of Spirit in a certain way, thousands if not millions will bend to comply to the ideal. If one does not comply, one is usually shunned and thus not accepted. If this individualistic tendency carries over in the consciousness, if you dare to think differently, well you are really in a pickle. Then you could be dangerous to *the norm*. When one is different one is made an outcast and is turned out into the wilderness, to survive alone amongst the beasts of the night....hopefully to disappear and die off.

"If one does not fit the ideal of what is the commonly accepted norm, the temporal standard for beauty, then one is to be ridiculed. Yet, beauty is such a nebulous thing, is it not? Even amongst the different cultures of this world! Beauty is an enigma. It is an illusive concept that can only be realized in the eye of its beholder. Creator sees beauty in all things, for all things are an expression of Creator's dreams and desires.

"You, my dear Angelina, are a splendid example of the outcast, the rebel, the unique one. You are the apple in a line of plums, and therefore do not *fit* into the picture. The countless faces that pass you by each day are little more than slaves to that ideal. They live their lives struggling for someone else's approval. They will never become that ideal because they, in the end, will be but a mirror of what they believe is society's expectation. They will consider themselves less than the ideal, and therefore manifest the lessor but dominating thought of themselves. We must never compromise our true essence and character to please someone else's reality, never.

"You have a beauty within your Being that is very personal and a gift from Source Itself. Your radiance is your individual expression of Source. It is your uniqueness. Without that expression, you would become like a leaf at the mercy of the wind. Eventually you would cease to be, and your Spirit would wither and die.

"I assure you, beloved one, that when you leave this plane your difference shall become a glory, which shall bathe you in eternal light. Love the Self that exists within your heart and do not strive to please anyone at the expense of your Self, ever again. When you place yourself in a position of compromise you will lose every time.

"Compromise is an action that can only result in self-destruction, for you negate the ideal that you are and split yourself into fragments. You will never be sure of yourself in a fragmented existence. For one part of you will doubt the sensibility of the other. Doubt is the culture in which fear is born and the true Self-vision collapses within the confusion of lower consciousness. It is like a ship without sails, sailing endlessly, helpless into the oncoming elements.

"God, the Source of all things, will never forsake you, for you are a part of God.

God is within you and you are within God. You are the face, eyes, ears, hands, heart and Spirit of God. That is forever. Love yourself because of you, and for no other reason. That truly is being close to God. That is being as God IS. God, the Source of all, loves the *ISNESS* of being for the sake of the IS. God loves all that IS, for all that IS, is God's creation, and thus is an expression of Divine thought."

FALLING VICTIM TO KNOWING

"While in this reality we struggle with the freedom of choosing and directing thought. We are in a sense learning how to function as flesh in absolute freedom. All experiences we encounter are a direct result, or manifestation of our thoughts. We are the creators of this reality. The elements, the beasts of the Earth, the plants, trees, even the waters and the Spirits of the Earth, all respond to our thoughts and emotions. Our thoughts, without exception, create the nature of our reality.

"The conditions of this world and its people are a result of our thoughts as well. Some experiences are not so good, and some experiences are good. That also is a result of our thoughts. The result of thought is found both in the action as well as the non-action that we take. We can choose in this life to be the dancers or we can sit on the sidelines and let it be someone else's responsibility and pleasure.

"This is what ordinary people seem to choose above all things. A lot of people like to come to the party, but only a few are willing to prepare for it. The others, it seems, would rather criticize the efforts of those around them. It is often only a ploy to cast the vision off of themselves for their lack, and deflect the focus upon the human frailty of others.

"This is often a good sign that they are caught in patterns that they cannot break. They are victims of their knowing. They are still under the influence of their conditioning. The hard thing to understand about their dilemma is that they enjoy their life of being the victim. It justifies their inability to take action and be causal, thus masking their fears. Rather than dealing with fear, they prefer to cast criticisms and blame upon the world around them. They are trapped in being reactionary."

"Falling victim to knowing? Don Lobos, I don't understand," Angelina added with a hint of frustration, her beautiful face emanating her state of confusion.

"The pettiness of people can set us back if we allow it. This usually occurs when we are suffering from our own doubts and insecurities. Then we lose touch with Source, and the webs of *IT* start to spin around us, choking our Spirits. It is a trap that we have to be constantly aware of falling into. Monkey mind, that's all it is."

"How can we keep from getting lost in that trap? I mean, is it not when we are unaware of our actions that we fall victim to our own circumstance?" Angelina questioned.

"Ordinary people are not aware of Divine Law, nor would they ask the kinds of questions you ask. That in and of itself is an indication that you have substance and that the consciousness of Divine Awareness is running through your veins. Those who seek to do the work of the Light cannot hide behind the excuses of the simple folk. Nor can they lord it over the simple folk because they know. Yet another trial that the aspiring Light worker must contend with constantly is falling victim to knowing.

"The path of learning to the Master, is a road less often traveled. It can have its moments of appearing pointless, with endless frustration, yet eventually if we keep at it, the doors that we search for appear and begin to open for us. We are, in the beginning, and continually along path, subject to learning how to deal with all that we see. Remember, there is a constant swinging back and forth between the real Self, the Spiritually Aware Self, and the intellect of the Altered EGO......where we are simply Always *Edging God Out*. Some suffer from this condition their entire life without ever moving beyond it. So they come back again and again to get it right.

"What we see when we enter the world of man, are many inequities and contradictions in what they say and what they do. People appear to be overlays of conflicting images trying to project onto one screen.   It is like they package themselves as an individual motion picture production. The visual of them is that which they try to sell, and what others buy, and the reality of them is that which we have to struggle with in everyday relationship…..and the two can be as polar opposites.

"Relationships are the true test of being on an accelerated path to learning. The friction of relationship will quicken the pace, and intensify the education, the awakening. Although it is a challenge to be in relationship, it is also the shortest path home if we can navigate through the emotional and intellectual obstacle courses that relationships create for us. The challenge is well worth the effort.

"Living this experience in the dance of everyday mundane reality, we can easily become cynical in our perceptions, if we do not remain aware of our own center, and focus only upon our dilemmas. It is important to strive to create space during the day where we come back to our center, and ourselves. Meditation is an essential discipline. Remember the formula for getting through the illusion of our 5-D reality, *Discernment, Discretion, Detachment, Desire, and Discipline*. Proceeding ahead through the drama without balance is like speeding down an open highway on a motorcycle in the rain.

"When we are learning to willfully direct and filter our experiences through the heart, the residue of sifting everything through our intellect can leave hazy films that color our perceptions, and therefore effects the attitude we take on in response to a given situation.

"We can become morose, saddened, and eventually reach a point where we become a part of *the turning away* and get lost in the apathy. We can see conditions as a hopelessness that seems to fall upon all experience. The landscape around us then can easily become the land of broken dreams, as most seem to live behind the veil that shuts off all heart feelings and Divine perception.

"It is a frustrating time during this transition period. A time where we must constantly be on top of the tricks of the intellect which is always trying to rationalize to the heart the reasons for its conclusions, which are almost always relative and two dimensional.

"This is the point at which most neophytes give up and return to the ordinary world. There they find themselves at first very powerful and effectual because of their previous disciplines. However, it is only a temporary feeling. Once they have re-entered the world of the ordinary, they quickly find that they are once again subject to the reality of common man, who is lost in temporal values, and temporal perception.

Their energy drains and they are worse off than if they never opened their eyes. For the memory of Divinity will never leave them. Once the mind has been opened it remains open.

"We must understand that our Intellect, having been separated from the totality of what we are for so long, has become a part of the cause of the separation of us from the *IS*. The Intellect had to separate in order to make sense of the limited reality it was experiencing. It became the main tool of the *Image* to play control games with our God Head.

"Living in the *Image* creates the Altered Ego manifesting very early in us, an artificial *Image* of what we actually are. This *Image* or false perception of self is one of the *Images*' strategic points of applied pressure to manipulate our true Spirit Self. The *Image* is the Tyrant in the Box. Caught in limitation, it fears anything that might change its circumstance. For its existence is limitation. Everything beyond itself is unknown, and appears as a threat to its existence. After all it is the *Image*, not an essence. It is merely a concept. Thus it is without Life Force.

"If there appears to be a conflict brewing, and the Spirit Essence is going to make a move that decreases control by the *Image*, or perhaps might even fracture the perception of the *Image*, the *Image* creates feelings of doubt to induce fear. Its purpose is to undermine any sense of self-esteem. It is a proven strategy, worthiness issues are always good to throw up in front of your face, a show stopper that always works, doesn't it?

"We have become fractured due to this process of thinking, and living continuously in our separate realities. The present reality we are experiencing now is an initiation, a great initiation. We chose to participate in this game long ago, in another lifetime. We have all chosen to experience this reality of limitation so that we could understand *IT*. We could then gain control, master our emotional expression, and remain in contact with the Source within and thereby move on to the next part of our evolutionary experience. How else do we perfect the physical expression as a Divine form? Do you remember being an Angel?"

Angelina responds in amazement, "Do I remember being an Angel?"

"Yes, do you remember your beginnings?"

Angelina gazes off into the Heavens, calling to her the ancient memories of her soul. "Do I remember being an Angel?" she almost whispers. "I have always had dreams about being this magnificent essence. There were others there, and we were playing with Light." She struggles to see her own vision…" Yes there were these sounds, like tones, swirling around, and well… ….. I believe we were creating this world. I guess somehow I have always known deep inside, I was an Angel ……perhaps somewhere far off in my beginnings."

"Your understanding of the Divine Truth of your origins is quite contrary to that taught by most religions," don Lobos replies, his sparkling eyes revealing his delight. "And I commend you for your clarity and ability to step outside the present paradigms."

UNDERSTANDING OF DIVINE TRUTH… THE CIRCLE GAME

"Isn't the understanding of Divine Truth supposed to be the goal of all religions?" Angelina asks, with an almost satirical note in her voice.

Don Lobos sighs and pauses thoughtfully before he begins his reply. "Divinity was never meant to be misconstrued as it has; fed to the people as a philosophy, a dogma masquerading as holy, ambiguous words promising some mystical pathway to the stars. Divinity is a choice. Divinity is a conscious choice to exist, maintain, and express in certain octaves. This is the plane of action, nothing stands still, all life is inertia. Mastery is achieved by balance in the flow of life, not the stillness of it.

"Prophecy, is only a prediction. 'Based upon present circumstance, this is the projected potential outcome.' It was for those who had the gift of seeing to give fair warning of impending danger to prevent disaster from befalling the People. *The People,* Angelina, they are the ones that many of those who spout out new age teachings are forgetting these days. Their gift, is for… *the People!*

"In order for one to speak to *the People*, and to be understood by all the levels of Beings, one must understand *the People*. Yet one must not get lost in the conditions of confusion that most are subject to. To do so can be fatal, and always leaves our embodiment with a mortal wound. Which is why there is an ancient wisdom that every Master learns the art of '*being in this world but not of this world.*'

"As an aspiring Life Master one must endeavor to understand that the five levels of Being, as well as each personality type projected into the hologram, all play their parts through their character manifestations in the drama we call life. In that understanding, much of life and the behavior of the players is predictable.

"It is the dilemma of humanity to continually repeat its past over and over. They keep coming back upon the wheel of reincarnation for hundreds, even thousands of lifetimes to repeat the experience, until they remember. There is a grand blockage to that learning process to be sure. But a blockage can be removed if it is understood.

"We can transmute stagnation of Spirit with a little guidance and applied discipline. First however, we must become aware of another point of consciousness to move towards, a new point of reference that is born of experience. Our natural tendency to gravitate towards the unknown will then take its own course in the events life offers.

"How we become this elusive, Divine principle in living expression upon this plane, is a matter of remembering yourself. To overcome the levels of Beings and the entrapment into neuronal pathways that we have unconsciously created for the purpose of the drama, the brain in many ways is merely a program manufacturer. We are the program designers. Presently we are designing a program that brings us back to the Oneness of our totality.

"In order to progress one must become the Oneness that *IS* the *ALL*. The *ALL*, that you are. The *ALL*, that you express in one cohesive expression of the Divine Source upon this plane. One must stop dwelling in the fragmentation of self, and remember to hold on to the Oneness of what we are within, according to the original program. We are struggling to become whole Beings.

"That energy would translate into the universal healing we hear so many speaking about. As whole Beings we are the Living Temples of the Living God, embodiments of the Living Light. In our wholeness we are proper vessels through which the energy and the great plan of future reality shall unfold. In this way the Christ consciousness shall once again be embraced by Hu-manity, and the prophecy of the second coming shall in Divine Truth be realized.

"One must live fully in the moment of the *now*, for in that moment is where we find the foreverness and wholeness of our Being. In that moment is where we find the ability to become the expression of God I AM, manifested into animated action, which is applied reality.

"Many have tried, yet only a very few have achieved this state of Being with even partial success, because the force of duality within the consciousness of the collective is overwhelming. Then, in a moment, when the God I Am is achieved, you will no longer experience the pains of the illusion of separatism, of feeling apart from, nor will you dance in the arena of duality. You will in that single effort experience the Whole, being a part of the substance in the Sacred Hoop of Life. Once experienced, the Whole can never be forgotten, nor can the Self be forsaken ever again.

"Remember, Creator, God the Father, Hunab Ku, Wakan Tonka, whatever name we call the Great Spirit, is not one formulated thought or essence. That which we call God the Father is the truth that *IS* within all thoughts, the Source of all thoughts, and the passion behind all thoughts and is the Life Force within all essences. Live what you are, then in truth you shall perfect what you are, you will develop the ability to open the road to all that you can become. Your potentials are more limitless than the stars in the heavens, and your inner beauty just as rare.

"Once you can learn to listen to *you*, once you focus on *you* and begin being what you are, you are in connection to all that *IS*. By taking the action to accept the perfection of what you are, the *IS* of you shall be. Once this is mastered, all things therefrom shall manifest into the abundant river called reality, all in perfect realization.

"Thus you will become closer to God I AM, to the truth. First, however, you must learn to live your truth, to actually live it, creating a constant energy of the Christos in your life pattern. Once achieved, you automatically form the pathway you can follow into your foreverness and achieve the state of Divinity you seek.

"When you allow yourself to feel your own thoughts, to hear your own words emanating from those thoughts, you will find that you are able to correct all the confusion that has been placed inside your mind from lifetimes of listening to everyone else. You will then begin to live for the Self. You will no longer suffer the pangs of duality within your Being. You will no longer dwell in a state of self-doubt. You will have mastered the ability to still the mind. The stillness we all seek is being free from duality and inner conflict."

The Duality of Truth

"What of love, Don Lobos, what of love?" Angelina inquires with impassioned eagerness.

Without hesitation he responds, "Love is what you are. Love is all that you are. Love is the only constant reality. Love is Divinity. In this life we either choose to embrace love or turn away from love. If we look at the decisions we have made along the pathway to here, we will see where we have participated in this choosing all along that path.

"If we look at our life honestly and objectively we will see where we have made the choices. This we will see clearly, though perhaps painfully at first. For whatever reason we use to justify our actions, we have chosen either to be in the state of love, or we have joined in the turning away.

"We always maintain the ability to change any circumstance, that is our Divine heritage. The power that lies dormant within us is only a thought away. We are creators, after all. So few of us, however, hold onto our own truth. Instead, we tend to relent to everyone else's opinion. Most people are constantly altering their truth, compromising every step of their journey, surrendering truth, piece by piece until they are left one day wondering….. 'where did I begin to lose myself?'

"Most people are afraid to live what they know as truth, for what they know is greater than the truth they allow themselves to live. By taking the initiative to live, one would have to acknowledge that what they were living prior to that moment was, in essence, an illusion. Today we find that we are often criticized for living the truth. Truth and honor are considered by most as an unattainable ideal, and not realistic. The human consciousness has become so terribly corrupted, that it is difficult for many to see the Light. It is much easier to expound someone else's truth, to live the illusion - for then if you are wrong, well, it was their truth!"

"Yet," Angelina pauses to collect her thoughts, "Don Lobos, you yourself have said that there are many truths. That all IS truth.....that illusion to one may be the truth to another. How are we to know then, what truth *IS*?"

Don Lobos closes his eyes as if looking deep inside, "You know because you listen unto the God of your Being, and not the God of another's Being. You know because whenever you hear the voice, it is always pushing you towards your highest ideal.

"When you find yourself in doubt and confusion regarding any one thing, you always ask the God of your Being for the answer, the direction, or course of action to be taken. You will be answered. You may not listen, but you will always be answered. And more than often the answer does not come in words…" don Lobos continues with a sly knowing.

"If you find yourself lost in the energy of darkness, ask then from the God of your Being to be given the clarity, the vision and the power to move into the Light. Dictate not the conditions and accept the outcome. Always go to the God of your Being. This is the key. This will do much more than uttering chants and rhetorical prayers which are little more than the wailing of inner agony and turmoil that always reaffirms your position of lack. Utilize the God Force within your own Being, activate it. Call upon it. Give it recognition, and declare your position. Make it alive and part of your life."

"How then…" Angelina interjects, "How can we understand and know what force it is that causes us to follow blind patterns of behavior, which cause us to create

disharmony within our Being? What is it that causes us to sabotage our own pathway?
If we are *I Am*, then why do we seem so helpless to these invisible webs that cause us
to initiate self-destructive actions? Are we not more than the physical projection? Are
we not three fold Beings?"

"Yes, Angelina we are three fold Beings," he replies as he gently reassures her
by embracing her hand, pulling her full attention to his eyes. "However, we must come
to a point of self realization that we know this about ourselves without question, where
it becomes our second nature. Then we are free to move to the third attention, where
we learn to cross over into the higher octave, to accept our true essence and our
knowingness. It is the only way we can escape the webs of duality, which only leads
us to our self-destructive tendencies.

"We can transcend and transmute our imprisonment within the limited reality of
the first and second attention, by learning the Alchemical formula that will cause us to
act beyond the programming that we came into this life carrying, as well as what we
have been indoctrinated with in the present reality. This is the true Gift of *Kryah*."

BECOMING THE PROGRAMER

"We all come into this life with predestined programs that were created prior to
us entering the third dimensional plane. These programs or implants, if you will, cause
us to behave and respond in certain ways to our life's experience. They are designed
to awaken us to our original commitment to remembering, or the task we chose for
entering or reentering the third dimensional expression.

"*Kryah* is an understanding which has been lost to our present consciousness.
There are many reasons for this condition. The main point to the story is that at this
time we are being awakened to our cosmic heritage. The *Kryah* never could be
destroyed, so it is coming up like corn in a newly planted field. *Kryah* is an integral part
of the original creation and cannot be removed from the blueprint. Without it, life would
not be.

"The understandings we call *Kryah* were once taught freely in the mystery schools, to lift mankind to a higher degree of mastery of life here upon this plane. This knowledge can enable us to more deeply understand our true place in the cosmic reality, and adjust to our circumstance upon this physical plane. As we begin to wake up to our true essence, we begin to respond to the octaves of our origins, which is our signature frequency.

"This original programming, we are calling the signature frequency is something we received at the dawning of creation and it is personalized specifically to us. *Kryah* is what makes one snowflake different and unique from every other snowflake... Can you understand it that way? When memories of our wholeness begin to flood into our Being we must learn to deal with new awareness of the fractalization of our essence. This fractilizing has resulted from the impact of our manifesting in less than pure consciousness.

"We have to deal with the feeling of separation of our core, which is another result of entering into a density of third dimensional reality. The density of the consciousness, the awkwardness of moving in the body, and duality of thought, all add to the fractalizing of the Spirit upon this plane.

"Once this was not so, but we have degenerated as a spiritual projection upon this plane. We have only some distant memory of our past glories. That is perhaps why so many people keep coming to these ancient ruins. They are looking for a piece of themselves that they lost along the way.

"We can use the *Kryah* element for the healing of the physical. It allows for the spiritual to merge with the physical, and bring the elements back to a harmony and balance. In this state, disease cannot exist. As we utilize the *Kryah* element in the Universe, we are in the action of embracing tone, light, and sacred geometry. We can then correct the imbalances that have occurred to the DNA as a result of impact into third dimensional reality. The force of this impact in many instances has thrown our genetic codes and emotional thought implants out of balance, or even rendered them non-functional."

Angelina interrupts, " Don Lobos, what do you mean when you say codes and implants? I seem to lose you there. Are you talking about aliens who tampered with our original genetic coding?"

Don Lobos answers, " No, not aliens. I am talking of something beyond that. Something those aliens would like to know about our cosmic makeup. We are to many in this Universe a mystery, an enigma. We as the HU-man expression, are very unique and multi-faceted Beings throughout the whole of the cosmos.

"When we come into the physical plane we come with full knowledge of what our purpose is, and the why of our circumstance. We are not helpless victims of the wind. We all have contracts, with our higher selves. We have a specific mission and purpose to enter this reality. In many ways it is perhaps the most challenging plane of our experience.

"The movement of formless Spirit in the flesh is a very complex reality for one to master. The codes I speak of are the original signature programming we were created with while we were still in the mind of God, still in the Spirit, prior to our entry into any physical plane. It is like the programming of a dream.....a dream which dictates conditions and identity with self. A dream we find ourselves expressing through over and over again, with each lifetime, and each experience, on many dimensions simultaneously. Remember, I said we are multi-faceted Beings.

"Third dimensional expression is after all, a great experiment. We have encoded also within our complexity, the emotional memory of all our experiences. In the Soul, we can find the entire emotional record, from lifetime after lifetime since the dawning of our Being, in every form of expression we ever took on. There is a back-up file, which is locked within our cellular reality as well.

"The memory I speak of is literally impacted, stamped by our experiences, and the result of the actions we took. You see, it is all choice, our actions result in our outcome so the finality is always that we will *always* have free choice.

"We are always coming from the *Kryah*, the formless part of ourselves. There are those essences that have chosen to never leave the *Kryah*. They are called the

Kryon. These essences remains capable of conscious thought communication, but not having the ability or desire to merge with the physical. These Spirits are very ancient. Some would call them Angels, yet they are different. I do not believe anyone knows how old they are, or if they ever had a beginning in our memory of creation. Nor do I believe they themselves would care. The *Kryon* are surely a very ancient manifestation of the God Force, perhaps older than the Angels."

"Are they the ones that we refer to as the Grandfathers then?" Angelina inquires insightfully.

"No, not exactly. The term 'the Grandfathers' refers more to those from whom we directly descended into physical expression. We are connected physically as well as spiritually to the elders. We are connected spiritually but not physically to the Kryon. "

Angelina brushes the hair from her face as a soft breeze begins to blow. "So are you saying, we created our destiny in the *Kryah*......that our fate is immutable and predestined?" She asks.

"No, I am not saying that, for there is always free will...free choice.

" We are all connected to The All, through the *Kryah*. The *Kryah* is a Divine state of consciousness, which exists, within the spiritual reality of ourselves. It is in the void, in the realm of light from which all knowledge comes, and all of life's potentials are created by Source. Strangely enough, as we go within we find that the Universe gets bigger. And the external world gets smaller. When we learn to always come from within we become truly unlimited Beings.

"*Kryah* is, " He searches for a word..."an essence..... a dimension of holographic reality. It is a state of hyper dimensional consciousness. It is an *energy* of such high frequency that it can only be accessed on this plane by humans, through the heart. For only the heart is capable of such intensity until we learn to sustain our existence in a constant state of love. The concept of consciousness we call *the Mind,* would shatter in this octave. Only the human heart is capable of accessing this level of consciousness. Yet in its outward expression upon this plane the *Kryah* is simplistic. It is the gentle purifier, like the Breath of God."

"I think I understand it a little better now. I mean……the Breath of God….. " `frrrrrrrrrnnnnt' ……don Lobos lets one rip. Angelina gets a whiff and then bursts into a fit of uncontrollable laughter, her giggles light up the evening, causing her to break wind herself…… 'fffft'…….now don Lobos erupts into spontaneous laughter, his flow of thought instantly broken, as he holds his nose in an exaggerated gesture. They both fall down with tears in their eyes, caught in the energy of joyful hysterics.

"You see Angelina……. even Nagual's are human!"

Angelina begins to compose herself, her eyes still sparkling with amusement from the incident.

Don Lobos starts to address her, wiping a tear of laughter from his eye. "I want to thank you my dear, these intense conversations usually leave us so humorless, unless we associate with one like yourself, who has not forgotten Divine humor. What would the Gods be without the Goddess to interject her humor and make light of the day?"

Angelina gets an intense glow in her eyes as she becomes lost in the creation of her next question. "Don Lobos, how do we manifest? What does *Kryah* have to do with Alchemy? Where is the connection?"

"*Kryahgenetics* is the heart science. By going through the heart we enter upon the highway to the soul, so to speak. Through the understanding of the *Kryah* we can apply the theory behind the thought. Then we would call the process *Kryahgenetics*, all other sciences were born from *Kryah*. For *Kryah* is in many ways the mother to the understanding of physics. *Kryah's* song is the musical code for the mathematics of creation. The secrets of 3, 6 and 9. The cycles of 7, and the Fibonacci series 1, 2, 3, 5, 8, 13, 21, 34, 55, and so on. Although if you want to see this easily just look at the way the root of a tree grows, it is right there."

"But don Lobos," Angelina interjects perplexed, "What if one does not under-stand mathematics? What if one just sees the world with the eyes of a child, in complete innocence. What if one has not suffered the blows of life, and has therefore stopped to ponder the meaning of it? Is all innocence lost to us in our adultness? When we reach adulthood is our ability to go forward ended?"

"Angelina,"…… don Lobos interrupts her by catching a falling tear from her cheek with his fingertip.

A silence over takes the two of them as don Lobos seems to look into the emptiness of the night sky for an answer to an unanswerable dilemma.

"I think I see it now." Filled with inexplicable emotion don Lobos sits back and stares off into the evening sky in silence. Both of them are enveloped within a bluish light that seems to emanate from nowhere and yet everywhere at the same time. After what could be forever, or only a moment, he turns to Angelina. She is sitting with tears softly streaming down her cheek. Not sad, but caught perhaps in the flow of the absurd paradox of the human drama.

"Angelina, you remind me of the truth we learn through relationships. You also touch my heart, bringing me once again in contact with the humanity that I am. You are correct, more correct than perhaps you know. What we experience here is a folly, this is true. But as Masters we struggle to make our existence a controlled folly. Controlled by our knowingness, of what we are and why we are here. No matter how hard we try, that control is always slightly out of reach. I believe that is the condition here. Or else we would grow too content and there would be no meaning for this experience any longer.

" In the recalling of the story, we often forget the mystery and the magical qualities of the Source from which the story springs forth. That innocence is so important for us to remember, so that each moment is a first moment. The innocence, that is God in flow. It is the emerald that touches each leaf, the red in the petal of the rose that gives us our perception of color. It is the song of the birds, without which we would only perceive the emptiness of silence. It is life celebrating itself.

"We all need each other. What a shallow world this would be if we could only hear our own voice. The story of what we are must be heard by another, to be appreciated even by ourselves. Without the relationship of male and female there is only one eye that sees, and no one to tell of that perceiving."

" My wonderful, dear don Lobos, it is quite all right to be human. After all, is it not you who taught us that to be the Master we must become fully hu-man.... more than 100% human. For in experiencing those feelings without limitation, we would birth the new consciousness of HU-Manity! Is that not the reason for the friction we endure? You said that we allow the friction freely so that our feelings are on fire."

Still filled with emotion, don Lobos takes her hands into his own. Their eyes touch like lover's fingers in the magic of the night, reaching for those parts of the soul that only two connected people could know between each other.......a knowingness earned after lifetimes of being in each other's innocence and exploring the secrets of both hearts.

" My dearest Angelina. You are a most remarkable woman. How you teach me with so few words, the wisdom of Mother's love. How the Mother gifts her daughters with abundance of compassion. Each woman is an expression of her Divine femininity. Each being another facet of the Mother herself. Through you, she always shows me the endless sea of creativity woman has when looking at things. All of you are unique....... yet all of you are mystically in many ways, one woman.

"Ahh, so much wisdom delivered with such simplistic accuracy. Perhaps *Kryah* is the feminine understanding of the Universe. Perhaps in our ponderances, we have only rediscovered what was taken away from us so that we might not complete the puzzle. The love that might exist between two people, man and woman, in its simplistic, uncorrupted form, without agenda, is indeed the fifth element.

"Love is the very element that can lift us to Divinity — For within the mysterious essence of Love we can access a sense of eternal knowingness. Without this element, without the drama of relationship, which is our mirrored self-reflecting back to us, we can easily slip into one-dimensional reasoning. Life quickly gets flat and we lose our passion for living. The male female relationship is the physical symbolism of Christ Consciousness, the essence of the Christed Soul, which has achieved the balance of the male and female energies. This is the purest essence of Christ Consciousness. If we are to progress from our present dilemma, we must stop the conflict between the genders, both externally and internally. We are I believe, in this experience learning to merge as one, once again.

"Surely life becomes the passionate dream it was intended to be, when we again merge and become the whole of the dream. Without the passion we simply exist, searching for an eternity for the piece that is missing.

"Relationship accelerates our growth. We have through relationship, the oppor
tunity to experience all aspects of our self. Without the balance of male and female one cannot hope to master this game we call living. To attempt to do so, is like a bird trying to fly with only one wing.

Angelina is stilled by don Lobos's words. She slips into silent contemplation for a moment, seemingly to be gathering her thoughts. She then renders a question to don Lobos with piercing accuracy.

"If we could do that don Lobos, if we could heal the war between the sexes....can you imagine what we would find? Could it be that the war between the sexes is somehow preoccupying us, and keeping us from realizing something else that is going on? Perhaps ......I know this sounds crazy, but is it possible that this wart between the genders was an imposed condition that is not entirely natural? Are we somehow perhaps being manipulated, directed into this cycle of friction that serves absolutely no greater purpose than to keep us divided from our other Self?"

"Yes Angelina, your assessment and interpretation is correct!" don Lobos asserts seeing that she is struggling, and yet right at the point of Self realization...."But to understand the answer to your questions requires that you take the next step.   You must come to terms with your own conflict, and the war within yourself.

There is much of the ancient knowledge that I have not yet shared with you. There are certain events that are occurring at this time, which cannot be averted. You might say that the wheels have already been put into motion by our actions as a living, expressing, consciousness, that are changing the nature of our reality. We, and by that I mean the human race, acting as a holistic consciousness, have caused certain energies to be unleashed which now have a life of their own.

You will have to do some serious thinking and make your commitment to the path of the initiate, if you choose to truly understand and learn to Master the *Kryah*. For what I speak of has to do with what I call, the days of destiny. We have altered reality far more than we ever thought would be possible, even by the ancients. We have played with technology and distorted the threads of reality. Yet, how could we have ever known about this time coming, without the ancient knowledge intact? It seemed hopeless that we would ever remember who and what we are, or that we would realize this incredible transition was coming. There was concern that we would ever have the opportunity to transform into the dream that we are........or......? Don Lobos falls into a silence which penetrates the night air, making everything perfectly still. He looks out at the evening sky almost as if he were searching for something that he might read in the stars. As he stares off into the void of the night, it is almost as if for a moment, he were detached from everything, including Angelina.

" Or what don Lobos?" Angelina's voice permeates the thick stillness that is emanating from don Lobos. Although he holds within himself the emotions of whatever he is thinking, she can feel the ominous vision that must be appearing in his mind.

" Or else my dear Angelina, many will create their own hells. They will not be able to tear themselves away from the patterns of illusion, they will fall victim to fear, and will create the nature of their nightmare..... rather than the Light that they are.

"You see Angelina, life is so intricately delicate. The fabric of the dream is so incredibly fragile, like the desert prairies, where we can see the trail of one who set out upon their journey 100 years ago, a trail that still remains embossed upon the frail ground....... long after the footprints have vanished ..... along with the ones who made them."

Angelina leans against the little wall that surrounds the garden, disquieted she takes her next step, almost as if she knew that the evening was leading her to this destination all along........

"Don Lobos.......days of destiny....... if I had not spent the time with you that I have, the sound of those words alone might frighten me. But, I understand more clearly now. I see farther than I once could, or cared to. I believe I am prepared to follow my own path regardless of what it might appear that I am losing, or leaving behind. You know it's a funny thing, but I have found out this much..... everything is always changing. We are always moving from one place to another, changing jobs, and changing partners. We can get lost in that, or we can focus on the miracle of it all."

Now it is Angelina turn to get reclusive and drift off to her own secret place. Don Lobos turns to her with an element of curiosity upon his face.

" Miracle?" He asks......

"Yes the Miracle! We keep pasting our lives back together through the exultation and calamity. We so often feel that everything is lost and there is no hope of resurrection from the collapse of our broken dreams. Throughout all our dancing, playing, and crying......we are recreating ourselves over and over, and over...so that we often forget the Miracle. The miracle is, that there is always a resource from which we can pull this magical substance.....thus allowing us to reweave the dream anew. It is always there, and never runs out of itself, no matter how many seek its nurturing.......this is the *Kryah,* isn't it don Lobos? The Miracle I speak of is the *Kryah."*

Don Lobos is glowing, with the grin of a true Cheshire cat. "Yes that is the *Kryah.* The *Kryah* is the source from which we weave our dreams. It is the magic of creation. Without *Kryah,* nothing could be..... for there would be nothing to draw upon to spin the fabric of life. For it all begins with our desire to express."

They both simultaneously sigh, and then laugh amusingly to themselves.

"Well," Angelina exclaimed excitedly. "When do we get started? I have a lot to learn...and can be impatient when I feel I'm on the edge of Spiritual awakenings."

"Tomorrow, we can begin tomorrow," replies don Lobos. " I have a friend, she is a very old friend, and she is a woman of great insight and extraordinary power. I believe that it is time for the two of you to meet. It would take a few days out of our lives so everything else will have to go on hold.......then again time is a no thing, correct?!"

There is a joyous almost childlike spontaneity between them. Angelina is exuberant and begins talking to herself as she starts making plans for the journey.

"What should I wear? Are we going on one of those journeys into the middle of nowhere?
....No.... she must have a house... . I can see the house....

" Who is this woman you are brining me to?"   She blurts out.....resurfacing from her self dialogue.

" She is a magnificent accident," replies don Lobos.

" Accident? What do you mean." Angelina asks, as she is already halfway down the garden path to her casita, to gather her things......

" She is a perfect Being.....She is like a diamond. She is also a Nagual. "

" Isn't it amazing that just a few months ago I believed that Naguals were only people one read about in books. How wonderously strange and magical life is.......I will see you at first light."

"At first light!" responds don Lobos.

He becomes aware of the silence that seems to fill the air as Angelina's presence dissolves. Thinking to himself he engages in a deep conversation. "Oh Lobos, you have done it now. Angelina will never be the same. You are taking on another initiate.

"Yes, but this one will be different. Angelina can make it all the way, she has perseverance.....and she is going to need that quality."

Don Lobos blows out the candles and walks down the pathway through the garden toward his house. The sound of night birds again begins to fill the crisp air. He looks up once more at the moon, which is sitting in an almost perfect circle of branches, beaming her phosphorescence upon him, and lighting the path ahead.

He thinks about his own life, and the many dramas and magical experiences he has had…… the wonderment of knowing made his, a life of fullness. Feelings of gratitude fill his heart, as he heads off into the night merging into a cloak of invisiblity in the forest..

TO BE CONTINUED...

Authors Note:
You will have to decide for yourself if don Lobos is real or fictional. I will say this much, to some he is both, to others……. well, those are the ones who have forgotten how to dream, and feel the magic of the night. The ones who's lives have become very flat. So as you go along life's journey, take a good look at yourself, and be sure not to leave any spot unviewed. For that just may be the spot where in your life as you walk away from the tales of don Lobos and begin to make hard reality out of your external life….. that is the day that he just may show up on your doorstep. You might also meet him at the supermarket, or while walking alone one day in the woods…..*he tends to show up where he is most needed!*

I shall continue in this series with five tales about the Nagual, for that is my personal contract with destiny. The time has come that we, as a species, are merging with a very different type of reality. I believe there are many who will benefit from the lessons of don Lobos, as his amazing story unfolds.

There is a great amount of knowledge that is available to mankind if they have the courage to step outside of their limitation and be the wholeness of what they are. Knowledge which has been hidden for many, many generations is now being presented to us once again.

Circumstances are making themselves know to some of us now, that the *Emergence of the Fifth World* is already occurring. There is more to prophecy and myth than is often comprehended by an uncultivated mind, for truth has always been right in front of us. This is how it survived the holocaust that swept our planet and destroyed centuries of accumulated knowledge. There are stories that the ancient ones foretold of in their prophecies and legends, that speak of another reality we would one day inherit..... when we would come to know *the end of time.*

As we walk together into our new tomorrows, perhaps these pages and the subsequent stories of the Nagual will rekindle the fires of awareness within you, the fires that have somehow grown a little cold. Perhaps in your struggle between the reality born of reason, and the struggle of keeping the creativity of the God-Child that plays within, there is still enough of the elements of magic that will entice you to leap across the abyss of limitation that now imprisons you.....and find the freedom of the Master within.

For that end I have agreed to share at this time these poignant words about the Miracle called *Kryah*. We are headed towards some incredible changes, and there is not one of you out there reading this book, that does not long for the memory of what you are. There is not one of you who has ever given up on the possibility that perhaps, once again you will remember how to dream, or wondered if you could take the next step, as Angelina is about to.

For what I have received from don Lobos, there can be no repayment, only the continued commitment to myself that I will walk the pathway of heart, I am already manifesting my destiny. For I am again as free as the wind, free to be the dreamer who dreams the dream..... fully conscious of my power. I hope you do as well. For from this point of power, we shall all meet the days of destiny that don Lobos speaks of.

Currently there is a sequel planned dealing with the adventures of don Lobos which will be release all things allowing during 2004

THE PRINCIPLES OF KRYAH

THE EMERGENCE OF THE FIFTH WORLD

It has been said, "With the emergence of the Fifth World, even the flowers that lie as seeds deep within the darkness of the Earth, shall push their way through the surface of the Earth to reach the light that comes forth on the day of Emergence. The day of the Awakening, the day of Destiny."

It is the inalienable right of every human Being to participate in the Emergence of this day into the planes of consciousness. The day when our Spirit Self and our physical self are united once again.   Almost every culture on Earth has prophesied that the day of Light will arrive with the millennium. The day when mankind becomes Hu-man, or man-kind Divine. In this manner we shall walk forth from the winter of our experience here on the Earth plane. The cycles of darkness shall slowly pass away, and the Light of Love shall prevail into forever. Thus, we will be able to know and access the Christos within us all, both individually and collectively as a People. The Day of Emergence is at hand, as we rise from the vibratory reality of the Third, to pass through the Fourth and enter the Fifth World.

Five is the number of man. Five represents the world of man, and five are the characters man plays in the drama. There are five aspects to our personality. The senses of the beast within are five, which shall transform into twelve. The five pointed star is their shield, the star of man. Mankind will achieve *Hu*-man-ity when the souls of man are able to join their masculine and feminine aspects, learning to make the one from the two. In that moment the road home will be opened to you fully and the mysteries of the Universe shall unfold as if by magic.

It should, as we approach this grand emergence be understood that Universal Law is older than time itself, and in actuality exists beyond our concept of time. Through our understanding and use of the Universal Laws we literally created time as we now experience it. Time of itself has no motion, it is the stillness in the river of thought. Time only holds the concept of itself, and has not texture till we as the artists, touch it with our light of creation. For we are the motion in the mind of God. We are the energy of God feeling Itself, as God plays out all Its potentials throughout the mad diversity of the Hu-man drama.   We are the co-creators in a grand experiment in which we created time as a concept of itself. This can be difficult to grasp at first, but as the process of understanding true Alchemy through the breath of Kryah that evolves within you, it will become second nature.

So persevere, and allow yourself to absorb the information presented here without judgment. The truth will stay with you, equal to the level of your capacity to absorb knowledge. This book will not grow old, and it will never cease to give you new information with each continued reading.

Many wonderful things are available to us through the understanding of the *Kryah*. You are invited to understand the principles of this Divine knowledge. The gift of *Kryah* will enhance your life, and bring you in touch with the beauty that is unfolding every moment all around you. When you can stand in the field and hear the color of the flowers being released to the morning Sun, when you can hear them growing under the light of the moon, you will begin to understand the true wonder of this place we call Mother Earth, as well as the deeper meaning to being HU-man. The mysteries of who you are, and why you are, will begin to become your knowing.

The wisdom of the *Kryah* will not be comprehended by those who would attempt to understand its secrets but do not approach *Kryah* with open heart. *Kryah* is like Divine Law, it can be followed but never controlled. Nor will the intellect alone be able to open the keys to *Kryah*. This is a journey of heart, of the Hu-man dream as it has been from the beginnings.   It is a journey that began long ago. Longer than memory will allow...... once upon a time in the void when the thought of the possibility of having two aspects of the Divine Self was first contemplated.

As the first God Woman looked into the Spirit of the God Man, and the concept of eyes was conceived so that they could capture the sheer beauty of each other's light, the sense of physicality was born that they might feel the wonderment of each other. Locked forever in an embrace they dreamt of being with each other. They dreamed of the worlds they could create together. In that magical moment the dream of Hu-manity was conceived, we are the children of that dream. The hope and the outcome of that dream, is now in our hands and in our hearts. *Kryah* is the key to under-standing Alchemy. Alchemy is the final necessity to understand, to truly transform ourselves into a forever expression of the original Divine Union.

Living in an existence where we are separated from our Spirituality, we slowly begin to lose our ability to communicate. We no longer interact with playfulness, losing our spontaneity and are then reduced to mere robotic modes of predictable animal behavior. Here, we regress to a consciousness of survival mode, becoming creatures without dreams. After awhile we can no longer see the Divine as being humanly attainable. Nor do we see ourselves as graceful expressions of that reality. Without dreams, Human Beings wither and die. Dreams are to our consciousness what the rain is to the land. As a humanity we are suffering a drought.

Only our *Will* can change the outcome. We have to choose life with every action we take, and every word we speak. There is a choice before us. We can stay on the old road, stuck in judgment, anger, fear and greed, and slowly die off like the dinosaur, or we can choose the path of compassion. We will all come face to face with this choice sooner or later. Compassion is where we make the choice, as well as learn the healing power of forgiveness, and the miracle of love. For L O V E is the only reason we are here at all. We are the Masters of our destinies. For what we think, so shall it be!

IS Vs. *IT*

There is a story of IS and IT. It is a long story of when Spirit became matter. It is a creation story. For our purposes here I will render a simplified version. IS, is the state of Creator. Creator IS for no other reason than being I AM THAT I AM. There IS not time in the higher realities. Everything IS in the state of ISNESS. There IS not polarity in the higher dimensions. Everything just IS. There IS no more than or less than.......higher or lower, good or bad. Source simply IS. Spirit comes from IS. When Spirit elected to experience matter, a way to merge with matter had to be conceived. So the IT was formed. Laws were created for the IT so that Spirit could express through an IT. ..... Spirit has no form, yet it IS the essence within all forms. Why was this?

When Spirit creates an IT to express through, the IT also must have an IT to express within, because IT cannot express without form. Therefore, we are caught in the physical expression, a constant struggle of IS to keep the IT from being corrupted. This would be like creating software for Spirit. Unless the program is pure we are always having to deal with corruption, and the program, (the IT) sometimes must be reloaded, or removed in order for the IS to express properly.

Mind riddle….. In purist concept, from the aspect of Divine reasoning, IS always IS, but IT is not always in alignment with IS, in other words IT isn't, there is only IS…….

In our struggles to attain access to our higher selves upon this plane, we are attempting to achieve the constant within the C h r **I S** t, the *IS*. We will eventually come to understand that the *IS*, peruses itself with constant friction to create the *IT*. Hence the term the dance of life.   The *IT,* is the canvas upon which we play out our human drama. The problem therefore, is in creating the proper nature of the *IT*, learning to give *IT* proper guidelines for developing, to meet the needs of our ever changing *IS*. So whatever we create must be based upon Divine Laws of metaphysics, and be allowed to be elastic enough so that it does not become ridged and fixed. For by our very nature we will destroy any cage we construct for ourselves. We are free Spirits, and that part of us which is one with Creator shall not be corrupted, and that fact truly IS immutable.

This is why the Alchemical process of applying the principles of *Kryah* through *Kryahgenetics* can be a vital tool for us during this time of transition. Through its understanding, we can thus achieve Christ consciousness upon the third dimensional plane of reality. It is our destiny. *Kryahgenetics* is the vehicle by which we can achieve the art of self-transformation.

Along the pathway of self-transformation, we often find that we reach certain plateaus in our understanding. Places where we feel like nothing is happening, and there is a stillness in our achievements. We have reached a place of dead space. It is our instinct to be rebellious that we are dealing with. We love to create the friction. For the friction allows us the chance to feel ourselves, and know we are alive. We love to feel who we are.

These plateaus are necessary for us to achieve mastery over our knowledge, where we apply our teachings to everyday existence.   The stillness is where we gain the opportunity of experience, where our teachings go beyond being simply a philosophy, and become our truth. Teachings are never more than potential reality and they are never truths until they are experienced, and incorporated into life. Then the philosophy changes into manifested destiny.

One must consume what they have learned, and knowledge must then be applied into our everyday action, and thought. Until the new reality is manifested within the pattern of our everyday life and becomes integrated, the teachings remain merely a philosophy of potential reality. A potential, is not absolute..... it is not yet a truth. Thought possesses the potential to become truth only when tempered by experience.

Achievement therefore, is our recognition of the sense of progressing (*Action*), but It takes time. It takes time for the physical body mass to untangle itself from the time space continuum and become motion or action. Manifestation comes from moving thought through the veil of physicality. Moving mass through physicality with conscious thought is like trying to run through Jell-O. It is slow and arduous. This is the old way. It is cumbersome, and can take lifetimes of experiences without guaranteed results. So in that sense we are all gamblers.

As human Beings we have arrived at a place in our progressive evolutionary experience, where *time*, by its own nature, is dissolving. Our experiment with limitation is coming to a conclusion. This could be considered *the Winds of Change. .....the Quickening, the Purification*. There is a paradox to this however, in that *Time* being realized as *a no thing*, soon becomes *a very real something*, an *IT,* that we are constantly running out of. *IT* is an illusion you can never hold on to. We are always losing *IT*. The experience of time no longer serves the purpose it once held in our evolutionary experience. We are in fact, approaching *the end of time*, as an experience in limitation. This eventual destination in the evolution of consciousness has been prophesied in every culture.

"Till the end of time." How often have you heard that phrase? In how many sacred writings, and how many books? The nature and outcome of prophecy is dictated by the octave of thought, or the ability of one to move thought into physical manifestation upon this plane. We can either wait, and do nothing, watching from the sidelines until the prophecy occurs, or we can make the conscious choice to be in the moment and take action to either change, or bring on the foreseeable outcome.

This entire reality is the sum of our experiences upon this plane and is the direct result of our thought processes. Our thought processes are dictated by our nature, or personality, and the nature or personality of humanity as a whole. Thus far, it has been a process of repeating history over and over again. There is no human upon this plane that has been excluded from this experience. Some however, have gone beyond this merry-go-round of recycled ignorance to become those who we refer to as Masters.

We are running out of the time experience….. the very thing that affirms time as being an *IT*. We are repeating our past patterns of consciousness in a constant manifestation of the collective thought process, and living through a continual recycling of situations, in order that we might experience our own patterns so that we could have the opportunity to change them; reliving the relationship game; breaking up and dealing with our codependency issues; gathering material wealth and releasing it; creating dysfunctional families that we then must escape from; moving from one location to the next; changing our jobs, houses and partners until we find out that what we really need to do is change the patterns of our lives. It may be necessary to find a new adventure and a new career, one that is in harmony with the real Self, our real desires, our real dreams. But first we have to own who and what we are. We must remember who we are. So do you understand the meaning of the term "to know God, is to know yourself," a little better now?

How then can one escape the trap of limited, repeated experience? How do we break the patterns of self-destruction? How do we break away from this wheel of re-incarnation, the circle game? How do we become Masters of our own individual destinies, instead of the victims of our repeated failures, and imperfections manifested by our corrupted thought patterns? By first realizing that through the chaos, if we can activate our third attention we will see that we are at a turning point, a place in the dream where consciousness can be rebirthed. It's like moving from one circumstance in the dream to the next......where you are one place, surrounded by certain people, and then in the next moment the entire fabric and story line of the dream changes. Have you ever had that experience?

Life does not have to be a repeated cycle of pain and suffering, corruption and tyranny. That is all just so much recycled ignorance, *the merry-go -round of the dead.* We have the ability to change our circumstance. We all possess the knowledge of self-transformation within our cellular structures, hidden within the coding of our DNA. *Kryah* is the key to understanding the DNA coding, as well as our *holographic signature frequencies. Kryah,* enables us to ignite the DNA encoding, setting free the original signature frequencies, allowing us to become free of the programming of the altered EGO. Thus taking us to where Source placed them so long ago, hidden within the very mathematics of our Being, the sacred geometry of the body itself. Often we see *Kryah* referred to by the ancients when they speak of our sacred cosmic proportions, literally speaking about the Divine aspects of the body, and how it can be used as a vehicle for this miracle we call the God-Force.

This knowledge has been hidden within the heart chakra, wherein lies the secret of the frequencies we have come to call the Holy Grail. The Holy Grail that Arthur looked for, was never the physical object, it was the Divine principle, lost. The secrets of self-transformation lie within our ability to initiate the transformation within our own consciousness. It is an Alchemical process that can be released through mastering our emotions. In this time many are struggling to learn how to expand their consciousness beyond the present restraints of limited mind, to merge once again with unlimited thought..... Divine thought.

In order for us to realize a true internal awakening, it must be achieved through life experience. Only through emotional experience can we cause the gateway of limited mind to fly open and release us to realize true awakening. This is why for eons the practices of the ancient schools always brought their initiates through the rite of initiation. Through the rite of initiation, we are given the opportunity to experience a reality of greater vibration than the reality we have come from. Today we are experiencing a global initiation where everyone can and is participating. Therefore we must become courageous enough to open our hearts, and minds to the possibility of *new thought.*

New thought has no boundaries except what we dictate through pre-determined belief patterns. Thought is neither trapped within, nor generating from, the limitation of our past experiences. The students of *Kryah*, will become the mystics of tomorrow. They will represent the living alchemy through which the whole of the present humanity may enter new vistas *of*

Hu-man realities......realities where we awaken to the God Force that *IS* within us all.

To create the manifestations of our thoughts or dreams is the Divine gift of Source to humanity. It is part of what makes our species so unique throughout all the cosmos. It is the inalienable right of every soul embodied in Hu-man form to manifest our thought processes into physical and conscious realization. This is to glorify Source, the Father-Mother principle we refer to as God. Events are occurring at this time to bring us to a face to face confrontation with our imbalances so we can deal with them once and for all and be free of them. We are being pushed to open to our clairvoyant abilities, and allow them to express in their own unique manner. We are learning to recognize these qualities in ourselves, as well as in others. We are being pressed to express all we can be in the Oneness of the Divine Principle becoming the God/Goddess of our Being without reservation and restraint.

We have our origins in the ethers of the great void, from which all things potentially arise, yet no thing materially exists. All potential things that make substance and consciousness can be designed and bent by thought and *Will*, to be pulled into the gravity of thought. If you can become in consciousness pure thought, without condition, in the state of Divine observation and love, you would then become that thought in its conception, as well as its application.

In that moment, you would become the new symphony of Life Source from which the *IT* would derive its new energy and pattern. In essence, you would create a new reality of unlimited potentiality, a new state of *ISNESS*. That is the wonderment of understanding the *Kryah*!

The Spell of Mortality

There lies deep within each of us a cosmic flaw. It is the foundation of all our fears. In this teaching, we shall unveil this hoax which we identify as *the Spell of Mortality*. We, who were once the Divine Archangels of God, find ourselves believing (for reasons unknown) that we have lost our immortality. This fear has caused the Great Archangels of God to dwell for what seems an eternity, within the confines of limited existence.

In our memories, there is the tale of a time when a veil of darkness fell over Man-kind. Women surrendered their right to their connection to the Divine Goddess and God-Men became tyrants, who were reduced to monkey mind reality, performing in the three-ring circus of procreation, pain, and power.   Kings no longer ruled by initiation into the Light, and were no longer valued for their wisdom attained through experience, but ruled by physical might and the manipulations of fear, to control their Kingdoms. A dreadful time…… for the Goddess and her Priestesses were driven out of every land and magic became something only spoken about in fairytales. Eventually, we were left to believe that Dreams as well as the Dreamers themselves were something to fear, rather than something to cherish.

The social order of the day that is presently dictating the conditions in which exists the reality of mankind, is regressive and discourages Spirituality for the most part. It dismisses it like an unruly child, asking of us to be silent, and unseen. As we continue to suffer its dictates, we watch as our children, and ourselves slowly become little more than slaves to a synthetic social order……an order that persists in maintaining a synthesized environment to perpetuate the illusion of itself.

Without discernment in our impassioned quest to reconnect to Spirit, we are too willingly drawn to the charlatan, and fortuneteller. Humanity will seek its true state of Being, as the salmon must return to its place of birth to be reborn. Without knowledge of how to access our true Spiritual natures, we are doomed to limited existence. We are little more than prisoners of *the Spell of Mortality*.

We have become trapped in a form of reality, which is far removed from our true natures. Life has in many ways become alien to our nature, people feel detached and disconnected, abandoned and unloved. There is little sense of community and everyone is a stranger unto us. No wonder everyone is depressed!

Alchemy is one of the oldest sciences of higher knowledge existing upon this plane of reality. *Kryah* is the mother principle of *Alchemy*. It was known and commonly exercised by our ancestors on a global level, even a galactic level. For once, we Hu-mans also traversed the stars. We were travelers of the Light, which the surviving Mayan and Inca records will affirm. We were, of course, in their time still connected to our memories of coming to this plane from the stars. In the European cultures from the temples of Solomon to Stonehenge, Alchemy was a driving force in the accomplishments and aspirations of Hu-manity, which until recently were regarded as being Myth and legend.

Somehow there was a break in our evolutionary path due to some un-remembered circumstance. Something happened that caused us to embrace a regressive rather than progressive state of consciousness. The wisdom schools were lost to us for an extended period of time. Even the star knowledge became lost and inaccessible to our memory. We have become what I have referred to so often as *Gods in Amnesia.*

There remains a wealth of information that is still held by peoples indigenous to Mother Earth, especially here, in the Western Hemisphere of our globe. We have casually come to term them in the America's, as the "*Indians.*" This is an imposed terminology having little to do with the present day descendants, nor the ancient glorious civilizations that once flourished here from Alaska to the Amazon, and Peru.

Shamans can be found throughout all indigenous cultures. Shamans are unlimited. The term Shaman is not confined to just male or just female. The Shaman understands the powers of mind and is an experienced journeyer in the worlds between the blinking of our eyes. As both male and female they have always been aware of another reality just beyond the ordinary. In a very true sense they are *Voyagers of the Light*, exploring another reality, just slightly off set from this one It is thus termed a separate reality. This reality is perceived only by the naturally empathic through their clairvoyant abilities and accessed only by the purest of hearts.

The knowledge of this extraordinary level of reality has been absent from the consciousness of the masses for many generations. The knowledge has remained protected from the onslaught of organized religions, as their crime lords spread fear and tyranny across the globe like a plague in this war of light and darkness, *a war of the Angels.* Over the last two thousand years organized religion has almost successfully crushed the Spirit of mankind. Now, the seasons of change are once again upon us. These structures of oppression and debauchery are passing. Their time is at hand. There is a rumbling throughout the forest, the remote villages of China, again in England and Ireland and from the mountaintops of Peru to the Canadian Valhallas. With an unexplainable illumination, across this globe the minds of mankind are being lit once again.

The powers of the Mind I speak of are available to everyone, if they choose to open to the Source of the God Force that is within them. The indigenous people of Earth still hold many keys to these mysterious powers of the Hu-man Mind. Their knowledge can neither be stolen, nor contrived. It can exist only within the state of *most pure Mind,* the Mind of the child, the Mind of Creator, the Mind that knows not, nor accepts concepts of limitation. As we reach up to the highest level of conscious light, we find the more that we begin to understand higher consciousness, the nature of the God essence is indeed child-like.

Once opened the Mind cannot be closed. Once touched by the Light of the Divine presence, the Mind will never again become lost in the shadows of illusion. Truly, the pathway to the stars is through the heart of a child. The gift of our Grandfathers and Grandmothers is accessed through dreaming and the understanding of the unlimited potential that exists. Through that expanded awareness, we have created the whole of third dimensional reality with a sense of space, time, and matter in all its forms. We are children of an unlimited Source that knows no restraints. This Source is quintessentially lawless in Its nature for It suffers not the consequence of polarities. Source *IS* that it *IS.* This dream in which we walk is only the experience of a moment frozen in the landscape of forever. Seek you the truth, and it shall free you. Forever is the pathway of heart.

In all of Its forms, the Source is universal. It is the One that is the All. Therefore, It is omnipotent in Its Beingness. Which is why It is oftentimes called, I AM THAT I

AM. The nameless God, is all Gods, and all concepts of God, as It is all things. This Source has no form, yet It is all form. Nor can Source ever be contained in anyone's dogma, or expressed truly in a religion. Source cannot be contained in a language, for Source is beyond language. Source is formless. Neither can it be proposed that the Source is within any particular living thing, yet not another. For Source is within all things..... all races.... all genders..... all species. It is even within the rock, as well as the stars that light the heavens. Source is with the Tibetan Lama, as It is with the streetwalker and the thief. Source was with the Priestess at Delphi and the little peasant girl in the Andes Mountains of Peru. Source is the rivers, the mountains, the lion, the eagle, the condor and the butterfly.

The knowledge of how this God Force works, how it can be accessed and applied in everyday life, is accessible to everyone. The wisdom of the *Kryah* comes from understanding what is termed the Universal Laws. This law is encoded within our DNA, thus through applied *Kryah* or *Kryah-genetics* we can begin to transform ourselves, and thus transform reality. The Laws act as a guideline when accessing this Greater Knowledge. We are fast approaching a time when this knowledge can and will no longer be held by only the few.

THE NATURE OF REALITY

In becoming the *initiate*, we learn to become the empty vehicle, the hollow bone through which the God-Force expresses. Therefore, we become servants unto the Supreme Cause, which is the Christos. There we realize our true cosmic purpose and destiny... to consume the unknown. We are *voyagers upon the light*, learning the laws of creation. This we do so that we can serve the purpose of the God-Force that is within us. For the God-Force has no other purpose but to perpetuate and to fulfill Itself. From this basic principle, all we call life is created as pure thought potentiality.

The God-Force can be no secular thing, for to elect to be one or the other is a form of judgment. The moment that the God-Force judged, It would no longer be. Therefore it would be ludicrous to think that the God-Force would express only through a specific gender or a specific elemental species, for the God-Force is all these things and more. Likewise the Creator, can neither be good, nor bad. For in the moment that

God would be either good or bad, judgment is born. In being the supreme elemental force of All That *IS*, in that moment of judgment, All That *IS* would cease to be. Life as we know it would end.

You could say that the God-Force is Lawless, for there are no fixed rules that the God-Force follows, only Divine Principles. Rules create form and structure. The God -Force is formless. Hence the essence of our Being is also without form and cannot be contained in the rigidity of dogmatic thoughts. For in the moment our thought realizes itself, thought changes. Like Father like Child.

God is the infinite unknown we call the void. Space itself, as we conceive it, is the river upon which the thought of God Supreme travels through the millenniums of universal existence. And like a river it has its sounds and nature to be understood. It is ever changing, and thus remains the constant from which All That Is springs forth into being.

The God-Force cannot be measured in terms of *Light* and *Dark* for in truth there is no darkness, there is only God. And what are we? We are the expression of God manifest upon this physical plane. We came from God, because we came from the thought of God. We were born of the Light and remain the Light into our foreverness. We as particums of light travel through Divine thought and manifest upon the various planes of reality as thought evolving. We are eternal light expanding into every part of the Universe. When we pass this plane, we again return to the thought, the Supreme Source. Thus the cycle continues in its forever process of God realizing Itself through creation. It is endless, for God is unlimited.

The process called creation is the Divine gift of The Source, initiated unto the children of God, Children of the Sun, we that are the Christos. For Creation is but a thought of Itself in a constant exploration of Its own potential, always seeking Itself, moving like a serpentine energy through the cosmos. Evolution and growth is presently realized through one's ability to create reality. Hence the time space continuum is perpetuated so that we can identify with that essence that we are. Experience is our touching stone, our remembrance of ourselves.

The thoughts of our creation reach out into the cosmos, through the planes of realized experience. The Divine thought seeks us with full passion, just as in the end of each cycle of our own creation, we return to the Source Itself. It is called valued life, all things seen and unseen. All things potentially, unrealized and realized are born of God. All is Divine, for all is from God's purpose, and born of Love in a state of perfection unto the thought of God

The God Force is eternal and touches us through the breath. The Breath of God manifests always into perpetual life. It can and will transform, but it can never end. Thus, God as we perceive It, is *Egoless*. For we can know not the true nature of *EGO* until we are no longer *Altered EGO*. We have become the reflection of the Light, believing that of itself, *IT* is the Light. Thus we walk in darkness, for the true Light is within not without. We have created a reverse polarity in our manufactured state of consciousness.

God is the purifier. To perceive that *the Source Of All That Is* would judge, is not based upon the Laws of the Supreme Being. It is based upon the laws of man, man in his state of limitation, living in an adopted state of reality, what could also be termed an *Altered State of ISness*. What we have perceived through limitation as *Ego*, is in fact, the *Altered Ego*. God of Itself is *pure unaltered Ego, I AM THAT I AM*. Man in his floundering has perceived himself to be, "*because.*" But, there is no *because*. There is only ISNESS. This then is the perpetual state of God, ISNESS. BECAUSE, is the reaction too, and not the CAUSE of.

The manifestation of the miraculous is seemingly unknown to most of us simply because we deem it so. We deem it to be beyond our reach. It is out there instead of in here. Because we are living in denial of the Supreme Being as being a part of us, it is illusion. For God is all that IS. "*Because*" is born of judgment. In the state of judgment as most of us are, we have separated ourselves from the Supreme Being. Thus we are in denial and being so, we negate our own creations. We are lost in this state of illusion from which we perpetuate our existence through pain, and limitation. The cause is, that our Dream Creation process remains unrealized.

We have as Hu-manity allowed ourselves to fall into patterns of behavior whereby we are creating the nature of our reality from an incomplete perception of ourselves and the Universe, thus manifesting reality in conflict with its true nature.

Through this process we have become the *reaction to*, rather than the *supreme cause of*. In our altered state of reality, we perceive the Source of Life as being external, rather than internal. Thus we are trying to create from a portion rather than from the whole.

We are the participants in all that is, Co-Creators in the game of life. In most cases, what we have come to call miracles, are simply the experience or witnessing of something we do not yet understand. This is because in most cases we do not yet possess the knowledge of what is making things occur, we do not understand the *Kryah*. The reasons why we do not have this knowledge is simple. There no longer exists the great schools of life. We are not taught the Divine principles of life in our present educational institutions. Look anywhere in the educational structures of western society, it becomes evident very quickly that we are not being taught the fundamentals of the Life Force, and how Universal Law applies to our everyday life. Thus we have become graceless and stiff in our expression of self. We need psychiatrists to tell us who we are, because we have lost touch with ourselves, and our connections to Source have been broken. We are being bred to become little more than feed for the corporate machine that in the end devours us, and cannot allow us to have our own individual expression. "Everyone is expendable and no one has a real friend."

In our neoteric society we are becoming almost completely reliant upon the use of technology to solve our problems. We continually seek the answer to a situation by going outside of ourselves. For the most part, the majority of the people working with modern technology do not have the slightest grasp of how or why anything works in the first place. They are operating in a space of robotic consciousness.

Our neoteric society is built upon the premise of logic, rationality, and the explanation of things through intellectual *Mind*. Everything is linear, our thought process goes from point A to point B without question, like a horse with blinders. The Universe is spherical, as is time, as is the true nature of our Spirit. Our Spirit-Self is not linear.

Linear thinking is two dimensional, as is intellectual *Mind*. There is something beyond *Mind*, called Consciousness, and beyond Consciousness is *Awareness*. The explanation of this phenomenon is easy. For example, let us suppose that you are involved in some sort of trauma, say an automobile accident. You suddenly awaken in a hospital room. You know that you are in a hospital, but you do not know why or how you got there. Further, you are unaware of what is going on or why these strange Beings with masks are hovering over you. At this point you have come back into third dimensional consciousness.

You are not yet in possession of your *Awareness*. Awareness occurs when you remember what event or events brought you to the hospital room. Consciousness becomes utilized. This activation of Consciousness, where it transmutes into Awareness is what gives us the ability to achieve action. You could say that *LIFE is a Verb*, and not a noun, for this indeed is a great truth.

What is occurring around us, in the experience we call *LIFE,* is the result of Awareness activating Consciousness. The entire nature of our perceived reality is the result of this process. These ancient laws we are talking about are infinite, and therefore imperishable. The elements that are constricted to this temporal plane have little affect upon them. So, the Universal Law that was in effect fifty thousand years ago is just as applicable today, as it was then. What Merlin accessed and drew upon can be utilized today. The understanding of this Mystery is achieved by opening our *Mind* to the realities of Metaphysical Truth.

We then enter the world of *Quantum Reality* through right use of *Will*. We quite literally become contemporary Alchemists. The problem for the most part, is that even though these very basic principles of *Kryah* exist, we are not aware of them, and we take little responsibility for our actions and words. We have little understanding if any of the Universal Laws of cause and effect. We feel we are hapless victims of chance circumstance. We are caught up in the results. We are unaware that reality is being manifested unconsciously and constantly by our thoughts. Creation is a natural law that is occurring with or without our conscious participation. It is akin to breathing, we never stop to wonder why or how it occurs, do we? Therefore one could say, most have fallen asleep at the wheel.

There is a limitless Source of Divine Power that is available to all of us. It is waiting there at our total disposal this very moment. We just have to learn how to tap into it. That is the purpose of this revealing of the *Kryah*, to show you how that can be achieved……..not in some distant future, not a nebulous tomorrow, but right now. These simple understandings can completely alter your life…… if you are ready to accept the responsibility of reclaiming and owning your own Divine Power.

THE SECRETS OF KRYAH

STEP ONE: ACCEPTING METAPHYSICAL TRUTH

The first step is to understand that *Kryah* is a process. Universal Laws dictate conditions for experiencing, as well as perceiving the Nature of our Reality. The participator transmutes their limited reality, accepts the results of what is presently thought of as a mystery, or miracle, and reality becomes applied knowledge. One must be able to deal with unknown outcomes. It is actually detrimental to your path to get hung up on the outcome of events.

What is going to happen, is outside of your present sphere of awareness, therefore it is unknown to you. It is a science and you are the apprentice scientist. The experiment is to journey into, and know the Self within. To take that knowledge and through applied experience, understand your true relationship to the whole of the Universe.

What is it that makes a flower? What is the true nature of physical matter? What is Creation, and what is the nature of the God that creates? What is my relationship to all of it? Why are there causes and effects? Why do things happen the way they do?

To answer these and the other questions that will occur along the journey, you must alter your present level of Consciousness.   Expanding your Awareness enables you to accept more than is presently acknowledged as your reality. You must go beyond limited Mind. Anyone can learn. The rudimentary requirement is your desire to know, combined with your commitment to completion. You are going to go beyond your present limitations. You cannot create something new from the same consciousness that conceived it. In order for creation to occur, the manifestation must be the result of an expanded consciousness. In other words, a consciousness that is greater than the original thought. A new thought!

So, the first step involves the understanding of how to transmute your present state of Consciousness. You need to identify what is keeping you locked in limited reality. Then you must come to understand the principles that are involved. So, let us begin with four basic elements, *Mind, Consciousness, Awareness, and the Soul.*

MIND: Is like a computer, waiting to be programmed by Consciousness. Of itself, Mind is a no thing. It is strictly mechanical, possessing no heart, no emotion, no reason. It is not capable of grasping the abstract. The Mind is simply a tool that we program. It responds likewise. Its abilities are severely limited to its user, which is activated Consciousness.

CONSCIOUSNESS : Exists in the great void, it is the Source. Here is where all things potentially lie...... yet no thing materially exists. This is the realm of Creator, yet not the completeness of Creator. Consciousness of itself is likened unto a dream state, constantly flowing like a river full of ideas, and possibilities. It is ever changing, yet remains the same to our primal perception. Asleep Consciousness, is waiting for the user to tap its unending knowledge, much like the empty canvas of the artist, waiting to be given life.

AWARENESS : Is an energy, it is the flow of the river realizing itself. It is powered by desire. Awareness is the recognition of a self-purpose, the elemental essence that distinguishes the difference between the rose, and the dandelion. It is personality. It is the individual essence which makes us unique. In its self-fulfillment, it merges with Consciousness and becomes the ultimate desire. In its commitment to fulfill itself, its only desire is *To BE.* As it expands it becomes the cause, and is realized. It is that which consumes the darkness, making the unknown the known. From our thoughts, all things materialize into reality.

THE SOUL: Is the embodiment of our memory Awareness. Your *Soul* holds the emotional memory of every experience that the Awareness has explored since the beginning of creation. The *Soul* is unemotional in its function, and totally impartial. It is the program that holds the knowledge of Consciousness, programmed intuitively with the knowledge of the *Kryah*. The *Soul* is used by Awareness to fulfill desire. It is the program, the computer chip of the Mind. Herein lies our every experience since the beginning of time. The Soul possesses the individual memory, as well as the collective memory. It is the God of your embodiment.

The Mystery that aligns these four elements together is the *Kryah*. It enables us to recognize and read the frequencies of the Universal Life Force, and Universal Laws. The Egyptians called it *Ska*, as do the Lakota people here in North America. Some would call it magic. Some call it God. However you define it, *Kryah* is the Mystery Intelligence that makes up the embodiment of all things. It is the very nature of existence......The Master Dreamer.......Spider Woman weaving her web.

STEP TWO:
UNDERSTANDING THE CIRCUMSTANCE OF LIMITATION

This Universal Life Force is eternal and limitless. Consequently, we all possess within us this unlimited energy, or power, if the word suits you. Manifesting in our reality is simply a matter of identifying with this Universal Life Force. The key element in this process, is in *knowing* that this God Force exists *within you*. A simple declaration can consciously apply and activate this eternal force from within. For example:

" From the God of my Being......*I declare that I AM* the perfection of God's desire, *I AM the child* eternal. *I AM* the expression of beauty that God desires. *I AM* the perfect expression of God's desire, *I AM* that *I AM*. Great Mystery behold me, for it is my desire that the God of my Being be realized NOW.   SO BE IT."

If you really want to change, say it while looking at yourself in a mirror after meditating for 15 minutes each day, until you love what you see in front of you.

This declaration becomes Universal Law if it comes from the alliance of our entire Being, BODY, MIND, SOUL. We must own it and desire it completely, and it must come from within our very core with full passion. It cannot be simply said for it to have an effect. It must be our truth. Then it must and will manifest. Practice this *every* day for 30 days. Own the attitude. *Hold the thought throughout the day*, repeat it before you go to sleep. See if your life changes.

We constantly allow our thoughts to come forth with no understanding of their origin. Within an hour, we have already forgotten our prior thoughts. This is unconscious thinking. The result is the reality that we experience around us. Whatever you think, whatever you express, so shall you call it to you. Think well before any thought is embraced, before any word is spoken. For the Universe responds to our commands, the *Kryah* is impartial.

The Soul is impartial and objective...... it is the God of our Being. From it comes forth the command to all creation to respond to our every desire. However, the Soul has no way of discerning what it is you want. It cannot discriminate between hopes and aspirations. It does not know right or wrong, or how much is too much, how much is too little, or what shade of blue you want in your landscape. The Soul is pure energy, it is alive with God energy, the energy of I AM that I AM. Whatsoever you communicate to it, it reflects back unto you a hundred fold.

It works much like electricity. It taps into the Universal Energy, which is the Law, and the Law is blind. It will give you anything you ask for, equal to your perception, equal to your emotion, no more and no less. Therefore, a very important element in the process is to clearly define your thoughts, and see what you are declaring in its entirety. Your thought patterns are mostly processed in the Mind. The process of this can be understood as the internal dialogue heard inside your head, and the spontaneous words that flow from your lips.

These thoughts are first connected to the collective consciousness. You must consciously give your chosen thoughts clarity and create definition and discernment. You create the color, the experience of life, through the language of emotion, outwardly expressed as feelings. You give substance to your desires......take charge of your life. If the experience is not quite right at first, it is OK. Have another go at it. Get the right shade of blue this time.

The moment you are born into this plane, your feelings and your thinking processes are unlimited. You are like that empty canvas in the artist's studio. You have committed to this plane, and are affected by it. You are influenced by the laws of physicality, but you are not yet bound by the restraints of any other Being's belief patterns. Internal core belief patterns are waiting to be created throughout your life experiences. You are still unaware of physical limitation and may dream of flying, of playing with Angels, of talking to animals, and other "imaginary" friends.

Newborns do not know the concepts of race, color, or creed. No one has told them that God exists outside of Self. So, Awareness is coming from pure *I AM*, pure Consciousness. It is not being strained through the filter of the collective consciousness. The limitations start the moment one begins to comprehend through language. The *I AM*, The God of your Being communicates through emotion, through feeling, not through language.

Here is where you begin to set up boundaries that can last your entire lifetime. Here is where you begin to establish the concept of external limitations. Through language, adults taught you their fears, their belief patterns, their limitations. Most of which is nothing more than recycled ignorance handed down from one generation to the next.....beliefs based upon superstition, rather than fact. This is when you were introduced to collective consciousness. You were taught the perceptions of the masses, "This is a Tree." "This is God." "This is Evil." "This is blue." "Don't do that." So on and so forth.

Most children experience adult teaching by an archaic method of punishment and reward. "If you listen to Mommy you'll get this." "Do like Daddy does." This molding process of collective unconsciousness gains in velocity as it progresses through our development. It is Pavlovian conditioning. Eventually the concepts of each generation become more and more rigid and inflexible. You are programmed to live the limitations of the faceless millions that proceeded you. These limitations have nothing whatsoever to do with your reality.

The rules that you experience and are expected to adhere to, are simply the madness of existential Pavlovian reality. Most of this reality is based upon incomplete information and superstition. The boundaries of your life have been created through the unenlightened, intellectual process of an unaware Mind. Intellect is only one of the aspects of the Mind, only one.

The rigidity of this behavioral programming does not allow the inner genius to unfold. It does not allow for individual expression, nor does it allow for your Being to engage reality on its own terms. You are locked within the limited reality of someone else's creation. You have become imprisoned by invisible bars of someone else's intellectual concepts, which may be no more than conclusions created by a superstitious collective consciousness.

We are entering a time where the fundamental infrastructures of this kind of limited reality are being swept away by the tidal waves of change. There is an avalanche of Awareness that is entering the planet. The path of the initiate is not for most people, because most people would rather stay asleep. Most people do not want to change, they are afraid to change. If they changed, they would not know who or what they were. They would have to assume responsibility for their actions, and that means their creations, as well as their life's circumstance. For we are the sum result of our collective thoughts. We are the creators of our own destiny. It is much easier to blame someone else and keep hiding your head in the sand.

The path of the initiate is the path of the Spiritual Warrior. You are going to have to leave behind everything you think you know. You are going to have to go beyond your present realm of limitations and step into the unknown. You are going to have to take this journey alone. You are going to have to commit to grow beyond the Body-Mind Consciousness….. to the greater reality. Most people have not come to this path. It is safer to stay at home in the illusion of the preordained dream, someone else's dream, at that.

Rules are created in the Mind. There are no rules in the greater understanding of Universal Law. All things are possible through the application of the Universal Law. Defined rules, are a prescribed Code. They are guidelines for conduct. Law is an applied principle. Principles are fundamental truths. It is upon the interpretation of rules that society's laws are imposed upon us.

Dogmatists have quarreled over their beliefs for centuries. They have even murdered because of them. In the reality of all these centuries, they do not know if their beliefs are true or not. They are not allowed to test them, yet out of fear they must defend their beliefs to the death. Why? For the most part they are dealing with phenomena and superstition, not Truth.

Did you ever wonder why, sometimes when millions pray to God, nothing happens? Have you accepted, "it 's the *Will* of God," as the answer? With Truth one does not wonder, because in order to know the Truth you must become the Truth. The Truth can be tested. It is constant. Truth stands of its own virtue. Truth is the fabric of the Universal Law and needs no defense, because it is of itself. The interpretation of the Law and the use of the application of the Law, is a matter of choice.

Consciousness is the *Will* of the Father, *Action* the gift of the Mother, and *Expression* is their child. This universal truth proclaims the Oneness of it all. In the realization of the consequence of this great truth, we realize our only mission here on the Earth plane is to awaken the God within and evolve from mere animal experience, then reconnect with the Divine that is the Source of us all. Thus we become a conduit for the God Force upon the Earth plane. That is a true definition of *Kryah*. It is being consciously in balance with the Universal Law and the outward expression of Metaphysical Truth upon this plane, as intended in the great plan of Creation.

We are not our body or mind or our emotions, nor are we anything we are experiencing around us in any given moment. We are like a dream within a dream. We are not even the dream, we are the one that is having the dream.

We are an infinite part of the Great Mystery, the force of the Great I AM. We are a part of God having this special experience, participating in a grand experiment called the Human Drama. We are on an endless journey of which this existence is only a part. What we are and what we are experiencing is actually occurring on many dimensions and time frames simultaneously.

You choose each experience that you have in this life. It unfolds in precise accordance with the next experience required for your spiritual evolution. If something happens unexpectedly, you then chose for something to occur which would expand your horizons. At that time the experience is created by the elements in accordance to the realm of consciousness to which you have access. Life is allowing you to experience exactly what you call forth, as you like it, because the Universal Law demands that you become fulfilled to your greatest potential. In this way, the Force of the *I AM* becomes an even greater expression of Itself in Its own evolution as the Living Spirit within all things.

To some this could sound like utter madness and their resistance will be high. "If that were true, I never would have chosen this place, this relationship, this life. I would have chosen to be wealthy. I never would have chosen to be a Black in South Africa, or a Sioux on the Pine Ridge reservation. I would have been smarter, sexier, thinner." These are merely the expressions of the *Altered Ego*, the voices of the illusion trying to justify itself. Pure *Unaltered Ego* on the other hand is God creating the Dream.

If the *Altered Ego* allowed you to realize you were God *I AM,* it would have to acknowledge that you were in control and it would be out of a job. Then how could you explain over 35,000 years of recycled ignorance? "You mean I've been stuck in this Dream for no reason? The bars aren't even real? What about all those generations of our *His* - story, you know, I have all these reasons I learned why and how to be this way. I have tradition."

The answers to the riddle waits just beyond this plane. Hu-man existence is just slightly out of focus. Just beyond the physical plane lies the source of your consciousness. When you entered this plane of third dimensional reality you engaged upon a heroic journey. The nature and memory of your decision to accept this mission is engraved within the deepest part of you. It is the blueprint of your physical existence...... it is *Epigenetics*. What you are today, regardless of how stuck you have become in the dream of it, was determined long ago by the God of your Being. When you, as co-creators, conceived of the *Epigenetics* of material existence, the blueprint of life in physical form, you were on the fourth dimensional level of consciousness. You created this whole experience and all of its infinite probabilities the moment light became matter.

The following is a brief explanation of the difference between Kryahgenetics and

Epigenetics.

Epigenetics: is the sacred knowledge of form. All That Is, is Light. All that is seen, is form that light is expressing through. In order to have form, in order to express upon the third dimensional plane, the concept of form was created. The Universe is crystalline in nature, meaning all light expresses through crystal form i.e. sacred geometry, the structure of cells, the nature of the atomic structure. Epigenetics is how light creates the form it express through….. .or we could not be.

Kryahgenetics: is the sacred knowledge of energy and frequency, what some would call the holographic Universe….. in other words that which is *Spirit*, that which is formless. What is it that tells yellow to be yellow? All matter is composed of the same elements, so what is it that tells the elements to be the rock, or the rose, or the fish or the human? It is the *Kryah*. What draws one element to another? What causes the force of gravity to be? *Kryah*. When one understands these Universal Laws, then they can apply them to action, bringing about cause and effect. This application of the knowledge of *Kryah* is called *Kryahgenetics*.

At the dawn of Creation, your Soul began recording events and thoughts through emotions and feeling. Your Soul understands the journey and its purpose. Your Mind began only at birth. It does not understand the journey. You see, the Mind is attached to the body. Where the body goes, it must go. When you leave the body, you return to your Awareness, to the Source from which you came. If it is desired, you may then create a new body and continue on the wheel. It is all choice. The Mind doesn't inherently understand the Universal Law. It cannot conceive of unlimited potential. It does not see *the God I AM……* because the Mind of itself is a no thing.

The Mind was created as a result of our taking on the physical embodiment. It is like a base component in an elaborate computer network. All being part of a perfect design, we must now assemble the rest of the components to suit our specific needs. This realization should not be interpreted as the Mind being inferior or a lesser part of the Dream. If the Mind could understand the nature of the journey, if it already had access to all of our emotional experiences, past and present, then there would be no evolutionary process. We would not be desirous of experience. We would be asleep in endless contemplation, existing only within limitation…..never knowing there was something more.

The Mind is only capable of working within the confines of the amount of information that is placed into its memory banks. The ability of the Mind to access the unlimitedness of that information and its perception of that information is determined greatly by the quality and pureness of that information. The interpretation of the knowledge is the job of intellect. The intellect accesses the memory bank. Our memory banks have, for the most part in this physical reality, been influenced and limited by Humanity's limited understanding of Metaphysical Truths.

For eons, these sciences have been restricted to only a privileged few. The Mind itself is being programmed with each re-birth. With each re-birth, we program our core belief patterns. Due to cultural and social experiences, we fall under the effect of the core belief patterns of the Social Consciousness of the day. This has changed vastly since the year 1972. Now as we approach the Millennium, we are developing at an ever-increasing rate of speed, we are approaching a global environment critical mass. Something new must occur, there is no other direction to go. We are becoming a Oneness, and world political bodies are in a fast panic to keep their control over consciousness.

This constant re-establishment of limitations in our consciousness is, for the most part, based upon tribal and religious beliefs that do not reflect a total picture of the ancient knowledge......what I call Earth Medicine. Most of the physical embodiments of this knowledge have been destroyed. The last great functioning schools of this knowledge vanished with the libraries of Alexandria and the destruction of the Mayan and Inca Temples. The rest of the knowledge that was in the form of text, was absconded with and hidden within the catacombs and vaults of the Holy Mother Church in Rome, where it has remained for centuries. Much of it also was taken by the Nazis during WWII, and has been hidden in obscure locations throughout the world.

Today what remains of these ancient schools of wisdom, appears to the ordinary eye, as crumbling pyramids, and scattered writings upon the living stone. These remains are much more than they appear, for they are keys to a holographic reality, just beyond the edge of the veil, that prevents ordinary Beings from awakening. Soon we will witness the reopening of their doorways to another reality. As we witness the unfolding of the prophecies," All that was hidden shall be revealed." Something very dark in our past caused the truth of what we are to be hidden from us. As I have previously stated there was a break in our evolutionary process. A definite unexplainable break.

We are preparing at this time for the Awakening. Events that are happening in our Universe are bringing into alignment something very special and unique. There are planetary alignments that are occurring to orchestrate certain frequencies within our solar system, amongst Earth's sister planets, that will realign the Holographic patterns of Earth and her expressed reality, placing her back into harmony with her own signature frequencies. Thus the Holographic patterns through which the light expresses is the living theater we call, the human drama.

The Earth herself will be set back to her original frequencies and that which has been holding the present holographic reality will begin to dissolve, as the original frequencies are reinstated and the overlay is removed from our consciousness. During this process we will awaken once again to our remembrance of our original teachings. For encrypted in the cosmic geometry of these ancient sites was the encoded knowledge of the *Kryah*, the holographic imprinting of our cosmic origins.

These ancient forms are energizing once again and receiving the frequencies from the outer cosmos, that which exists beyond the veil. Yes, the buildings could be destroyed. The beautiful paintings that once adorned their walls…….burned. The incredible crystals that played such an enormous role in maintaining the level of frequency upon which our consciousness was sustained, could be destroyed and pillaged, but that which kept the energy alive.

Yet the *Kryah,* lay dormant until this time of awakening. Those who destroyed these ancient universities of light did not have the capacity to understand that the energy could not be destroyed. The *Kryah* was eternal, and would outlast the temporal closing of the veil, as the Angels fell into darkness, and believed that they were created to experience little more than mortal existence.

With what is now occurring in our heavens, these ancient living buildings which hold the keys to our cosmic awakening in their Sacred Geometry, are being activated by the emergence of the higher octaves into this plane. They are being charged with new life force and once again they have begun transmitting their own Divinely engineered frequencies, and the consciousness of humanity is being steadily raised to unparalleled heights.

These frequencies are permeating the present degenerative dream of reality so that it might continue with the process of merging with the new consciousness that is birthing. Remember, "Our thoughts create the nature of reality."

We are about to realize the impact of that teaching, as the reality we are holding on to, changes before our very eyes and we are wakened from the dream that presently holds us prisoner to the Spell of Mortality. The locations of these ancient sites, including the ones where there exists only petroglyphs, were specifically chosen by our ancestors, when they still possessed a level of conscious awareness that has for the most part been inaccessible to us during our experience in the darkness since the fall of Atlantis.

The Mind which exists in the lower vibratory fields of the present condition, is being prepared to rise and merge with the higher octaves of creation.....octaves so high that these frequencies would shatter all presently conceived paradigms of acceptable reality. We are talking Wizards, Dragons, and Star Wars all the way here. These ancient sites in many instances act as antennae for receiving the cosmic codes from the outer Universe and are essential to our existence. They remain the keys to our origins, and the ability once again for accessing the state of Divine Hu-man consciousness.

As my Hopi Brothers say, "We will have to remember our original instructions from Creator that were lost to the other Brothers. These teachings we all knew, before we set off upon different pathways into the four directions.....before we split up and became many different people. Before we had the need to create re-legions, we had a way. Today, many are struggling to remember that way, because they are beginning to see that without that knowledge, we are lost."

What the Hopi are talking about is the remembrances of a knowledge that is being born again in Maya Land, which is the surviving remnant of the original Mother land of HU-manity. For it is here in the Western Hemisphere that the remnants of the original Lemurian knowledge still exist….. what some might call the teachings of the Garden of Eden. We are in essence experiencing the sequel to the Western Theological myth of Adam and Eve and their fall from heavenly grace. The ancient Mysteries were the teachings of the galactic understanding of the Universal Laws. This knowledge is universal and will be brought to the surface of our consciousness once again. The ancient universities did not create religion(s) aimed at dominating one point of view over another's.

When the ancient Maya saw the conquistadors coming upon their shores so long ago, they thought one of two things. They knew that history would take one of two turns. Either this reappearance of the Younger Brother meant that the Younger Brother had returned home to embrace once again the Knowledge of the *Kryah*, or a great period of destruction would follow his sudden reemergence from the mysterious lands to the East. For his nature if not evolved was one of war and destruction, he knew no other way.

Until most recently, these truths could not be spoken of openly, for our knowledge base as well as the language base itself, could not effectively articulate with the delicate intricacies involved for understanding the Universal Laws of cause and effect on an Earthly level, let alone the Galactic concept. Therefore, as a global society, it has been impossible for us to develop accurate holistic perceptions of the true nature of our reality. The belief patterns of the European or Judeo-Christian experience, since the demised of Egypt and the libraries of Alexandria, have been based almost entirely upon *disinformation* at best.

Having lost the ties to their roots here in the Western Hemisphere, the humanity that was surviving in the European frontiers was in a state of despair. The sense of separation was too much to bear.   So, a new myth was created by those in power to solve the dilemma. The doctrines of all surviving Spiritual expressions were to be altered and modified and brought into the sanctified mold of the ruling warrior society of the day, ROME.

These new ways of educating the people to their connections to GOD were to have no ties to the old understandings of Gaia (Maya). As a result, the degree of separation between mankind and Creator became even greater. Spirituality was homogenized and made consumable for everyone…but only under the supervision of the ruling power of the day. The differences between peoples would be acknowledged to keep everyone content, so that they most assuredly had their own uniqueness. Thus the formation of Organized Religions was created and then engineered and developed for centuries by the Emperors of Rome.

There could not be allowed any Spiritual body or group, that spoke of the connection to the original teachings, for it would only caused descent in the camp and most likely lead to rebellion against the political order. During this time it was decided that any remembrances of what *WAS*, that might link people to the past and their connections to *Caga Maya,* would be destroyed. This was simple and decisive, with predictable results. Plus it was a fairly known factor that ideals and philosophies can be bred out of a people within four generations. Then, there would be no remembering, and therefore there would be no conflict…… no opposition to the control of the populace. Then, there would be no chance of an awakening of some initiate that would bring the house of cards down.

Dealing with those who still had the knowledge of these teachings was simple enough, just drive those who possessed the memory of the original knowledge out into the wilderness, away from the protection of the tribe…..let them be *Pa gons* (Pagans-those who lived outside the city, outcasts). Then amongst the people themselves, there was created a systematic program of *separationism*……a separation from Creation Itself, a separation of church and state, which created separation of the classes. God was even separated from us!

Because of the deliberate restraints employed by the many sanctioned organized religions, which were politically orientated, the masses were more easily controlled by the select few. Any organization which did not heed the rules and conform to the new homogenized theorems, was labeled heretic and burned to the ground with its leaders meeting a less than desirable ending, which included public ostracizing and dehumanization. And the lords were free to go about their business of enjoying the fruits of the land. Sounds like Robin Hood in reverse, does it not?

The execution of this strategy of divide and conquer has continued to successfully keep Humanity frozen in the throes of separatism. One could call it the patriarchal influence of Roman rule, which has greatly influenced Western Society. This is the reason for the corruption we are witnessing in our society today. If one side got too close to the truth, well, then just begin a little Religious War so the imposed philosophies of superstition would not be discovered for what they were. Besides it was good for commerce, and filled the lords coiffeurs. The lords could then rape and pillage with the blessings of the church.

Remember we were controlled, as we still are this very day, by the warrior societies. This is the way of the Younger Brother, it would seem. They would always shout out, "If we do not get our way, we shall all come out of the castle and kill everyone." This is what we have grown up with isn't it? In many ways life is like living in a Monty Python comedy.

These policies were carried over by the Holy Church in Rome, after the religious leaders successfully brought down the decadent warrior lords and the Roman Empire fell. The church of Rome did continue these policies with their barbaric conquest of the New World, by the Armies of the Inquisition and also the invasion of the Americas by European settlers. The policies of *Churchianity* were executed all along the line until almost no trace of the original teachings could be found. Those who knew, were too frightened to speak or even elude to the fact that they might have a knowledge of the ancient understandings.

While the tyrants pondered, hidden behind the public face of decency *in their secret societies*, they were actually scrambling around, trying to figure out how to access the ancient knowledge themselves. This is affirmed by the fact that most of the information was obtained through the pillages of war, and to this day what survives the ravages of time is hidden within the underground vaults of the Vatican in Rome, and in the castles of the Illuminati. One can steal the books, they can even incarcerate and crucify the messenger, but this does not gain them the ability to access the wisdom of what to do with the knowledge.

Organized religions have employed the practice of sanctioned genocide throughout the history of our civilization for what seems to be nothing but war, building to ever greater destructions. Any people who opposed *The ORDER*, or who were inclined to have a different belief pattern, were simply exterminated. The madness of

Churchianity has evolved by creating a society which could more correctly be called the *Evangelical Church of the Spiritually Dead and Unaware*......governed by the Spiritually Blind, praying to a God that has become little more than the Wizard of OZ. It contains doctrines preached by the unenlightened, lost at sea in the storms of conflict, dying from the diseases of over indulgence in limitation. It is truly a *Ship of Fools*.

Let us resume, and return to the subject at hand. Know that your desire in life is to accept full responsibility for who and what you are......to learn to love yourself as a Divine Creation of the great I AM presence. Let us also assume you accept that you have had an infinite number of previous experiences here on the Earth plane.

Perhaps in some of those experiences, you were weak and indulged yourself by relying on someone else's experiences rather than coming to your own conclusions about the true nature of things. If you knew of this experience in advance and did not have access to the Universal Consciousness, did not apply Divine *Will* and the desire of your Spirit to seek Spiritual Union with the Divine, it would have seriously altered your personal path through the evolutionary process......your path to the awakening.

Yes, most likely you would have intellectualized yourself into creating the exact positions and circumstances you wanted to achieve. You would, however, be devoid of Spiritual Awareness. You would only be working within the confines of Mind. Which, is again, part of the collective consciousness and would have dominated the outcome. Most likely after seven and a half million years of existence you would have developed the consciousness of an expanded Neanderthal.

Without access to the whole computer network, evolution of the species simply could not occur. You cannot intellectualize your way out of circumstance, you cannot overcome weakness by ignoring it. You must engage it. We exist in a participatory Universe. This is a plane of action, where we learn through experience.

You can only overcome a weakness by owning it, going into it, becoming it, thus understanding it from its perception of reality. By accepting responsibility for it and then leaving it behind, you can then say to yourself, "Well that was an interesting experience, glad I don't have to do that one again." If you never experienced it before, you only need to experience it once. The second time is always by choice. This course of action expands Awareness. If you are experiencing a weakness, you are being given the opportunity to understand what in you, has the tendency towards negativity and self-abuse…..that which does not support the principle of Self-love, or your acceptance of Divine perfection within your Being. It is a matter of Self worth.

By dealing with the weakness, you can hope to understand the nature of the problem. More importantly, understand its source. Once this understanding is owned, you are free of the shackles and able to move upward, out of the collective unconscious….free to continue your journey home to Self-Joy and harmony with Creation. You have employed a discipline of Self-empowerment. The danger for most is, they tend to dwell in the weakness. This is a world of duality. There are always two sides of the story. In one instance what could be considered tragedy, in the next, can be Divine Comedy. We are, after all, involved in the Human Drama, Drama, Drama.

Perhaps one of the biggest pitfalls of a new initiate is the tendency of slipping backwards now and again. Know that you are developing your *Will.* Once your have committed to the attitude of strength and the acceptance of Divine perfection in the effects of Universal Law, the knowledge will always be with you. Eventually you will learn to use these principles like the thermals that keep the Eagle aloft for hours, without ever once flapping its wings. It will be effortless. The time spent in learning and staying focused in your journey is the discipline. One day you will just fly and not even think about it. It is like riding a bicycle.

Becoming is a process. Becoming is not an event. This is why we refer to our Earthly experience as evolution. One has to train the Mind to understand the principles of Universal Law. The Mind, of itself, does not possess this aptitude to access unlimited thought of its own accord. It must learn to merge with the Awareness of unlimited potential. The tendency of the Mind is to find the rational solution. It will want to rely upon its intellectual abilities, always.

The Mind likes routine and habit. It is fond of making Body-Mind Commitments. Intellect is only part of the Mind's capabilities, less than one-percent. Your Mind has the capacity to access unlimited consciousness. You were designed that way. It is in your blueprint of Epigenetics. You will accomplish this when you learn to allow your Awareness to carry you over the hurdle. It is a matter of allowing and not achieving that brings us to enlightenment. And it is allowing everything along the journey and embracing it all that brings wisdom.

STEP THREE: Revealing the Web of Life

The human species, above all the creations on the Earth plane, possesses the unique ability for Dream Creation. So powerful is our development of this natural ability within us, that we even possess the power to alter our perception of reality...... to reweave the fabric of the dream simply by changing the way we think. We can alter the nature of our environment with our moods, and emotions. The whole of the Earth responds to us, and the whole of the animal kingdom is in awe of our ability. We can alter our consciousness to the extent that our perceived reality, will actually bend the light. Then in a manner of speaking, reality will conform within its allowed awareness and comply with our demands.

On more than three occasions we have literally changed the nature of reality for the entire planet, and some say the confines of our solar system as well. Yet for the most part, mankind remains asleep and unaware of our former realities through most of our journey. There are those among us who are not asleep, who have removed themselves from the web of social consciousness and have become the caretakers of the Light as well as the darkness.

There are Grand Masters who have walked in their original form for untold thousands of years and continue to do so, and are among us from time to time. You could say, "But this is impossible." Yes it is, if you were caught in the ordinary manner of perceiving the time-space matrix of conceptualized reality. In order to accomplish this, each of these Masters learned to think in *extra-ordinary* ways.

They broke the rules and went beyond their own limited thinking. They learned to hold the frequency and even perform this wonderment at will. They have moved out of the first and second attention and now are creating for themselves *extra-ordinary* ways of Being. These illuminated Beings have unlocked the doorways that separate the dimensions, and are able to access the fifth dimensional understanding. Further, they are able to come and go at will, and perpetuate an immortal state of Being here upon the third dimensional plane.

The how and why to this phenomena is seen in its simplicity. These Beings who were once just like any other Being, have expanded their Awareness to the extent that they have moved beyond the limitations of ordinary existence, the existence of the collective consciousness. They have embraced an extra-ordinary existence by choice and maintain their own Separate Reality.

They are no longer caught in the consciousness of the masses that tells us if we go out into the rain, we will catch a cold, and so we do…...the consciousness that a human Being can only jump so high….. when you get older you die….. life is temporal. And so the whole of Humanity responds to that established belief pattern. People have for the most part bought the program, and they follow the street signs and never break the rules. Within that reality, we much like bacteria, collectively get caught in a unified field of Body-Mind Commitment. We are not free Souls, unless we have exercised and owned our right to Divine heritage, and we take the courageous step and start living for our own reality, clearing out the useless programming and making the space for the miraculous ……the space to manifest.

An example of the entrapment of Body-Mind Commitment can be observed in the training of a horse. If one were to set up a corral of electric fencing, the horse would soon discover that if it attempted to go beyond the electric wiring it would receive a shock. After awhile one only has to tie a simple string resembling the wire, and they would be able to restrain the horse. The horse could easily break the string, but it has made a Body-Mind Commitment that it cannot.

We are not unlike that horse in our devotion to dogmatic teachings of the limitations of the Human species. We can see this in how easily we accept our theorized separation from the God Force. You are making a Body-Mind Commitment to a duality of being less than. Life, the Light of the Universe, will conform to affirm your reality conception.

At the moment you enter this Earth plane, you accept the commission to expand the relative patterns of established beliefs that you will personally effect. Your Spirit is charged with breaking the collective Body-Mind Commitment. It is the condition of progressive evolution of the species. This can be evidenced in the natural rebellious attitude displayed throughout the youth of the entire world. Youth must push against the boundaries established by the previous generation. It is this friction that is called growth. This attitude is what allows us to effect change. It can be seen in every culture in our intensified world societies. We are experiencing expanded consciousness on a global level. It is truly a time of a great awakening!

It is the action of the God Force within us to seek Itself. Once this union is achieved, one will meet their own destiny. If met with spiritual balance, it will be their true destiny. This fulfills a commitment you have made from the God of your Being.....the Source from which all life comes, the great unlimited I AM presence of the God Force, the part of you that is God, upon entering the Earth plane.

Ordinary existence is living in the limited awareness of Body-Mind Consciousness. Body-Mind Consciousness tells us that we have these five senses in which to perceive the reality around us. These are our tools for participating in the game of life. When you are in the womb you still have a direct connection to the Source of all life, the original Consciousness, and respond with all your senses.......many more than five. The process of this original Consciousness and how it works, could be scientifically explained as non-referral, self-reliant, self-acting, data loops, communicating through light particums that move through matter by way of little fibers called neuronal connectors.

These fibers function very much like fiber optics in the physical. Thought in motion becomes light. Light is activated by emotion which, in turn, is communicated through electricity. These patterns of bio-physical behavior, being the viaduct of the Great Mystery we call God, make up the Universe of the human body.

We possess much more than the five senses that facilitate the awareness of Body-Mind Consciousness. There is also intuition, reason and the eighth element, which we shall call Divine Awareness. When we understand that these three additional senses also compose part of the physical body, we enter a place of true perception. This is the path of the initiate in achieving Mastership.

We need to think of ourselves as being able to go beyond the consciousness of those who came before us.....to become more than the paradigm of being limited to five senses of Body-Mind Consciousness. Limitation is the embraced reality of billions of human Beings who are caught in the trap of living in the ordinary existence. The limited existence of accepting the menu of sanctioned belief patterns is very difficult to break away from. It is for most, a very difficult task to break the Body-Mind Commitment, which has become our devotion to ignorance. We are after all, creatures of habit.

To go beyond, requires that you develop objective Mind, the Mind of Self. This can only be realized by the God within us, acknowledging this Great I AM Force. It is learning that we are the image of God, and not the image of ourselves, and that truth is alive within us...... in every part of us. We are a part of this unlimited energy that streams forth into the Universe in a constant process of creation. We have to overcome this entire lifetime of programming by our elders, our educational system, the standards of the society we live in, our cultural belief patterns, and our perception of the differences between the sexes, and the races. Virtually everything that has been told to us, can be applied as sanctioned reality. We are caught in the spider's web of the collective unconscious.

We follow the patterns of this net of social consciousness with pre-determined behavioral reactions. In short, we have been programmed to live a limited existence that results in a predetermined linear reality, having a fairly predictable beginning and ending. We are programmed to respond to a concept of limited existence. Therefore, it is hard, if not impossible, for the average human caught in this spider's web, to see the unlimitedness of their potential.

We have in many ways become enslaved by mysterious Phantoms of Darkness, imaginary demons that we created. They are actually our shadow self. The dark side of our nature, which everyone has, feeds this shadow self. We follow the dictates of our programming to be subjugated as slaves lifetime after lifetime for the perpetuation of an illusion. Which is why we never see ourselves as being equal with anything. The thought patterns of the ordinary Being is constantly reinforcing the thought of being less than. This fact has been clinically proven time after time in laboratories. It is a flaw in our genetics. The pattern will remain unaltered unless we learn the keys to releasing our inner Being from its pre-ordained prison.

We have been caught-up in these patterns in countless lifetimes that preceded this experience. It is no new battle to us. We are only reaffirming the limitation of our reality in this experience. It is seen in the unconscious drive to conform, to be like the others.....to be the same.... to look like the ideal.....to dress like the ideal. And isn't it funny how after all the struggle to conform, the ideal changes anyway. You see, it is an illusion. It is the phantom dream of illusion, which never allows you to see the beauty and perfection within Self. Everything in the program is designed to make you look away from yourself. So we need to go beyond the program, to something new.

Only a very few have gone beyond the collective consciousness. It is a consciousness that is addicted to its past, perceiving reality from past experience. It is always coming from the past, never from the *Now*. So are you committed to go round and round the wheel of life, spending lifetime after lifetime, reliving the same experiences, because you can never see the pathway in front of you? That is living life backwards!

Now comes the part that is hardest for most of us to accept in the beginning of this journey. All of this Earthly experience we choose to experience, is done of our own free *Will*, so that we could develop every aspect of our consciousness through achieving Awareness.....accomplishing our goals by moving Christ Consciousness through physical form. Have you heard the phrase that we are Spiritual Beings, experiencing Hu-man existence? This is God realizing Itself, through our Beingness. We are learning the Awareness of Self. For creation is of itself, and simply that. It is I AM that I AM. We are the hands, eyes, and heart of Creator.

The ancient Masters have already developed this understanding. We need only follow their footsteps. They have become aware of a dimension that exists right here on the Earth plane, where the miraculous is common place. Here they access and apply the Universal Laws of creation, through focused *Will* to create the conscious nature of their reality. They have changed the pattern of the Wheel into the pattern of the Spiral. You call them The Trans-Himalayan Brotherhood, The Great White Lodge, The Grandfathers, The Grandmothers, The Ascended Masters, The Council of 12 (not the Mormon Church). Well, be advised they, for the most part, are made up of women. And they are positively your brothers as well as your sisters.

One's ability to perform the miraculous is predicated upon the extent to which you allow yourself to remember and enter the energy fields of your true reality. Enlightenment is a process of remembering. Attainment is a process of becoming. We become Masters when we have learned to allow ourselves to access this unlimited Awareness of the universal field. Mastery is learning to detach from the past, not moving and getting caught up in the future, but being fully in the now which is where creation is occurring. As you simply allow yourself to remember, your perception will gradually expand to accept the higher vibratory language of thought, unlimited thought. You will begin to see that what others believe is their truth, is not necessarily your truth, and you will also begin to realize that, that is OK.

Their dream is a part of their experience in the evolutionary process, but it is not by any stretch of the imagination the sum total of the vast amount of knowledge that comprises the whole of reality. These individual perceptions are but windows through which we can perceive portions of the reality, for reality is creation in process. It is endless and it is forever. It becomes a matter of one's Mastering the perceiving of the manifestation of thought through participation.

One of the perplexities of the collective consciousness is that, as it is created now it is predicated upon anticipated rational outcomes. This sagacious outcome is based upon the reliance of a two dimensional intellectual perception. Intellect is a tool of the Mind, which is a creation of Body-Mind Consciousness. Remember the Mind in and of itself, is incapable of perceiving unlimited thought. The concept is not in its programming. The Mind does not know what forever is. The thought must be placed there by our Awareness, which we gain through experience. Intellect is the dewy decimal system of the Mind. It is the collection, if you will, of knowledge obtained through past experience. Up until now it has been a library of *his-story,* rather than the personal experience or *my-theology.* Through the filter of intellect, we are perceiving the world via the acceptance of someone else's summation of collective experience. Intellect is a very important and essential part of the mechanics of the Mind. But it is only a very small part of its machinery.

Through the Alchemical process of self-transmutation, one's Consciousness expands. Through Divine Awareness, it connects with the other parts of the computer that it was designed to work with co-operatively. Intellect alone cannot decipher emotion, only that the existence of it is possible. Yet, emotion is the language of the God-Force. Emotion is expressed through feelings. One emotion can cause in us many feelings, on many levels of our reality. Experiencing the feeling is the action of our intuitiveness, or our empathic abilities interpreting the emotional plane. The action of this is caused by energy. The *I AM* that I AM energy of the God Force. The God Force is directly connected to the Soul. The Soul is the interpreter of the I AM Energy through our physical embodiment, thus creating our reality. It is the God of our Being. It translates our desires into physical manifestation, by the use of the God Force.

By gaining mastery of our emotional thought processes, and altering our brain patterns through *Will* so that we ignite both hemispheres simultaneously, we can change our perception of this reality from mundane to ecstasy. We can easily switch from anxiety or anticipation to fulfillment, from anger to laughter, in a moment. We can stop the movie and even enter into multi-dimensional realties if we desire. Each of these dimensional perceptions affirms to us that our normal perceptions are in fact many times deeper than the ordinary existence that collective consciousness would allow us to believe.

Remember that the ordinary perception is experienced within Body-Mind Consciousness, and limited by the process of the Mind. It is also stuck in Body-Mind Commitment. It is not capable of accessing that which is established beyond the constraints of the collective consciousness. It is capable only of perceiving mass, for it is a creation of the mass. The greater reality that composes mass, is energy. Energy is part of the original consciousness. It is in the holographic fields that surround mass. It is the very stuff that creates mass, that holds it together and expresses as form, which is coagulated, thought. Thought realizes itself through feelings, that manifest into action, that creates physical reality. This is Simple Stuff. It is the Universal Law, but remember, the Mind is not naturally aware of Universal Law. But it can be taught.

The Mind relies upon intellect. Both are caught in the laws of physicality, the electrical forces of positive and negative poles. This translates to duality. You say, "I will be abundant, I AM becoming all I can Be," but the Mind says, "You are not." Because you still have lack in your formula. You are actually stating that you have not yet arrived. You are creating exactly what you are declaring, but your thinking process cannot detect the glitch. The Universe will and must respond to our desires. But the

Universe does not understand the present language. The reality around us responds to emotion, energy, and frequency. Dream that you already are, that you have arrived so to speak, and get into the gratitude of receiving, is the secret for the layman. *Be there and you are there.*

Unless you shift into a gratitude mode you suffer from the endless conflict of polarity. We are creatures of polarity, existing as it were, within an electro-magnetic reality. How is it that you truly think? Do you own the Divine within you, or do you wallow in *Self Doubt?* You are, for most of your life, constantly creating opposing energies. " I want it, but......" " I want to be more than I am." "I want to have power" "......I want this........ I want that......." "I am God." "Why is this all happening to me?" These are thoughts in conflict, and not the state of *most pure mind.*

The Soul is sitting there trying to read your confused communication. The Soul is very much like a Carpenter that works off the blueprint of what you as the Architect have delivered to it. It will build exactly what you have designed, no more, no less. It has no will of its own except to be. It only knows the Universal Law. It must execute your plan. "What do you mean this is not what you wanted? This is what you told me to build." When you create from lack you manifest greater lack, when you create from confusion you manifest chaos.

Remember, the Consciousness that is required to create something new must be greater than the Consciousness that created the reality in the first place. Creation happens in the middle of the neutral zone. For in that space there is no friction, no resistance to something manifesting into the holographic space, from which all form is pulled into three-dimensional expression. Everything is light, absolutely everything....so create the space for the light to *BE*, and things will happen, *matter of factly*, so to speak.

You must develop within yourself the ability to live Consciously. To be clear, very clear and precise with your expressions of what you desire. Your Soul communicates through your projected feelings. Feelings are, of themselves, very simplistic by nature. Keep it Simple. When our "feeling picture" gets out of focus or we start to overlay too many " feeling pictures" over each other, it becomes a complex matter. Then the Soul can no longer interpret the blueprint clearly. It is receiving conflicting information.

This kind of confusion also occurs when we accept the illusion and deny our true feelings, as when we live by the allegorical dictates of someone else's doctrines. Feelings do not understand language. Language was created in an attempt to explain the feelings and express our desire. The *Soul* comprehends energy, not words. It is the energy behind the words along with the intent that commands the elements to respond to the *Will* of the God-Force within.

In a way, understanding *Kryah* is like learning how not to make the picture too real, verses not real enough. It is a question of balance that can only be realized through our Divine Awareness, which created it. We must cease being the *creation* and reawaken to the fact that we are the *creators* of our own realities.

There is a very powerful sense of clarity that comes when we expand inwardly. For it is within, that we are able to access the Consciousness, the original Consciousness of Creation. The Consciousness of GOD I AM. The doorways to the dimensional realities are not out there some place, they are in your inner worlds. The myriad of expressions that are occurring throughout the Universe are occurring within you. The God Force is within you. It is the God Force expressing Itself from within you, through the eternal process of creation, that is the result you experience.

So everything you experience around you is the result of that which you perceive yourself to be, and the condition you allow yourself to feel. Your innermost thoughts dictate the very nature of you exterior reality...... that is Universal Law. The nature of the dream is up to you. You are what you Dream. The Dream is the drama you live through your experience. But no one can have the experience for you...... *it is a self help program.*

If you perceive that you do not have a role in the outcome of matters, then you are embracing the consciousness of self-victimization. It is giving away your power to something, or someone outside of you. Worse, it is not taking responsibility for you. To do this is to say to the Universe, I am less than. In that moment you disengage from Source, you feel you are no longer a part of. You begin to fractalize your reality from there, and the geometry that holds the manifestation of your thoughts, ceases to exist, making your landscape an empty void.

It is all a matter of worthiness, this God stuff we are talking of. And Love is the glue that holds you and your manifestations together. It is so simple that it eludes you. Can you see how you are always doing it to yourself? If you feel less than, you will feel that you are not a part of. You will enforce the separation, and the power goes out of your creation like the air out of a balloon.

If you feel separated from everything, everything around you reflects the inner world of self-reality. You will then realize the experience of being apart from. The words you run in your head, the endless chatter, can fool you. They can speak of conflicting realties. Remember, God is feeling, not words.......so listen to your feelings. Your emotions speak the truth of how you are. Because you're only as pretty as you feel, get it?

Whatever you conceive, is in a state of *constantly becoming* outward manifestation. This realization can totally alter the concept of "Holding the Thought." If you hold the thought that abundance is in your life, if you adopt the attitude that you have all you need in the moment, you feel gratitude for the very fact that you can conceive this feeling. You will eventually become that feeling. You create the feeling of abundance, which is the environment for the thought to exist. The Universal Law will take charge. If you arrive at the answer to this riddle, remember the secret, *Love is what holds it together*, without Love your thoughts are but dust in the cosmic wind.

Through discipline we can teach the environment within Self to accept the feelings of abundance, and hold the frequency. In the Native world we call it gathering power. By making declarations each day, no matter how silly it might seem at first, you are gathering power. You are activating the Laws of Attraction. Life will affirm through the manifestation of circumstances, experiences that confirm your emotional feelings. When you don't feel good about yourself, and you look into the mirror, no matter what you do for yourself, you will appear less than acceptable. Pay attention to this for a few weeks, and you will get the idea.

So you have to facilitate change here, change of mood, don't allow yourself to lock up. Commit to change and activate your adapters. You can commit to changing your feelings. Simply take that walk in nature, interact with a friend, paint in your studio, take up the action to cause the change of mood. The experience of looking into the mirror will change, as if by magic. Through this simple exercise you can experience the process of *Kryah* first-hand. But you have to make *the commitment* to change. You are also teaching yourself the process from conception to completion. It is the magic the artist knows, the understanding that makes a Mary Cassatt or a Claude Monet.

DEEVELOPING WILL AND OUR SHIELDS OF PROTECTION

By taking command over your feelings and not allowing yourself to be as a leaf in the wind, you will soon develop an attitude of assumed strength and Self-esteem. You will be ready to receive success and abundance when the Universal Law delivers it. It won't just be given to you. You have to work at it. You may be shown a path. Life will bring a new opportunity, a new experience that will say to you through feelings. "I can achieve this. Why didn't I think of this before?" If you think it will be hard pressed in the coming, well then it will be. If you adopt an attitude of grace and poise, so shall it be. The Good Red road is oftentimes not a straight one, and the shortest distance between two points of perception is not necessarily a straight line.

Grandfather once told me to observe the Eagle. He is constantly developing his patience with applied consciousness. The Eagle is not just sitting there without purpose. The Eagle sits in the tree for hours watching the water, seeing into the valley of transition. The salmon suddenly appears after the long vigil, right there in front of him, but if the Eagle does not rise up and take hold of the moment the fish swims away, and the Eagle must begin its vigil all over again.

So make yourself ready for the moment, and the moment will be realized. Like I said, it will take work, "nothing for nothing" as the saying goes. You take the action, life supplies the experience.

The space between the conceiving of the thought and the manifestation of the thought is the process of becoming. Traveling through the valley of transition, can be a time of tremendous Self-realization. This is where we redefine our feelings, as well as our reactions to those feelings. We get the opportunity to discard that which does not enhance our growth, and embrace that which enhances our vision. We are continually developing our discernment. It is where we develop the sense of Self- determination. We are adjusting our attitudes, opening them up to accept change. Often we travel through the unknown as we experience transition.

This is where we get to develop wisdom. The knowingness of why we are doing what we are doing, or choosing not to, is being in your power and not leaking like an old can. We no longer feel separated from the Force. For we know the Force, the power of the God I AM, is alive within us and we are a part of this Force. We are simply on a journey......a journey that takes us into forever. We are Voyagers of the Light.

When we go within we become closer and closer to this inner power, of unlimited Being. We learn to trust our feelings. Always along this journey, we are developing our ability to communicate with this inner Self, this expression of God I AM, expressing through us. We begin to accept that everything outside of us is merely the result of the inner feeling, the inner world.

This process will alter our outward perception, and in turn our inner perception. We begin to accept all that exists outside of us in the wonderment in which it was intended and stop taking things personally. The interactions of people and events, are simply the Universal Law manifesting in outward expressions of the collective consciousness' dream. We stop taking the world and the outward expression of reality personally, realizing that for the most part it is merely the expression of the collective unconscious.

The events happening outside of us, which seem confusing, the madness of the drama, the occurrences of insanity, are for the most part, simply the results of unconscious thinking and uncontrolled emotional expression. At this point we begin to develop our *shields of protection*, rather than walls of separation. The *shields of protection* are the result of Self-realization and clear perception.......realizing that this I AM energy is in all things, that it is manifesting for them as well as for ourselves. We can then participate in the game, exercising our own boundaries.

The game is called Dream Creation and it's fun. There are no rules and the losers are only those who choose not to be creators, those who choose not to participate, those who live out the dramas of others and not their own. We are learning to utilize Divine Awareness to decipher our experience. Our method of defense against intrusion of another's reality is our developed Conscious *Will*.

This realization can open many doors for us. For in reconnecting to the God Force within, we become limitless in our potential for creation. We are creating a new *Awareness*. Realizing every moment that it is the nature of this God Force within us to create the Dream, it becomes an automatic process. We all do it anyway, most of us just do it unconsciously.

By choosing to participate consciously we can learn to create the Dream by exercising our Conscious *Will*. The learning process is simple. Allow the God Force to teach us how to create new core belief patterns by putting our feelings out in front of us and allowing ourselves to follow. We use our awareness and listen to our feelings, shutting off what we have come to think of as linear rational behavior. Stop the little voices inside your head that your Mind doesn't know. Put your Dream in front of you and walk the sacred pathway. Just dare to take the next step.

It is essential that we reconnect with the God Force within us to successfully complete this process. For that is what is eternal within us, that is what is limitless. *Kryah* is the common ground between the elements and us. *Kryah* is literally how we are able to communicate with them. All other concepts are born of the altered ego and are subject to limitation. Altered ego is the *IT*. Altered ego exists only in the exterior world of the Dream......the world of duality.

When we focus on the exterior world, it will distort the process. *Kryah* is accessed through the inner, and experienced as the outer. If we forget the balance and lose our ability to switch gears, we can get stuck in the web. We will then be coming from an image of the outer world, a reflection, a part of the whole, and not the whole. This has been the dilemma of Humanity for eons. We have been allowing for the intellect, which is born of Mind to logically reason out what is GOD. Allowing the Mind to become the only component in the computer and making the intellect God.

Mind does not possess the information or the ability for deciphering reality. It comes from the exterior reality and it is only one aspect of our physical reality. The Mind is in charge of the maintenance of the Body. Mind alone is limited to physical third dimensional reality so it can only create from within the limitation. Through creating from limited awareness, we have manifested an entire world of disharmony. A world full of disillusionment, devoted to the perpetuation of ignorance.

For once the mind discovers that there is an alternative to ignorance, like turning to the God Force within, the Source of Eternal Light is again rekindled within the Human Spirit. We no longer turn to the Dream for the answer. An enlightened Being knows that the Dream is no more real than their reflection in the mirror. Take away the Source of the Light, and the image is no more. We are the Source of Light. We are, in essence, the Light Itself.

We can have anything we choose when we participate in Dream Creation. We only need to make a slight perceptual adjustment, realizing it is the accessing of a natural energy......the I AM energy of the God Force that comes from within. In our embracing of illusion, we conceived ourselves separate from this great I AM presence...... the same presence that is in the leaf, the river, the ant, the rock.

So, in this manner, we accepted a superstition. The superstition was that we are not part of the God I AM, and that The God I AM, had a gender, and He was out there living in some piece of real estate called Heaven. Furthermore, He who was all-knowing, created us to be doomed to failure. We desecrated Heaven and were cast out to live forever in pain and separation from the I AM of His Being. That is when Earth became Hell. A detention yard for bad spirits.

The story of Adam and Eve is truly a creative fairy tale. But it is very far from being true reality. This story has taught us from childhood that we are unworthy, the bastardized children of an angry jealous God, cast out of paradise, unprotected and vulnerable to the evils of physical existence. Our entire existence here was punishment. The only hope for salvation was to serve Churchianity.

Commit to a life of indentured servitude, and contrived ignorance, then at the end of your life of penance, the Priests as God's chosen ones, decided if you are worthy to go to Heaven with the good little children. We are growing up now and this fairy tale no longer answers the questions of the new consciousness. It cannot withstand the scrutiny of Divine Awareness. It was not born of Christ Consciousness, it was conceived of man. Immature man. Patriarchal man. Man who embraced fear, rather than Divine Love. That kind of thinking is dogma, it was someone else's Dream. It is born out of duality, and unworthiness. It is self-destructive thinking born of ignorance. It is a road that leads to nowhere. It is the consciousness of Pavlovian Dogmatism.

Does this all seem negative to you? Good. It is important to look at all of our negative feelings. This is how we learn. We expand through the friction. Since the Creator of all things, the GOD I AM is absolute perfection, we are also created in absolute perfection.

Our only special sin was that we forgot that we were the children of this I AM Presence that it is within us, and is the part of us that is eternal. Use your other senses and reason it out. What does your inner Soul tell you? Why would God create you less than perfect? Yet this God Force created the Eagle, the Crystal, the Flower, the Cloud in a glorious display of its perfection of the I AM that I AM.

Let no one Dream you. Know that you are not the Dream. You are in fact the One, the I AM who is having the Dream. You are the Dreamer. Dreams are not logical, so the last thing you will need is logical advice from the Mind. When you hear that kind of advice speaking from deep within the logical caverns of your Mind, thank it, acknowledge its effort and declare, "I AM the God of my Being, I AM the I AM, I AM the Dreamer. Be gone." Affirm your inner vision, affirm the existence of the I AM presence within you. Embrace the feelings of the God Force within, reconnect to Life, listen to the music of the wind and be in your Truth. Persevere and know that the Force is with you.

Each time you reaffirm this Magical Presence within, you will get a renewed feeling of existence and strength will fill your entire Being. This Infinite Presence is so powerful, so magnanimous, so much more than the limited Mind. It will dissolve your illusions and self-doubt. You are accessing another dimension that the Mind has no understanding of, for it is limitless. The Divine Awareness will come and whisper the proper course of action, so be prepared. Learn to listen to the subtleties of Its expression.

Great power is silent. Creator is silent. It is moving beyond light speed and our preceptors have grown slow through lack of use. The God I AM never abandoned you, you simply got lost in your perception of your relationship to It. You got stuck in Mind. Through your over indulgence in the intellectual process of Mind you became lost in endless duality, the world of the image. It is time to move forward now, into Awareness. Remember, you are the Dreamer. You know, the one who is having the Dream.

Before we move ahead into STEP FOUR, *Manifesting Your Reality*, let us go over some essential points. Consider going out to the wilderness, a garden, or a field, and find a great tree, sit down at its roots, under its great branches, and feel its connectedness to you. Contemplate upon these things, before you take this next step.

The God force of the I AM that I AM, the Great Mystery, is the Source from where Universal Law comes. The Universal Law only works when we are in alignment with this magnanimous presence. This presence is within you, therefore, you have immediate access to it. Meditation is an excellent vehicle to get out of Body-Mind Consciousness, to escape the internal dialog of the Mind.

This Universal Law is impartial and unprejudiced in its actions. It does not seek to find fault. It will manifest precisely what you ask for. The totality of the manifestation is directly related to the extent of your conviction and your clarity of expression. Keep it simple, one thing at a time.

You are not your Body, or your Mind. This robe you wear will one day be discarded for a grander garment. You are a manifested individual expression of this Great Mystery. You can call upon this I AM presence at any time, regardless of your seeming circumstance. It is the real you, the you that is your eternal living Spirit.

You can literally create any circumstance you desire through application of the *Kryah*. Manifestation cannot occur, however, if we draw the feeling from illusion. For instance, money is not real, it is an illusion. Being in abundance is not about having money. Money is the result of something else. It perhaps is the desire for success in your work, your skills, your energy. Money is a creation of the altered ego. Abundance is a state of Being. It is a feeling. It is an attitude.

You are the child of the Earth. Your very body is made up of every element that comprises her embodiment. She is your Mother. Therefore, you possess the consciousness of each of those elements. So the elements are under your domain, so to speak. But remember, the elements have a consciousness also. They are also of the I AM. *The Key is in being in Harmony with them.* The elementals rule this domain. This is their home and they are very real.

You are the expression of the God Force upon this plane. This God Force is neither male nor female in gender. It is more like energy, a force. This Divine presence is expressing Itself upon this plane through you. It is part of you. Get close to it..... reunite with it. Become yourself, your True Self. Whatever you desire is there for your use. Always ask permission, respect all life forms and the God Force within them. Respect the laws of the giveaway, for each thing received, leave a gift that holds meaning to you.

Your manifestations are not manna from Heaven, they are your creations. They are yours to utilize and further express this Divine presence through your enjoyment of them. They are of you, therefore they are you, just as you are part of the Great Mystery. Rejoice in the God Force working through you. Become the hollow bone.

You are a part of an unfathomable whole, a magnificent force that is limitless and inexhaustible. All of life around you is the manifestation of Its presence, It will and does respond to you. Realize that same presence is in everything you come into contact with. Without it, nothing materially could exist. Acknowledge it and go forth with right purpose and proper action. For all is balance, all of life is a prayer. Walk the sacred path by making your life sacred.

Remember that the Universal Law, the effects of the *Kryah* is of its very nature, the state of Divine Balance and Harmony. So, as you begin to test the waters and participate in Dream Creation, you will not be able to infringe upon anyone's space, so to speak, or you will lose your canvas. They are also of this presence. The Universal Law does not allow you to dominate another, it cannot be utilized for the sake of tyranny without serious consequences to the originator of the Dream. Whatever you shall think, so shall you become it.

Whatever you judge, so shall you become. You will find in time, along the journey of the sacred path, that what appears to block your progress is simply the results of your judgments. Remove your judgments and the river of creation will begin to flow from the Source, as it was originally intended. The pain you experience along the path is equal to the love you withhold.

STEP FOUR: MANifESTiNG YOUR REAliTy

Within the Divine Source, the Great Mystery, the I AM that I AM, there exists no duality. Source is Pure Awareness born of the original Consciousness. In the beginning, the Consciousness of *Source* contemplated Itself and in that grand movement *Source* realized through Its own energy, Its potentiality, and all of the Light that is, was created. All things potentially were brought into Conscious reality. This Consciousness works the same way yours does, for you are part of this Consciousness. You are a particum of the original Light of the dawning and *Kryah* is in and of all things. It is the result as well as the cause.

Consciousness, is Thought lying dormant in the void of eternity. Awareness is the force that activates Consciousness. The Consciousness expands and realizes its potential. Energy is created through this process. Energy is how Thought moves and is felt, just like the waves of the Ocean. Awareness is the force the Egyptians called *Ska,* what we know as *Kryah.* When *Kryah* engages Consciousness it creates Energy. When Consciousness is aligned with Energy, creation occurs. It must, it has to. We are aware of our *Thought* through our feelings. When Thought moves, it creates Light. Light, in turn, creates tone and color. The degree of tone or color is realized through energy frequency.

All of life resonates to these different frequencies. The differences cause dimensional changes. The difference between the fourth dimension and the third dimension has to do with the rate of speed of light.....how fast or slow it vibrates. The Masters existing in fifth dimensional reality, resonate at such a high frequency that they can walk through walls. The walls are in our third dimensional reality, thus they are vibrating at a much slower rate of speed. This is also why we cannot see them, even if they are right in the room with us. At this point, it must also be taken into consideration that all things existing within a particular dimensional reality, vibrate within a specific energy wave, or rate of speed.

This means that we, the tree, the rock, the bird, the flower, although vibrating at our own individual metabolic rate, are co-existing within the wave of energy that comprises third dimensional reality. The Source is coming from an extremely high rate of vibrational existence. It is beyond light. It is, after all, thought.

As thought waves slow down or coagulate, they become light waves. As light waves slow down they, in turn, coagulate and become matter. In the manifesting process, we emit, so to speak, thought waves to the Source. As they commune with the Source, they return to us through the same process, eventually manifesting into third dimensional reality via thought, to light, to matter.

The closer we are to the Source within us, and the more we learn to remove our judgments by seeing the interconnectedness with all of reality around us, the quicker the manifestation can occur. Hence, the emphasis is on moving our perception beyond embracing the thought patterns that create separatism.....separatism between Beings, as well as our Spiritual reality. The sense of separatism is but an illusion. Its cause is our own choosing to live within the state of illusion, or what we call *the image*. In many ways, we perceive our world from the opposite side of reality. *Hu*-manity has gotten stuck on the wrong side of the camera lens.

The reality of the ordinary human Being is caused by an extremely slow metabolic rate. This is caused by a number of situations, but mainly distorted thinking.....sort of like looking at life through the opposite side of a telescope. We therefore compress the frequencies that we have at our availability. Therefore we have a constrained perception of reality. We were originally created to read the different frequency bands through our feelings. Our brain, for the most part, is likened unto a transducer. We are simply receivers and interpreters of the Light.

Feelings are an aspect of the pure Consciousness of the God Force. Feelings are impartial and do not possess the quality of discrimination. In fact, they have no ability for discernment. They simply are, once again I AM that I AM. You have the power to allow the existence of feelings in your reality or deny them access. But you can never have the ability to destroy them. They are like nerve endings of this eternal God Force. They are part of the communication process between Creator and you, allowing you to express upon this plane.

In this expression there are no accidents, no victims, and there simply does not exist the probability for mistakes. Each Being is responsible for their own evolutionary path, as well as their actions and reactions along their chosen path. Each attracts or repels circumstance that facilitates the Dream in its creation. This again has to do with frequencies......like attracts like.

The Dream itself is the result of our Emotions. Taking our thoughts and embracing them or not embracing them, is a process of utilizing and connecting with energy, not discerning personalities. Personalities have to do with the Dream. They are holographic projections of our chosen dramatization. We each by the manifestation of our emotional feelings, create patterns that dictate the very Nature of our Reality. It is all energy, physical mass is nothing more than coagulated thought, or Light in slow motion.

Another key: Understand whatever energy creates the thought, is not the same energy that creates the manifestation. It will take a greater energy to manifest. The process is called expansion. When you have the conception of the Dream, it is a slow process at first in becoming. The journey from the moment the thought was pressed into your awareness, until it actually develops into physical manifestation, is the learning.

Most people just want to get on with it, let's see the Miracle. It is very difficult to manifest expanded thought into third dimensional reality. It is extremely dense here. The success, or lack of success, depends greatly upon focus. To bring in the Light and merge it with the extremely slow rate of speed existing in this reality, one has to work at it, come up to speed, so to speak.

Again it must be understood that what you are undertaking is a process, not an event. The manifestation is only equal to the understanding, which determines the magnitude of the Emotion embraced in the contemplation of the Dream. The Emotion expressed can be no greater than the God I AM.

Therefore, one must align themselves to this great I AM energy and allow themselves to become as a hollow bone. The power demonstrated is again equal to the depth and perception of the Divine Awareness we have developed within our Being.

If you want to sail a great schooner you first have to learn to row a little boat. So, in the beginning make it easy on yourself. Let's not try to create a fourteen-caret diamond or turn water into wine. If this sounds ridiculous, that's good. There are countless people who would try to make this occur. Upon their failure, they would walk away with the only manifestation having been realized is their enhanced feelings of unworthiness. We must start by addressing *attitude*. We must change our attitude, and sustain the higher thought patterns that come from the heart center, or the fourth seal. Without the proper attitude it is impossible to proceed down the pathway. Meditation is the quickest way to the inner world. If you have not already conceived a process, I would ask you to consider this very simple and un-dogmatic method.

MANIFESTATION AND THE RIGHT USE OF MEDITATION

1. Find yourself a quiet place. It could be outdoors, in the basement of your home, or a special corner in your apartment. It needs to be a place where you go to have sacred space....where you go to be closer to the forces of nature and the God within. If you are creating it, then make it special. Prepare yourself and the area as if you were going into the holiest event of your life, as if you had invited Creator to dinner. Announce to the Universe to the best of your ability, what your intentions are, what you wish to accomplish here. This is your place, so other's ideas should not be allowed to influence you.

If you wish you may light a candle, acknowledging the flame of life within all living things.....the Violet Flame of eternal Beingness. Smudge the area with sage or your favorite incense and invite the Spirits, *all of your relations*. Ask for their assistance. It is too often forgotten the importance of the role that the elementals (Earth Spirits) play in our everyday existence.

Call to the six directions, (North, South, East, West, Father Sky and Mother Earth) always acknowledging the seventh, which is within. Ask for the protection of the Great I AM, the Great Mystery of perfection. Literally call forth a merging of the physical you, and the Spiritual eternal you. Acknowledge your Mother the Earth, and your Father the Sky for they have given you life, and an embodiment to experience this Divine *Hu*-man drama.

2. Make prayer ties. This can be a good form of meditation for those who might be unfamiliar with meditation processes. Prayer ties are small square pieces of cloth, made from a natural material like cotton. Take seven pieces of cloth, each one representing seven positive aspects of what you wish to create in your Dream. Think about the changes you wish to occur, the effects they would cause for the betterment of your life, and how it would bring you closer to the God Force within. Put a prayer into a small offering and place it in the center of each square, (the Native American tradition calls for a pinch of tobacco, cornmeal or sage). Fold the cloth around the offering and tie it with a cotton thread. Then tie them together in a chain.

3. Take another seven squares of a different colored cloth, and place a pinch of offering in each of these also. These pieces shall be the seven negative aspects you wish to discard from your life, the seven attitudes or conditions you no longer desire to embrace and experience. These are the negative influences you feel in your Dream that keep you from being more than you are presently experiencing. Take your time.

Be specific. Be simple. Be very clear. It doesn't matter if it takes you all afternoon, or evening for that matter, *where are you going*? . This is your life, you deserve this special moment with yourself. You must see the Dream through to its completion. The ties are tied together in a chain as before. For all of life and all of your experiences are continuing, like the flow of a river.

4. Link together the two chains of prayer ties when you are complete with your meditation over the aspects of change you wish to create. You will have fourteen ties when you are finished, seven aspects for the positive that you desire to bring into your life, seven for the negative that you desire to leave your life. This is the balance. Put these in your special place and for seven days think about each one of these ties, seven times during the course of the day. By the end of the week it should get very

easy. Your can do more, but keep it simple to start with. God is simple follow the ideal.

5. Each day that you have executed this simple discipline, you have been developing your ability to focus. Each time you thought about all the aspects that each little prayer tie represented, you declared that thought into the Universe. Pick a time, either each evening or each morning when you rise, sit in a comfortable position in your special place. If you can sit in the lotus or half-lotus this is fine. If you cannot, that is all right too. Intent is the most important factor.

6. Honor the six directions and the presence of the God force within. Take seven slow breaths. Upon the intake, acknowledge your connection to the eternal God Force within, envision yourself within a Great Violet Flame. On the out breath, envision this Great Violet Flame bursting into a great ball of light with you in its center. Feel your connectedness to all of life around you. Feel this Violet Flame and its light streaming into every cell in your body, see it there, become the Flame.

It can be of assistance in journeying if one chooses to listen to soft music. Flutes or harps are excellent. Also, one can truly journey while listening to the sounds of nature recordings, if it is difficult to get into the great outdoors. Make it music without words. They will only draw you into someone else's dream. The objective is to get to a place where you are not aware of your thoughts. You are awake, but drifting some-where beyond time.

7. Now, think about each of the little prayer ties that embrace each aspect of yourself......that which you wish to bring into your Being, and that which you wish to experience no more. Try to go beyond thought, and feel the feeling. See in your mind's eye the completed change and the person you will become when the change is com-plete. Actually live this change of attitude, walk around, meet people, interact with them in the new way you have created.   See yourself moving through life in the flow of it rather than against the tide. Remember, you are the Divine Law, you are perfection, you are harmony.

8. Set aside a time at the end of this seven day period, where you allow your-self to spend at least two full hours lost in the Dream of what you are endeavoring to create here. It is your life, it is OK to do this, you deserve this time alone with the God

Force within. So, give yourself permission. When you have done your discipline and achieved the state of mind where all there is, is you and what you wish to create, take the prayer ties that are before you, place them in a safe position and burn them in a small ceremonial fire. Mix some sage with them while they burn. Declare that you are committed to the God Force within and committed to walking in the Truth of the Divine Perfection. You are now letting go, allowing them to become part of the Universal Force, the God Force.

9. These changes that you have called forth are accepted from the God of your Being, they are so. Release them into the Universe. Let them go from your consciousness, for they are complete. They are consumed in the Great Violet Flame, as is the illusion in your life. As they burn, affirm yourself in your mind's eye as standing in your truth, being the changes you have dreamed about within your Being. Become the completed form of these creations. Walk into life allowing for nothing that is in disharmony with your declaration. You have just completed your first exercise in Dream Creation. Now go and do something that brings you joy. Playtime is important, it lets the child out.

Change must start from within. In order for you to alter that which is outside of you, you must first go within and expand your abilities within the inner world. You must go beyond the consciousness that created the problem and become more than the circumstances that created it. You must accept your responsibility for its creation, take from it its lesson to you and your life's path. Leave it behind you. If at first you do not complete all the desired changes, this is OK.

Just go back through the process, ask the God Force within to reveal to you what you chose not to release. Perhaps there is a situation that needs addressing. Then you will be free to continue on the path. Remember to the true initiate, life is never a problem. It is a never ending opportunity to develop our skills and to become the expanded Self.

Everything is energy......sometimes high energy, sometimes not so high energy, even the feeling of no energy is energy. It is like you are a magical fish swimming in a vast sea of endless energy, going around asking all the other fish where the ocean is. Well, the ocean is all around you. The reason you can't see it is simply because you are immersed in it. Your existence within this field of sacred energy, the God Force is no different. It is endless and all around you all the time.

Your ability to perceive this endless field of energy and precisely how it works, is determined upon how much effort you have spent on centering yourself in the reconnection of your Awareness of it and your connection to Source. This is accomplished by using it. At first, like a small child learning a little more each time, and then picking up speed with each experience.

This lifetime, this experience upon the Earth plane is yours. You created it by choice. You are involved in relationships and interactions with other people. But the experience is yours. No one is going to die for you, only you are going to do that. No one is going to live for you, for only you can have that experience. This is *your* evolutionary experience.

There are no incurable diseases, there is only restricted consciousness. They can seem incurable because of a senseless devotion to ignorance. The refusal to grow. It is called *A CLOSED MIND*. Your true inner nature is eternal and unlimited. Even your body was programmed to be eternal.

Death itself and the embracing of death is conscious choice. It is the conscious choice of the collective. Remember Jonathan Livingston Seagull*, and how he had to struggle to go beyond the pull of the collective, to go beyond limitation, just to become his own individual expression of life. He, like you, will succeed. It is your commitment to conscious choice.

You can spend the rest of your life trying to correct your imbalances through physical and mental methodology. You may even find temporary solutions like Band-Aids, to cover the wounds. But to cure the imbalance, to achieve harmony and leave disease behind once and for all, takes the conscious effort of going within.

Going within and reopening the doorways that you have shut down lifetimes ago. You have gotten lost in the Dream and forgotten that you are the one having the Dream. The doorway to the God Force, the I AM that I AM, the Great Mystery, is within, not without. The Source, the manifestor is within. Everything outside is merely the result of the inner, expressing or not expressing itself.

Now, is where you come into contact with the first Key, Compassion and self forgiveness. We all have made mistakes. We all hold the thought that there are things we would have done differently, if we knew then what we know now. But you see, if you had not done that then, you would not be where you are now. You arrived at this destination and place of realization because of all that you have done prior to this moment. So first forgive yourself, and then forgiving others will be easier. For you will have owned forgiveness in yourself. Now you are being God In Action G.I.A.

The changes that begin to happen from this internal process that you have just begun, as you assume responsibility for your life, will more often than not come about in an illogical manner. They will manifest in the strangest of ways. This is your inner Being's way of getting you to trust the Universal Law. You will know when it is occurring because you will feel it. It will reveal its existence through the communication of feelings rather than thought. Feelings are the experience. Thoughts in the Mind are merely the review of past experience.

You cannot control the manifestation. It is a process of letting go and trusting. The more you trust, the more the energy will come through. The more you say, "OK, lets see this eternal God Force work here. Let's see just how it manifests," you are in a sense calling it forth and stepping aside, or shall we say, getting out of your own way. Each time you are becoming more and more in tune. You are becoming more and more centered. This process of allowing the Self to become centered and to feel, is much more powerful than you may think.

Each time you declare your alignment with the eternal God Force you allow for more and more of it to flow through you. You will become an observer of your own life. The Dreamer seeing the Dream. You will begin, through the power of observation, to realize that you are in fact participating in the Dream. You are not the Dream. As you perfect the process and continue, it will start to dawn on the Mind that you were correct in your new programming. That in fact, you are the Dreamer, you are the creator of your own reality and your Mind will always respond to its Creator, it is the Law.

Remember, who you are, is not what you were, not what you do, and not how people conceive you to be. It is how you feel. You are your thoughts, not your thinking……your thoughts.

STEP FIVE: PROPER ATTITUDE

The laws governing proper attitude are important to comprehend in order to progress along the path of the initiate. We all too often spend vital energy in useless pursuits. This is a form of dissipating personal power. Thus when called by life experience to draw upon our power of focus, it is not there. We find our thoughts and emotions lost in a whirlpool of confusion, where we are desperately trying to focus through a labyrinth of conflicting perceptions of probabilities. This can only cause us to become reactionary, rather than causal.

This attitude causes the focus of creation to change direction. The inner Being contracts, and our consciousness which is likened to a cloud of light, implodes within us. We are then cut off from the God-Force and we begin to spiritually suffocate. This process is called *dis-creation*. When all of life appears to be coming from the outside rather than the inner world of our Being, we will experience the feeling of implosion. Our consciousness, in essence, is collapsing upon us. This state of Being is the doorway to Fear, and Fear shuts down the access to our Divine system. Fear quite literally paralyzes the heart chakra.

When the system shuts down, we get lost at the crossroads and are unable to choose a course of action. The feeling is confusion. Life gets flat and we lose our ability to "come from a position of power." This is when the demon rises within and we suddenly enter *the Valley of Self Doubt*. It literally causes an experience of insanity. To the aspiring initiate, this can be disastrous. If we give into the negativity of Self-Doubt, the Dream dissolves. The initiate can actually cease to be, by virtue of his or her own self-judgment. In simplicity, what is happening is that we are turning our power over to the Dream. We start to become that which is Dreamed, losing awareness of our center, which is the *Source* of the Dream. We have fallen out of sync with our life's natural rhythm. We perceive ourselves as viewing the Light, instead of Being the Light.

Being out of sync with the natural rhythm of life, we begin to experience feelings of lethargy, and malaise, both mentally and physically. We literally lose our ability to communicate with our inner Being, the God Force. We disconnect from everything around us, as we give into fear and shut down. This process again is called implosion. It is consciousness collapsing in upon itself.

Think of it like a computer that suddenly becomes disconnected from its source of power. It stops transmitting the picture after a few seconds delay, and then your visual screen goes blank. We have all experienced this to one degree or another at different times. If it occurs, it is all right. Retreat to within, the Divine Source. Surrender to your inner Self and then allow the Universal Law to take over. It knows what to do. Just go back to Source.

If you stay in the *NOW*, you can and will take command over these situations. And eventually they will cease to manifest in your reality. They are an indication of not spending enough time acknowledging your inner feelings. Spending too much time focused on the outside, too little on Self-realization.

Adversity of this nature can be a great teacher, however we must watch our tendencies to indulge in this space too long. Negativity is like the cancer cell….. if left unchecked it can consume you. Like the cancer cell, it is the direct result of a bad attitude on the part of the collective *Hu*-man consciousness. It is this poor attitude of the collective consciousness that is destroying the Earth and bringing mankind to the edge of self annihilation this very day. Is that not the nature of cancer, does it not destroy the very thing which affords it life?

Now, in the beginning of this process, you are going to spend the majority of your time adjusting attitudes. Making the garden ready for the planting of the seeds. You are going to have to make some very clear decisions here. You are going to have to take a long honest look at yourself and decide what is positive and what is negative in your life.

What allows you to stay connected to that inner Source and what breaks the connection. If a circumstance does not align with the inner balance, go into it. Look at it for its truth, and release it as no longer serving a useful function. Remember you are the Dreamer and not the Dream. If the Dream is cancerous, cut it out.

This will be hard at first because you haven't developed your *belief* yet. You have faith, you are reading this work. Therefore, you are reaching out because you have faith that there is something more. But you are going to have to develop *belief*. Remember the Mind does not naturally understand unlimited possibility. It doesn't know that it is only a part of the Dreamer. It has to be taught.

That means that you are going to have to commit to this undertaking and become the teacher. You have to first assume the attitude that you are important enough to care about. Even if you don't know all there is to know at this moment, you already have assumed the position of becoming.

You are going to allow the child within, the Dreamer, to emerge. You are going to allow yourself to feel. It has been a very long time since most of us have let the child out of captivity. So we are going to need to create a safe, loving environment. This can be accomplished through the attitude of allowance, and objective observation.

It is going to grow like a seed in this garden you are nurturing and preparing. If you dig the seed up to see what is going on, the flower will perish. So allow it to grow at its own rate. Allow it to feel, allow *faith* to become *belief*. Focus on the thought that the seed, the thought itself, was created through the original Source. It has been brought into manifestation by the God Force which is within you. The I AM that I AM, which only knows perfection.

Thoughts of imperfection are the creation of the external world, by-products of the Mind and intellect......good-bad, being more than, being less than. These thoughts of comparison and judgment create inner conflict and division of purpose. Until you develop within you, a love for Self, equal in vibratory level to the love that the Creative Force, God, is pouring out constantly to you, you will not be able to access the greater planes of knowledge that lie within. For you are in a state of denial.

Love is the very glue that holds your embodiment together. So to begin, we accept that like the seed, we are already complete. Everything we need is already there. We just have to learn to access it. This we will accomplish through proper attitude and thus the right use of will.

The seed does not know its next step in evolution. It does not know that upon completion it will develop into the wondrous rose. It simply follows the Universal Law. It grows, it seeks moisture, it seeks nourishment, it seeks the warmth of sunlight, it rises through the soil and rock, constantly reaching out towards the light.

You see, we are the only creatures that are afraid of change. The only ones! One of the most beautiful stories I have ever heard is the story of the Caterpillar, the little worm that spends its entire life consuming green leaves. It does not know that it will become the Butterfly. It cannot even see the Butterfly because the Butterfly is the next step in its evolution. There are no great wise ancient Caterpillars to consult and ask, "Why do I have this compulsion to spin this chrysalis, to go inside and sleep? What will I dream when I go through this process?" It just follows its own inner voice.

Do you think that when the Caterpillar awakens, it says, "Wait a minute, what is this. I do not want this. I want to go back to being a Caterpillar. What are these wings of Crimson and Blue? What happened to my hundred legs? Now I only have six. And what about these ridiculous black stockings?" Do you think it asks this? I don't think so.

We are imprisoned by the unopened Mind, which has produced the consciousness of the collective. The Mind unrealized relies upon intellect. Intellect is the robot that can only accesses past experience. The collective Mind is afraid of change, because (they) cannot see it visualized, into mass. The outcome is yet unknown, and the Mind does not possess of itself the ability to conceptualize, what you could become in thought, because what you will become has not yet been experienced.....not unlike the Caterpillar changing into the Butterfly.

So through exercising our communication with the inner Self, the unlimited Self, we learn to look at things as a child. Seeing only the infinite possibilities, not the unending limitations. Which is why children, when they are very young, are not afraid of change, and deal with it constantly through their natural development. They are more like the tiny Caterpillar.

However, as the child grows to adulthood, the spontaneous curiosity that sparks the creative ability to Dream and to believe in miracles, is suppressed. The "Adult" belief pattern of the collective unconscious is imposed upon the child to conform to the collective thought patterns. This creates limitations and objections to personal expression through ignorance, rather than heart felt understanding. The child is suppressed and the genius is placed in prison.

So keep the child alive, keep the genius free and living. Keep close contact with that feeling of enthusiasm you had when you were a small child.....when you played for hours and went long past the time when you should have been home for dinner. Remember the feeling you had when you looked out of your crib, and observed life, before you tried to apply the values of the "Adult" world around you....when your feelings were still yours, before you were taught to discard them for someone else's. Remember when you lost all concept of time and became the game.

Keep your thoughts pure and focused, do not allow yourself to be swayed by the thoughts of others. These are only the opinions of yet to be completed creators. Do not allow your creative process to be constrained by the limits of the material plane. Realize that everything in the material plane is the result of Thought. Good experience, or not so good an experience, it is a matter of choice.

The circumstance is the result of being the Dreamer or being that which is being Dreamed. Your thoughts are more powerful than physical reality. They are the very source of its existence. Physical reality is the source of experience for the Dreamer to evaluate, and determine what he or she desires to be Dreamed. The result of the Dreamer's dreaming is manifested into existence. It is law.

The swelling of desire and the conscious decision to act upon it, is our pathway through life. Place your dreams before you and follow. As you work with this knowledge, constantly developing proper attitude, and living in the *NOW*, life will have a way of showing you the next move at every turn along that pathway.

Once you make the commitment to be the Dreamer, your inner God Force is so powerful that it will literally pull you into adventures beyond what your current beliefs can presently allow. But it demands absolute commitment from your Being......so you are capable of handling the energy that you will merge with, once you reunite yourself with the Source of your Being......God!

That which is Dreaming you, is so Loving that it allows you absolute freedom of expression.   That which Dreamed the Dream of life, allowing you free access to the knowledge of the process, asks nothing in return. *Rules*? Keep it pure, keep it simple, dare, do and remain silent. Tell no one of your inner quest, or what is being revealed to you. If you have questions go within, not without.

You will not find the answer in the collective unconscious, they simply don't know. They most likely are hoping that you have the answer. *To do, to dare, and to be silent.* Keep your methods to yourself, and then speak only of the Manifested creation, not its cause. Your brothers and sisters, your teachers and guides will make themselves known along the Pathway.

At first you may not be certain of your direction. You might be facing terrific change. The tendency of the Group Consciousness is to avoid confrontation. It is hard to discover your own pathway in a world that is caught in *the spider's web of collectively agreed limitations*. You will be feeling things that perhaps no one around you has ever allowed themselves to feel...... nor have you.

Those around you who are still in the ordinary experience, are for the most part locked up in the prison of intellect, always coming from past experience. They live in constant fear, unsure of tomorrow because of the denial of the *NOW*. They have elected themselves self appointed ambassadors of the *"Have Not's."* They do not yet own themselves.

If you find yourself entering a space of confusion, try a walk in nature, a walk with your Mother. There you will find many answers. Everything that surrounds you has the God Force within it. In the quiet of nature you will become aware of the subtlety of the energies around you.

In nature you will be able to get in contact with your feelings. You will be grounded by her energies. She will actually take the negativity from your body. When the body is grounded you can experience through your senses that are beyond Body-Mind Awareness. Ride the feelings out......clear your mind of all internal dialogue. Get control over your Mind and center your energy inwards.

Get to where at first you are only aware that you are not thinking. Not thinking…..Get it? When you are not thinking, you are Being. When you are Being, your consciousness opens to Awareness. The Awareness follows Universal Law. Use your feelings to guide you through. You move through the Dream by pushing your feelings out in front of you. How does it feel? Where does it flow, where do you find resistance?

You may have some difficulty at first. Most of us have spent years shutting down our feelings. Push them out in front of you. You will find that you will be able to allow them to surface because *you* are not going to hurt *you*. Trust in that and feel your way through it.

After awhile the process will become easier and easier. Just ride those thoughts out and get to the place where the internal dialogue stops. That is where your feelings lie. That is where the Awareness is. There, in the silence. You can feel the energy of events that will occur in your life, weeks, sometimes years, before they manifest. Every event in your life is linked to the next.

Know that all collective consciousness operates from the past. It has no sense of now. In fact, the very awareness of the now dissolves it, and it will no longer have any power over you. When you can no longer battle against the outside forces that seem piled against you, surrender to Divine Order, allow the thought to be totally released from your Being. Dream it completed and let the Divine Force follow its course. Let it go. Do not hide, do not run. Stand your ground, stay in your truth and let it be.

Personal power comes from being in the now. Dis-empowerment comes from living in the past or trying to run away from the now into the future. Your pathway must address the present the *NOW*. Only from the present can creation of any kind occur. The reason you enter into a state of confusion at any given moment is the sole result of being out of alignment with the now. Then perception is clouded and there is no focus possible. The Master walks the middle road, meaning literally through the center.

This great I AM energy, the God Force, is always in the center. You have heard it referred to as walking the middle road. It was never meant to be construed as the state of complacency and being non-passionate. Consider it rather like a sliding scale of -10 to +10. Let's make +10 Positive, and let's make -10 Negative. Creation occurs in the center, at 0 point. That is where neutral is, that is *ISNESS*.

Remember the God-Force is neither Positive nor Negative. It simply is. " I AM that I AM." The Universal Law does not discriminate, it does not judge. It is of itself. It is available to anyone, even the Butterfly. If it is available to a mere Butterfly, why not you? Are you any less worthy?

You are no less than the Butterfly. You are just the Caterpillar struggling to break out of the chrysalis that you have slept in for seven and a half million years. Struggling against thousands of years of organized religions, governments, society, your parents, your traditions, your culture, and your friends saying, "It's hard out there alone. Come back into the fold, you know no one can make it alone. No one has all the pieces. You can't think for yourself. God is out there. Heaven is out there." They are patterns from your past. They are already lived Dreams. Although the present conditions may be different, the person within is still the same person, having the Dream over and over, and over.

Heaven, is and has always been within you. God I AM, is not outside of you. Heaven is not a piece of Real Estate out in space. The Creator of all life is within. So if God, the Supreme Being, whoever or whatever you perceive God to be, lives in Heaven, where is that? Reason it out. Where is most pure Mind? What is it? Where does it come from?

Developing Proper Attitude is essential to the path of the initiate. It can be one of the longest disciplines that we apply. We must re-adjust our perception of our entire reality to the original thought of Creator in order to continue down the pathway of knowledge. We must become one with it, then willfully live it out in our expression of everyday life in the Human Drama. Only through developing proper attitude can the initiate expand beyond the boundaries of the limited collective consciousness. The reclaiming of personal power can only be achieved by understanding what causes it and how to correct the patterns of the consciousness that created the situation of disharmony in the first place.

As long as we continue to give our power to external sources, Self-realization, which is Self empowerment, cannot occur. Enlightenment itself is a process of remembering what has always been there. It is a process of *awakening* from the Dream, through the process of becoming the Master of the Dream, through Mastering Self. Know thyself and you shall know God.

You can only be enslaved and controlled if you are in lack of knowledge. It is the lack of knowledge that keeps you dependent upon the external benevolence of some created God, and your destiny is subject to the mystery of fate. There is no fate, fate is a misnomer......it is based on the condition of not taking responsibility. There is only destiny. Fate becomes the result of *your* Manifestation, complete or incomplete. Destiny is the Self-realized Dream....it is the pathway of the Master.

By the continued affirmation that you are less than, that you are separate from, that you are in worship to some external deity called God, is a ploy of tyranny. Man was created as God's image, not the other way around. If your conception of God, is of a God that is all powerful, yet still must be worshipped by little old you, perhaps you should consider reevaluating where that concept came from in the first place.

The thinking process of humanity has been severely damaged by the dogmas of organized religion for thousands of years. It is the resuly of man's insane attempts to dominate his brother. That time is past. God, be assured, has no desire to dominate you. God could never condemn you, for in essence, God would be condemning Self. If that occurred, then Life on all levels would cease to be. For *All* that we call life is the Dream of the Divine Father and the realization of the Divine Mother.

A day is coming where *Hu*-man kind will no longer need to express itself in terms of power, or being more than. For the greatest power that can be experienced is experienced in the state of not Being. The state of ISNESS. There, we no longer have the need to justify our existence. We will come to know God, the True Source. The very fact that you are, is enough for God.

Why then, is this simple fact not enough for you? The Great Spirit that Dreams the Dream of life has never lost belief in what you could become. Only mankind has lost belief in himself. Only mankind can destroy himself. Only Mankind can recreate himself. Pain is caused from mass separation from the Source. It is the worst kind of pain. It is illusion.

We were created in absolute perfection. We are a Divine concept. We are whole. We were created complete. There have been some errors of judgment. We are children, growing. The Creator knows that. There have been genetic tamperings, resulting from outside interference in our development as a species. Our truth still remains, even after seven and one half million years of self-enslavement, self-annihilation, and blind devotion to ignorance.

You cannot ever bury the Truth for it is within the blueprint of life itself. It is the testimony to Epigenetics, the plan of Creation. It is the *Will* of the unknown God, the Great Mystery, the I AM that I AM.

You can never destroy life. No more than you can destroy a Dream in your slumber. You can stop dreaming, you can wake up, but you have no power to destroy the Dream itself. After all, life is the Dream of creation itself. You can choose to participate, or not to participate.

You can choose to know, or choose to walk in ignorance. You can choose to take on a dis-easement, or choose perfect health. You can choose to live in Self-Joy, or Self-Denial. You can choose to be powerless or the child of the living God. It is your choices and those choices are all a result of your personal attitude, your personal myth if you will. The difference between observing the Light, or being the Light, is attitude.

If you choose to walk the path of the *initiate*, it is a supreme commitment to Self Awareness. If you desire to manifest, you had best explore the reasons why. It is your attitude that dictates your choice of action. It is your attitude that dictates the thought you choose to embrace. And thought embraced becomes manifested reality. That is Universal Law.

Think on this to the core of your Being. Call forth the God of your Being. You can go no farther until you pass this gateway. Until you own it and accept full responsibility for your decision of your attitude, for it determines what you express upon this plane. Your input into the Dream is the result of your choices.

'"From the God of My Being, from the Source that is within me, to the Source that is within you.......may the mighty I AM Presence enfold you within the Violet Flame of forever. May you be empowered to be all that you can be. May you walk evenly with all your brothers and sisters in the Cosmos.

" May you realize your true relationship to all your relations here upon the Earth plan, as well as in the Heavens. May you come to see that all you walk upon, the water you drink, the very breath you take, the trees, the flowers, the four legged, and the fowl that fly through the sky, everything including yourself, is *SACRED* to this Great Mystery. You are the Dream of the Mother. You are the Dream of the Father. Know you are forever...... Know you, child of God, you are the Dreamer. SO BE IT

STEP SIX: Life is a verb not a noun

There are countless reasons we can manufacture for not learning. So many reasons for not expanding beyond what you are presently realizing are the dictated limitations of the collective consciousness. At best our present systems for higher education offer us the lowest of understandings.

As a result of this kind of consciousness, an adopted form of being, ignorance, has become a condition of malignancy upon this plane. Instead of the individual being inspired to engage the Mind, to open it up and explore its nature and its possibilities, so that the Mind becomes stimulated to seek its full potential, we have created a condition whereby the individual is discouraged from Self-expression and the potential for genius. Self-Awareness realized through that expression, has been stilted.

The natural process of Self-realization has been suppressed to such an extent, that today it is almost a no-thing. There is an enormous amount of programming which must be overcome. We are taught what to think and how to think. We are in fact, given a programming of socially acceptable preconceived conclusions, which are nothing more than the composite picture of a synthesized reality...... assembled by a collective unconsciousness we call society.

This society has created within us, through its educational system, governmental controls and religious dogmas, a condition whereby we have developed an attitude that fears change. We are told change is dangerous to society's established system of Material Divinity. In our educational institutions and social order, technology it seems has replaced God. We do not seek to live in harmony with ourselves or the world around us. We seek to dominate all that is the creation of the Supreme Source. It is madness.

To follow the path of the *initiate,* you must willfully develop an ability to not grow roots, not in the Earth, not in a belief system, not in the society, not in tradition. For tradition, more often than not, is no more than the expanded dogma of recycled ignorance. It can be a prison. Rather, you must develop within yourself the innate ability to have no strings that bind you to that which you create, or the process by which it manifests itself.

You must be able to allow yourself to engage a process. You must allow the God Force to work through you. The process by which we can come to understand this Divine Principle is called evolution. Through the applications of objective participation, we can develop an understanding of how to access unlimited Mind.

You are going to have to develop within you the ability to discover the perimeters of your consciousness, and then go beyond them....... to the expanses of the God Force, the realm of unlimited thought. Teach the Mind how to access the potential for unlimited power that is available to it at every moment.

To realize your own unlimited potential, you are going to have to develop the ability to go betond it, into the unknown, to go beyond fear. You are going to have to learn to accept and allow change. Not only allow it, but welcome it. "To boldly go where no one has gone before," and explore new Universes of potentiality.

In working with the principles expressed in the previous chapter, you will be more aware of your *attitudes* with the passing of each hour. You will find that by releasing your attitudes, you will become more and more aware of the subtle energies that are in every living thing around you. Coincidence will more and more become the *result* of your desires.

By dropping dogmatic attitudes, you will allow life to occur in its natural rhythms, instead of the perception that you force upon reality. The events around you are simply the expression of life's energy following the Universal Laws of attraction. They are not personal, they are objective. It is all cause and effect.

Did you know that light has rhythm? That color has rhythm? There are rhythms that are indigenous to various locations on the Earth, as well as our different positions within the Dream. Ancient drums once attuned to these various rhythms and were the driving force behind the movements of the armies mobilized by the Ramadama, Krishna, Genghis Kahn, Marc Anthony and other conquerors.

As we travel through different areas of the world we feel different vibrations. The dance of an Apache in Arizona differs from the dance of the Polynesian and the Mayan, and differs still from the Vienese Waltz and the Polka. never mind the African rhythms and how do the Australian Aborigenies dance i wonder? . These rhythms are tied to the land as well as our cultural diversity.

For instance, in North America, we live a vastly different life style and pace (rhythm) from those who live in India. Our rhythm is tied to the land, and the energies that come from the Turtle itself. The Native American Grass Dancer, again, has a very different rhythm than the rock dancer at one of your local Night Clubs in a modern city. The Grass Dancer's rhythm comes from cultural heritage, social perspective.

Just like an athlete training for the Olympics, you must as the aspiring initiate, learn to re-tune yourself to the natural rhythms of the Earth, as well as to those that naturally flow through your physical Being. This commitment will bring to you a sense of well being that can open one to the natural rhythms that every other living thing on the planet is in harmony with, except Humanity. We have fallen out of balance mainly because of existing so long in our artificially created environments and being separated from the Earth energies. We have become juxtapositioned to Nature.

The human animal in reality is a very finely tuned instrument. Everything, literally everything, in our environment interacts with us. The term web of life is not metaphorical, it is a literal reality.   That web is affected by everything connected to it. That means from the tiny plankton that lives in our oceans, to the Moon.

From the EMF fallout of our electrically dependent society structure with its high tension wires, sound and media pollution, to the cutting down of Grandfather trees. Our bodies are, after all, biological computers designed to perform as electrical transducers. Our physical bodies are biological machines, which act as housing units for the Spiritual essence to function in our Earthly environment.

Nature is the greatest of schools for Biological Spiritual units. Planet Earth is a school, one of the greatest in the Universe. For woven into her world of nature and expressed through all of her creations, lies the blueprint of all things that exist within the planes of physical reality. By observing Nature's rhythms and listening to the heart beat of the Mother, by observing how the tide ebbs and flows, and how the feeling of dawn differs from the evening in the forests, we are once again returned to the understanding of our own rhythms and the cycles that govern the Universe we call the Human Body....... our secret cosmic gift that we understand so little about.

Man is born of nature. Man cannot create nature nor will man-kind be allowed to destroy her. The stories of the attempts by mankind to become the Masters of nature, are being discovered in almost every location across the globe. They are buried deep within the Earth and below her oceans. The wisdom of the Tao, which is based upon the rhythms of nature, stands today. Centuries after countless civilizations that chose to ignore the wisdom of the Tao have vanished from the face of the Earth, and even our memories. There is more wisdom realized in coming to understand the *River of Life*, and its rhythm of life, than in all the universities that contemporary man has built.

As you progress in your understanding of these natural rhythms that are occurring around you, as you begin to heighten your senses through developing your ability to utilize *objective* observation, these energies will begin to communicate to your inner Being.....not through language, but through feelings.

You can learn to exchange feelings with a tree or a flower. After awhile, you will witness an occurrence and see clearly why a thing happened the way it did. You will understand Universal Law as the Earth communicates through your emotional body.

Here is where you begin to learn the higher language. Emotion is the language of the Angels and the whole of the higher realms..

A very simple overview of the Universal Law, and how it works through you on the Earth plane, can be explained quite simply in the following manner. There are three principles involved. **Thought,** which is your inactivated consciousness. Herein lies all things that are possible, yet no thing material. Consciousness comes from beyond the Earth plane. It comes from the great void, in other words...God. Which is also the place where your ideas come from, your ideas. As this consciousness contemplates Itself and Its possibilities, It does so through the language of emotion, which you understand as seing your **Feelings.**

As you move through the Dream (life), your feelings develop into desires. They actually pull and push you along the pathway of the river of life. This happens through a constant reflecting back and forth between experience, which causes feelings. Your thoughts on those Feelings, are realized by you through Awareness, as desires. Thus, you develop the desire to draw the Feeling to you or to repel it. This is done through the laws of Attraction, and Repulsion.

The conscious choice to follow a desire, creates **Action.** Action is the result of allowing our desire to motivate us into a course of motion, which we initiate by Dreaming. Thus, we assume the role of the Dreamer when we desire with the whole of our Being, a "thing" to become a reality. It is quite natural and occurs even during our states of unconsciousness. These then are three principles that are the cause and effect of the Universal Law regarding action and manifestation....... *Thought, Feelings,* and *Action.*

These are the elements that direct the Dreamer towards a particular course of action. The occurrence of interaction between these three principles is happening almost simultaneously, and there is never a moment that they are not occurring. That is why *Life is a Verb.* Life is energy and energy is always in motion. That condition is a constant, which is why we exist in a participatory Universe.

If you are not engaged in physical motion, the energy which is always in the state of motion will be felt within your Being as uncontrolled emotions or confusion. Because we exist in a participatory Universe, we must be in the state of motion to exist here. This plane is literally called by your elder brothers from beyond the Sun, "The Plane of Action."

These three principles of life can actually be seen in the first three layers of the human aura. The one closest to your body usually appears bluish in color. It is the field of **Action,** the life force holding your embodiment together.

Just beyond this field, is another field of pure light energy that we often perceive in colors. The colors are actually your **Feelings.** We perceive them as color because they work through the Universal Language of Emotion. Emotions manifest themselves as color. They are actually visible in the light spectrum and can even be observed with Kurlian photography. This is the field that is often identified, although not entirely correct, as a person's aura. This field is actually only a part of the Auric field, which actually can radiate out from your heart center as much as 55 feet.

Just beyond this plane of reality there is another reality that is merging with this one. It is sometimes called the Auric field. This field of reality is not quite as clear, and takes some time for most of us to be able to perceive it. This field, when visualized through what has been referred to as our "Auric vision," is perceived as waves of energy......almost like what you see when you look just above the pavement on a hot summer's day and you see a wavy energy pattern. Or you can see it as the heat waves coming off the hood of a car when the Sun is beating down upon it. We perceive this field of energy often with little lights shimmering within it, swimming about like little microscopic life forms.

These little swimming light forms are actually thoughts. Thought enters into third dimensional reality as light. This field in which the little lights can be perceived is where your **Thoughts** are coming from. Quite literally, it is where the thought of your form and Being, your experience, is conceived. That, which you relate to as your body, is much like a light puppet that is responding to the energy field around it. Therefore you are not in your body at all. Your body is the receiver, and the transmitter of your thoughts that emanate from the energy field around your body.

This field can and does have color. It is the holographic Universe. Your **Thoughts** are communicating with the other two layers of your Auric field and realized by your physical Being through Emotions. The colors will range from being primary or pastel in nature that appear in an array of very unique unidentifiable colors, to being muddy, sometimes taking on grayish, or brown tones.

This variation in tones is due to your mixed emotions and not so pure thoughts that you collect around you. Sometimes this field will appear to be merging like wispy clouds down into the second layer of your Auric field, just as the rain can be seen falling from the clouds across the distant prairie or descending upon the mountain tops. When this is occurring, you are in the state where you are anticipating the taking of action.

So, it is an actuality that someone who possesses the ability to see with Auric vision, can see right through you, so to speak. They have learned to decipher the colors. They understand the emotional language, and will know what you are thinking of doing even before you realize it yourself. Some of us do not possess such a developed ability of Auric viewing, but your inner Being, which is connected to the God Force, understands this form of communication. It will see and understand these occurrences, even though your *Mind*, which for the most part exists within the limitation of the five senses, does not allow you immediate access to this dimension.

Your Inner Being is directly connected to your Awareness center, which is connected to the God Force. It knows what is going on, and communicates to you through the mechanics of the body. The body communicates through the central nervous system, by creating interferons. Interferons communicate via aquatic highways to the physical Brain.

The Brain sends electrical impulses throughout the body which are deciphered by your Mind, which, in turn, registers through your "gut feelings." Through the intuitive senses (sixth sense), you experience the need to take an action. This need is called a desire. Once it is activated by consciousness, the doorway to manifestation of the experience is opened.

The nature of the action itself and your sensitivity to the other levels of consciousness, depends upon your level of mastery over the Body-Mind Consciousness and its reactive tendencies. The input of knowledge with which you have or have not programmed your Mind, determines the variations in the form of responses to probabilities that could occur in any given situation.

The ability to expand the programmed responses of the Mind, is solely determined upon your developed ability through *Awareness* to access your unlimited consciousness. You must teach the Mind that there is something beyond itself that it can access. The Mind does not know that you created it because the Mind is trapped within third dimensional reality perception.

The process of programming the Mind, getting in command of our Body-Mind Consciousness, is not as hard as it might first appear. First you must realize that you are the Dreamer, and not the Dream. You must realize this through feeling it, not intellectualizing it. The Body is like a complex machine. It utilizes the Mind for information and accesses it like a computer.

The Mind has a basic ability to determine what is going on in your reality at any given moment, based upon third dimensional perception. The Mind is like the caretaker of the machine. It is being governed by the Altered Ego, the image of what you truly are. The image or caretaker is almost a double of yourself without the God- Essence. The Caretaker or the Altered Ego is extremely fond of its position. It has been left alone in its process of operating the machine. No one has been telling it what to do. It has even grown to think that it is you. It is very much the wayward child.

Know that you own the Body. You are the architect that designed the structure of your present reality including its physical form of manifestation. Thus, in a manner of speaking, you have employed the Mind to do a job. You are its creator. The problem in your life, up until the point where you begin to awaken to the God Force within and decide to assume mastery over Body-Mind Perception as well as the Caretaker, is that for the most part you have been an absentee owner.

You have relied on the Mind's robotic abilities to operate *the biological machine*. The Mind, in your absence of Awareness, has been relying on its limited expanse of intellectual knowledge to get the job done. The job has always been to produce your desire. But the Mind itself has been trapped within Body-Mind Consciousness. It reflects back to you the madness that we all witness in our present day society. We know the madness is there. We know it does not work, but we feel powerless to change it. We are stuck in limited reality, limited perceptions.

You are, as the *Hu*-man animal, a consumer of desire because you like the feelings that desires can manifest. Your whole existence on the Earth plane is realized through feelings. Feeling comes from emotion, and *emotion* is the expression of God. It is the fabric of which the Dream is spun.

Our memory of a past life existence can only come from emotional memory. We can only remember through emotions. Now, back to our caretaker, who is not used to being told how to perform the job. It has developed methods of its own while you were away on holiday so to speak. It does not yet possess the understanding of multi-dimensional reality.

Easy does it it is like working with a horse... a few minutes each day and allow the process to grow longer and longer as the mind learns to head you commands. Else you will startle is and well   ever try to stop a horse from running by holding a rope?

If you try to bull dog your way into the process, the Mind is going to resist you. It will resist you with everything it has access to. Remember that it does not know who you are. It is programmed to *"caretake"* the machine, to defend it at all costs. It has been given a position of trust.

At first, you as the Dreamer, entering into the field of its limited perception, will be perceived as an intruder. You are coming with a whole new set of ideas on how things should be done. The Caretaker is very limited in its education. You are coming in with the concept of unlimited possibility. The Caretaker has never even heard of that concept.

A typical inner one-sided conversation of conflict or *"monkey mind"* would go as follows: *"How do I know your are the Boss here? This is my gig. Go away. Leave me alone, this is my domain."* The Mind is naturally paranoid you see. So you have to be non-aggressive in your approach. You cannot bully the Mind. It will outsmart you at every step. It becomes a chess game.

Remember you are the caretaker's *CREATOR*, therefore, the caretaker is also a part of you. It even has your personality, like a double. It has inherited your rebellious nature. It does not understand that you are coming from pure mind, for it exists in the duality of the physical plane.

The Caretaker is always running a tape of inner dialogue in your head. So you respond back to it with a new idea. You say to the Caretaker....

"Look, you've been doing a fine job here. I mean it is a beautiful reality you have created for me, but I have something new to introduce. It will actually enhance your job. You'll have more to do and it will be easier. You see, this machine has unlimited energy, unlimited potential. I can show you how to add new programs to your library. I can offer you access to unlimited information. You can become the best Dream Creator in physical reality. Now you don't really have to do anything but sit back and listen."

Simple isn't it? The Mind which has created the Altered Ego loves to be flattered. Also you are offering it job security. "Now, the way you've been doing things ...... well, they're OK. But there is always an ending to the Dream, and you're out of a job anyway. What if I could show you a way that the Dream could be forever? Then you'd never be out of a job. Wouldn't you agree that would be a better plan?"

You see the Caretaker is not your enemy. There is no enemy in the greater understanding of things. Everything in the Universe is made up of the same stuff. You're going to have to go slowly at first. The Caretaker is simple. It cannot grasp concepts, and abstract thought with great speed until it hooks up to the expanded program. It will not understand abstract thinking. So make it easy.

You are already applying the techniques for mastering your attitudes simply by desiring to read this book. That is half the battle. As you change, the Mind will change. It is part of you and will change with you. It takes time for the Body to catch up with our Spiritual evolution especially in this time of accelerated growth, where everything, including time, seems more and more abstract. Allow yourself the grace of making a couple of mistakes at first. Allow yourself the grace to change.

Kryah is a science. You are the scientist here. The Body, which is part of the Mind, is composed of cells. Correct? Well, each of these cells is like a tiny Universe.

Every single cell possesses consciousness. The Universe, being as infinitely small as it is large, is all connected. In each of these cells there is a caretaker, so to speak, that must be re-programmed and educated in the new process of Being.

In the Medical understanding, it takes a certain amount of time for the liver to reproduce itself, so long for skin tissue, so long for bone, and so forth. In the conception of time as it is presently perceived, it takes approximately one year for the body to totally reproduce itself in new cellular form. This process of regeneration can be understood very easily by reading one of the several books available by *Deepak Chopra**. His articulation is easily digested by the western mind set, yet remains inoffensive to one who might possess a more advanced metaphysical understanding.

The regeneration of our physical structure is in continuous motion and governed by Universal Law. It does not require thinking. As new cells are created, they will respond more and more to the Consciousness you are developing from your God Source. They are learning to take their orders from a new department.

So, the Mind, although it is involved with what is occurring in the process, does not need to calculate the actual process itself, it is automatic. As you expand into new levels of Conscious Awareness, as you take control over the Body-Mind awareness, the old patterns of inter-cellular behavior are transmuted to accommodate the newly expanded consciousness of God I AM.

There are circumstances where the Body, and therefore the Mind, can be catapulted into a new Awareness instantly. However this usually occurs in the circumstance of severe trauma. Getting hit by lightning is not the easy way to wake up, (just ask Dannion Brinkley*). After the experience of trauma, there will be a period of disassociation, experienced as a sense of disorientation. This is because the Body has been thrown into shock. It is nature's way of allowing the process of conscious assimilation to occur in the quickest possible amount of time.

Because the Body is programmed to accept the idea of time as reality, we are simply stuck in a concept of limited thought. The concept is very real, only if you believe in it. Whatever you think, so shall it be. You are not going to change overnight. This is going to happen over your experience of the passing of a period of time. That is how we experience evolution on this plane, through the passing of time.

As the initiate, you are engaging in a process of natural transmutation. It is called *Change*. The whole of our species is changing. We are evolving. You are learning how to apply and use Conscious *Will*. You will need to develop endurance and focus. Most likely, the greater portion of your life has been creating Karma. Now you are going to have to allow for the programming to be released. You need to change your direction and method of operation. It takes approximately one year for the Body to recreate its cellular structure. It takes that amount of time for the Physical structure to respond to the new commander, you, reconnected to the God Force.

Eventually you will learn how to collapse time. Through your journey into Consciousness, you are able to access the Greater Knowledge available through your unlimited Being. You are learning by experiencing the effects of Universal Law itself. So, let's say you begin to apply this knowledge now, today. Within approximately one year's time, you will be seeing its effects in your life as an absolute reality. Your entire Being will accept the **Thought** as being absolute because you allowed your **Feelings** to affirm its reality through experience brought about through conscious **Action.**

THOUGHT expressed through FEELINGS = ACTION = YOUR REALIT PURE INTENT = The QUALITY of that REALITY+ FOCUS + RIGHT USE of the GOD FORCE.

This formula allows Oneself to become the vehicle for the GOD Force......
Being Non Judgmental about The Outcome, we allow it to occur through our participation and understanding.

In understanding ourselves we will understand GOD.

You might be saying to yourself right now, "But I can't wait a year, I have to learn to manifest now." If you are committed to this change, if you sincerely apply these methods of perception, you will become what you desire. The amount of time it takes for the process to complete itself is totally affected by your attitude, desire and personal ability to allow. The outcome is based upon your pure intent, the *Will* of the elements to co-operate with your desires, and your ability to merge thought and emotion.

You are involved in a process. The road of the initiate is a great undertaking. You are changing your entire perception of known reality, and thus altering the outcome of that reality. The reason why it appears to be taking time is that you are still stuck on time. You still believe it to be a truism. One guidepost that you can use is to *SEE* the outcome, not the blockages. Allow the Supreme Force to move through you as a river. Do not try to control the outcome. Get rid of your judgments of how it should happen. Let the process itself guide you each step of the journey. Desire the feeling, become the feeling. The understanding of how, will come to you on a need to know basis.

Know that this Universal Law governs the vast expanses of our Universe, and in reality there is no time. Time as you experience it, is a phenomenon of the Earth Plane and it is relatively new in its creation. Life and the Cosmos are in continuous motion, and change is the natural order of things. Life is metamorphous. You are Creation in motion, time is a concept that is frozen, like a frame in a movie. Time never moves, you move through time.

It canbe predictable that, most of you will not experience instant manifestation of your thoughts. But take faith they will manifest..they always do. This is because we are in the process of developing oir Awareness, and as a species we have yet to develop the whole of our potential. So how xab we fully ecercies our will. The whole of what you truly are, cannot exist within the present limitation of our consciousness. However commitment and allowing ourselves to leaver the box, will bring forth thr fruits of labor.

We must learn to allow ourelve din this process and forgive ourselves a lot. It's a good exercise n compassion. We not only have to get out of the box, but when you start to get hard on yourself think about how far down into the box we have burried ourselves...So we are dealing with a double jeapardy situation and a long but not impossible climb back up the hill. any lace is going to be better than where you were..

It takes an enormous amount of energy to be the Dreamer. You must become impeccable in your every action and thought. Once impeccability is achieved through Proper Action, you will no longer wonder why you are waiting. You will not give into anxiety. Giving into anxiety, doubt and lack of self worth, opens the door to fear, which is illusion. Through Proper Action, you develop *Purpose, Focus, and Will.* What the ancients called developing the *Warriors Awareness.*

Why do I use the term warrior? .... Because we are a warrior race, this is our basic genetic makeup. We, as it is presently perceived are Animal Warriors. Through the exercising of the principles of *Kryah* we transmute into Spiritual Warriors of Light.

Through your process of becoming that Awareness, and Being the Consciousness experiencing that Awareness, every experience you encounter can and will become your teacher, and your guide to the future. Step by step you will climb out of the planes of confusion and doubt, until one day you will greet the Sunrise fully knowing who you are in this Universe. We too often want it all right now. We are addicted to *fast food and carry-out.* As we walk the Sacred Path, the Red Road, and cross the Rainbow Bridge, we will achieve our fulfillment of a task undertaken eons ago. Through the willful practice of *Kryahgenetics*, we will awaken to the God within.

Remember, this transition is a 5-D experience. It is the conscious application of *Discernment, Discretion, Detachment, Desire* and *Discipline,* constantly being exercised. We are breaking the borders of our limited reality. We are struggling through the programming of the last two thousand years of Spiritual destruction of the Human Spirit, by dogmatic religions, and the tyrants who were born out of our ignorance. We have become a race born into a consciousness of enslavement. We serve the wrong master. Our Awareness, as it expands, will allow the Truth to be known within us. We then must learn to deal with the increased energy that our new state of enhanced Awareness brings along with it.

It is not so much the output of energy, as it is the allowing of energy to pass through you. This is what is truly meant by, "Can you handle the energy?" The way to develop the capacity to "run" the energy is by working with the breath of life, bringing it through the seven great seals and developing our inner focus. You have to learn to keep moving towards your desire, regardless of the confusion that appears to be around you.

This is known as taking the *pathway of action.* You take that pathway knowing your thoughts must and will be manifest. As you develop clear mind, you will become increasingly aware that it is the Law, the supreme law of creation. Applying your belief along with focus, is your *WILL*. Your *WILL* becomes the sword of Arthur. Use of this *WILL* through proper action, can enable you to break out of the spell of the vision, to go beyond *left brained* realism and reach *right brained* realizations.

Consciousness combined with *right use of WILL*, creates Divine energy. As you learn to be flexible and release judgment, you become fluid. Remember that the Universal Law is not logical. You may be headed straight along the path your Mind dictates as proper, when a new pathway opens up. Take it. That is how the energy works. You will come into direct confrontation with all of your blocks along the pathway to your inner desire. As you overcome them by dealing directly with them, one at a time, you will open the doorway to your next step in evolution. The shortest way to your desired destination may not be a straight line. More often it is not. And more often it is the journey there that holds the jewel of experience, that changes the final outcome...... always by choice.

As you move into alignment with the God Force, there is absolutely no way of predetermining what will happen next. You are moving into uncharted waters, the unknown. Your focus will get you there, but you cannot be in denial. You can never outwit the Universal God Force, which is why it is called a *Great Mystery*. It is a process of allowing life to happen. Your Mind will argue with you every inch of the way. It will say to you, *"This is ridiculous. You don't have this much time to waste. This wasn't in the plan. It makes no sense. Look how tired you are. You couldn't possibly be Divine."*

If along the journey you are experiencing great trials and tribulations, you can make the estimated guess that that pathway is not the one for you, or perhaps it could be the way you are dealing with that pathway. Are you employing right action? The pathway is not supposed to take away your life essence. It should be a pathway of *Self-Joy..... always of Self-Joy*. If you have to get lost in confused deliberation over a course of action, it is usually not the correct one. The state of indecision is the Mind trying to retake control of the vessel. Miracles happen without effort and are always surrounded in an inexplicable feeling of Joy and sometimes awe. Just focus on being aware of your feelings. Learn to watch the signs, follow your dream.

Put your dreams out in front of you. They will be your guide. If you are confused, get quiet, become still. Go within. Practice non-Being, (unattached to the personality.....in the IS). The Universal God Force is like the wind. If you have ever sailed a boat, you know instinctively when the wind dies, that the wind will come again. Get quiet, know the power of the silence, and watch the signs, the ripples on the water, the bird in the sky. Is it riding a thermal? Within your Being, the signs are your feelings. In the silence we come in contact with them again. The process of dream creation is in the state of action, and the change is occurring on many levels. If you find yourself confused, it is just that you are not yet aware of all those levels.

To help you develop your *WILL*, your ability to focus in the Dream, it is important that you realize that you are not trying to control the process of the manifestation. In fact the strained effort of *trying*, can actually prevent you from manifesting. You are accessing it through expanded Consciousness. Creation is effortless, only our realization of how to create is a struggle, because we are so imprisoned by our own thoughts. You are experiencing a process governed by the Universal Law of Attraction. The God Force. The, I AM that I AM. Everything around you possesses Consciousness. It is governed by its own relationship to the God Force and the effects of the Universal Law. In order for you to manifest a thing, you first have to know the feeling of being one with it. By knowing the nature of a thing, you can call forth its occurrence. It, like you, is an energy. It is only expressing itself through a different form.

Use the principles of *Kryah* to bring about the effects of true manifestation. It is not that you are learning how to create matter, rather you are remembering how you can access the Consciousness that does. In the physical reality, you must never impose your *WILL* over any thing, or any one. You can only work in harmony with the Consciousness that creates the possibility of its existence. It is through our developing a clear sense of owning the feeling of something that will actually cause manifestation to occur.

You call forth the feeling into your inner Being and release your focused desire into the Universe. You Dream the Dream, and then let it go, be done with it. In the letting go of the thought and releasing the hold on it with your feelings, the Universal Law of *Kryah* will take over. The elements of *Kryah* make up what you felt, and what you thought, and as they are released into the Universe, they will draw to themselves like energy, in accordance with the Universal Laws of Attraction.

In accordance with the Universal Law, they must return to their creator, their source. They will return, manifested into your reality, with energy equal to the energy focused upon the feeling. Thought, embraced by Emotion, turns into Action. The Painter knows that red and blue make purple on the canvas. You allow and trust in the God Force, then release it into the Universe. You can own your feelings, but you can never own the elements whether physical or holographic. They own themselves. The elements will respond to your desire in their own way, of their own *FREE WILL.*

STEP SEVEN: DIVINE REASONING

As you undertake the Sacred Pathway of the initiate, one of the most difficult things you are going to have to overcome is the *Offensive Mind*, your own, as well as those around you. The Offensive Mind is the Mind that is closed...... the Mind that is bound by the webs of fear, immersed in its own prison of limitation. If you go around trying to tell everyone you know what it is you are working on...... that you are going beyond limited mind and accessing the mind of God, for the most part they will look at you as if you are mad.

By electing to take the pathway of the initiate, you have already committed yourself to walking away from the masses. They may try to compromise you and say they understand your struggle, but most likely, they will still oppose you. You see, they have no choice but to do so, because to them, everything you are trying to achieve, if you succeed, would nullify their belief patterns. It would mean that the borders of their reality would be false and they would have to change. Their reality would be shattered...... Like yours was before you started this journey.

Change is a personal thing. Most people are happy where they are. Why else would they keep perpetuating their predicament. Time after time, after time, we are always re-creating the same situation for ourselves. We are secure within our lack. We have come to know it well and identify with it. We have a deep fear of, and are often even angered by, the mere thought of change. Therefore, expect that those still caught in the slumber will try to undermine your every hope and prayer of going beyond limited Mind.

It is not so much that they enjoy being mean to you, they are simply following the pattern of animal instinct, ans being in the box thay only know reactionary thinking. Which only allows them to choose an action within the matrix of the unenlightened Mind. They are hopelessly lost in the labryinth, and don't know it.

In their *re-actions*, you will be witnessing this pattern of animal survival and it can be very nasty. They will attack you and you will not understand, for you are coming from the innocence of the God-Child awakening. Remember, the Universal Law allows their reactions, just as it allows for you to expand beyond the limitation. It's all about choice. Remember Jonathan, he had to leave the flock didn't he? Yet he was never abandoned, and never alone.....

As you travel down the path of the initiate, you will become aware that there are indeed many levels to what you once saw as two dimensional and flat. There are many different levels of Beings and they are all playing out their perceptions. They are, for the most part, processing the pain of living in limitation. They are not necessarily like you at all. In fact, being imprisoned within the walls of limited Consciousness, which is an unnatural state, humanity for the most part has gone insane from the pain. Limitation is very painful. You are going to have to develop a keen sense of *Divine Reasoning* to complete the journey through the maze and come all the way home.

A very important aspect of *Divine Reasoning* is to let no thing be accepted into your reality until you yourself know it to be truth. Knowing something and believing in something are two different realities. In other words, knowing is when you come to understand something as well as it does itself. When you have contemplated the nature of a truth and feel at ease in your heart with it, you will own it. This *is knowing*. You have within you the ability to become what you contemplate through the mastering of the language of emotion. It is through the emotional field that all things in the Universe can communicate. It is the higher form of communication, the communication of the GODS.

When you can view something objectively and allow it to maintain its own integrity, you do not feel the need to alter or manipulate the experience of it. The proof of the Mind's tendency to manipulate, is sometimes experienced as we see our relationships to people and places change over time. Remember the old adage, "Familiarity breeds contempt"?....or have you heard someone say, "It was so beautiful when we first got together, then the spell wore off...."? Have you ever remembered a person or place that you experienced in your past and when you return to it, it is somehow unexplainably different? The colors somehow seem to have lost their luster.

By allowing the experience of energy to possess its own integrity, by allowing it to express itself, you own the experience of it in your consciousness, through the principle of Divine Truth. You are therefore able to make the experience a part of your consciousness, and know that in the experience, a thing can be accessed or denied as you desire. You are free to let it go if it becomes necessary, and move on......returning to the process of your own journey through Evolution.

This is a form of multi-dimensional realization. It can never be achieved through separation, which is the result of living in a state of judgment. You see, in its purest form, everything including people, are just energy. The electricity or lack of it you are feeling in a relationship is merely the exchange, or lack of exchange of energy.

The principles of *Kryah* are not some fictional probability. It is an absolute science of the laws of nature and creation. It is important to maintain the connectedness of all things while attempting this process. Non-judgment is a state of mind, not a physically or intellectually dictated rationalization of an occurrence. Non-judgment is achieved through the realization of the state of non-Being.

We have oftentimes heard about the importance of stopping the internal dialogue. We have also been told that we must learn through meditation how to still the Mind. In the ancient schools, it is taught that one can never quiet the Mind. The information highway feeding the Mind is in constant flux. Energy does not stand still. Source does not stand still. If this occurred, the Universe as we now know it would cease to exist in a moment. It is possible for one to Master the navigation only of this highway, but it is not in the cards to anticipate getting off the grid or controlling it.

The quiet Mind is one that has learned not to sway too far into passion......being not in the negative or the positive, and never drawing conclusions on the outcome of events. It is one that is focused on proper action, and is at Oneness and in harmony with the True nature of the God Force. The miracle is never realized in our resistance to the God Force. In other words, trying to still it, causes extreme friction and paralyzes our access to the Life Force. The friction then creates a stormy environment for the individual who leans towards either extreme, and finds their life in a state of chaos. The quiet Mind is open to the ebb and flow of thoughts, aware of its own identity and energy at all time, it is the Mind that knows it is God experiencing.

This unlimited Mind accepts its unlimited power. Such a Mind is in tune with its Creator.....*YOU*. The relationship has come into proper balance and does not try to defend itself against the presence of the Master, the unlimited Being. This Mind takes its orders from the Awareness of the Consciousness of God, with whom it shares the body. Because of this, it learns to speak the emotional language of the Creator. It is objective in its observations, focused in its actions, and clear in its intent and purpose.

The gift it receives is the Awareness of its eternal nature and freedom to access unlimited Thought. It is aware that it is not limited to the five physical senses. It is not trapped in the illusion of temporal mortality. It knows that its source of energy, its power, is limitless and infinite, for it is not ruled by the Image, nor subject to reactionary reality. Thus, it is likewise aware that time is an illusionary concept that can be embarrassed, or not embarrassed. This small yet monumental knowing, allows the Mind to enter a space of timelessness. It has the ability to access muti-dimensional reality, where one may spend what could be conceived of as hours, or even lifetimes, on one single thought.

With this awakened ability, the *Hu*-man Mind can at last be fully utilized as it was intended at conception. When this doorway is opened within the individual, there is no limit to their potential in manifesting reality. As the Nazarene taught, we are not limited Beings doomed to drudgery and suffering. How could God the Father/Mother, the all powerful and all knowing, have created us less than perfect?

The Mind alone does not have the ability to access multi-dimensional reality. It only has the capacity to handle the coordinating of the program that you the Dreamer make available to it. That is all. The Awareness for creating the program comes from the Divine Self alone. Therefore Mind, anyone's Mind for that matter, has no power over you. The Mind is not the Master it is the tool of the Master. Only what you allow the Mind to have, will it have. You are, after all, something beyond Mind and made up of much greater stuff. The Mind is only a small component of what you are. When you leave the Body what happens to the Mind? What happens to you……. The I AM, that you are?

Yes, it is true, you create images in your Mind. The Mind is a blank computer graphics program upon which you dictate the method of expression. These expressions can be frightening or they can be beauteous in nature. Some real, and some not so real. They are only images and we are addicted to them. We love the creation game. The problem is we have little or no control over the images, until we open the Mind to higher thought octaves. These images we conjure are unlimited in number, as endless as the Universe. Images are but reflections of thoughts until they are qualified by the Universal Law and we learn to pick and choose them with discernment. They are but shadows, illusions, until you elect to make them reality.

We have yet as a species learned how to create in unlimitedness. Only a very few have managed to do that. They are the geniuses we hold up as our ideals, after we have tortured them in their own lifetimes, for being different than the norm. The Universal Law allows us to have choice in selecting from our billions of thought patterns, those potentials we choose to manifest as our experienced reality. *Discernment, Discretion, Detachment , Desire* and *Discipline* are very important aspects in developing our Divine Reasoning. They could almost be called the Golden Rule for the Spirit engaging in action within the Physical plane.

Before deciding on any manifestation of your desires, you need to be in harmony with that action completely. Not partially, not half-heartedly, but completely and passionately at one with it. You need to calculate its effects in every aspect of your life. Also the effects of your action or non-action concerning a particular manifestation in the interaction of other realities around you. In other words, you are assuming total responsibility for your decision and owning it.

Remember it is equally as important not to impose your desires upon any other Being in the Universe, as it is for you not to have your reality infringed upon by someone else. You always have the right to self-defense, so do not allow yourself to be abused. Let no one exercise their uninvited *Will* upon you. "As you do unto others, so shall they do unto you." Keeping in mind that one's Sacred Space is after all, their Sacred Space. To judge is the action of a fool, to allow is the acquired action of a God awakening.

In the mastering of the principles of *Divine Reasoning*, on the third dimensional plane, we mainly allow things to just be. ...to the extent where this principle becomes a part of your sub-conscious action, as well as your outward or conscious action. We could call it in its outward expression, the human art of co-habitation. We co-habitate in this physical plane with the trees, the whales, the wolves, other people of different cultures, as well as the worms, and the insects.

We also are immersed within an envelope that contains many different dimensional realities. There are Beings that co-habitate along side with you. Some are called Divas, others Fairies, they are the Elementals. Did you think that they are not affected by your actions? The Earth herself is a living thinking, feeling Being. She possesses a Consciousness beyond our own. The expanse of her Consciousness cannot even be realized fully by the Ascended Masters.

There is going to be a lot of realizations by *Hu*-manity with regard to co-habitation. *Aho Mitakuye Oyasin*. Which is Sioux for "All My Relations." We are all one family, regardless of your personal likes or dislikes. We are all the children of one Mother and one Father. We are about to find out this is a galactic truth, as well as an earthly one. We co-habitate inter-dimensionally as well as mono-dimensionally. There is but one reality. There are however countless variations of its interpretation. We call that free *Will*, or choice!

The Divine Plan calls for harmony. In relationships it calls for compassion. If we choose to walk this Earth plane and to express our reality within the Mother's Consciousness, we then must accept that we are the Dreamer within the Dream. If we annihilate other life forms without regard, just to fulfill our desires, if we rape and plunder the Earth, without regard for future generations, if we continue to live our lives in complete denial of the other dimensional entities that exist here, if we deny the God Force in our Brother or our Sister.......we deny it in ourselves.

It is like turning off the energy every time we do any of these things. The Mother and the Father want us to live in harmony. All that we need, they provide. When we get that part of the program down, there will be no end to the powers we will be able to access, but not before.

The Mother has given to us the gift of the body to experience reality within her Dream, to help us along in our path of evolution. We are here to be the caretakers of all her creations. We are visitors here in the Great School. The Mother and the Father with the exception of love and respect, have given us no rules. We are given the mystery of *Kryah* to apply with principles of the Universal Law in accordance with our desires.

E-volution is the process by which we realize the Universal Laws of Life through experience. We are constantly making the unknown known, through the experience of our actions. We are exploring the causes and effects of creation, as well as *dis-creation*. In history, you are remembered for your actions, the Universe itself responds to your actions. It is a participatory Universe. You are Divine energy expressing upon, as well as experiencing, the physical plane, so that the Creator would better understand Itself.

This is very important to understand for the evolution of your soul, as well as the species. We can only evolve if we are free from dogmatic rules, which were created by man to perpetuate a controlled Consciousness, all for the purpose of the dominance of one sect over another, so that mankind could rule over his brethren. If we look at even our recent history over the last five thousand years, we will find that whenever Consciousness begins to rise in the cycles of historical time, the emerging Consciousness always meets with strong resistance.

For whatever reason there is another anomaly that occurs. Just before the new Consciousness emerges fully into the Light, there is either a Great War, or Cataclysmic Earth changes that precede it. The chains of thought patterns must be broken so that the new perception can manifest. We all were created to be FREE BEINGS, *free men, free womb of men*. Only as *Free Beings* can we hope to fully understand the Laws that make up life's design and Divine purpose.

Only by freeing the Mind can we as a humanity hope to see clearly how reality is affected by each and every one of our interactions with other energy forms.....how it responds to our thoughts...... how exactly our intentions towards any energy, relates to creation or dis-creation. Consciousness can be likened to the web of the spider. The threads of Consciousness are all connected. Without the web of Consciousness no thing could exist. Even a Spider must have a web of Consciousness that encompasses the Earth in order for it to exist within this plane. Oh, how much of the ways of *Kryah* we have forgotten!

One could say that the purpose for our whole existence upon this plane is simply to experience feelings and emotions. Through the experience we learn. It does not matter what the nature of those experiences are, as long as we learn from them, that we own them and are able to move on, unattached, but in knowledge of becoming enlightened Beings moving towards our *Christhood*. The understanding of Christ energy and the emergence into this level of Consciousness is our inevitable destiny, for it is the true state of existence for the children of God and is our genetic heritage.

We have created for ourselves quite a web of illusionary reality. It is a virtual reality game that has corrupted, and is presently out of control. It has gone awry and is recreating itself in a reality based upon the limited Mind.....based upon the Image and not the substance. That is why we find life for the most part, unfulfilling.

Christ Consciousness is beyond the Consciousness of the Image. So the Consciousness of our struggle to rise above the mundane, to leave the world of the Market Place, where even our deepest feelings are bastardized for the sake of the Religion of Materialism, is manifesting and rising to the surface. It is a given in this process of the Purification, that we are witnessing the Emergence of the Fifth World, where mankind moves from animal consciousness to a Divine Consciousness of God-Man, God-Woman realized.

It is a process of remembering our eternal connection to the multi-dimensional, collective field of our Divine *Hu*-man origins. This field of Consciousness exists on all levels simultaneously. The "I, that is the All, that is the One," whereby you can develop your abilities of Discernment and Detachment to such a degree that you are able to understand reality from a different perspective. By reconnecting to your feelings, you are beginning the process of reconnecting to the Source of all Life. You will remember who and what you truly are in connection with this Source.

You are so much more than your five senses, so much more than your physical embodiment, so much more than your Mind. To think that you are less than Divine is regressive thinking, it is from your past. Your sojourn, within limited reality, and the spell of mortality is over now. You are part of the Original Source, the God Force. The I AM that I AM. Part of a whole. Everything you do, think, or feel, is felt by the rest of the whole, and the whole is there for you to connect to as well. It is how it works......it is the Great Mystery.

This perception can be difficult to grasp for the beginning initiate, because we have developed in our language no word, no mental reference for the simultaneous action of "the I, that is the All, that is One." It is new information to the collective Consciousness, who by choice has drifted into a slumber and become caught up in the delusion of I, My, Me, Mine.

Even in today's " New Age" movement, the humanity of the masses is far to easily caught up in the gratification of self, at the expense of life, all life and its forward motion. This time is ending. We have entered the Age of the Light and the Light shall be great indeed. For all that we know shall be transformed within the very next generation. The first quarter of the 21st century will see our galactic reality blossom once again upon this plane. We must prepare.

You are part of the God Force, which acknowledges you every second of your existence. It must also be acknowledged as a part of you, if you hope to access the Greater Knowledge, the reality of the Mystic. You have created your body as a Temple for the habitation of your Divine Awareness, your Spirit. You have manifested into physical form to experience the Dream of physical expression upon this and other third dimensional planes.

You are the nerve endings of an unfathomable Consciousness, exploring through Hu-man perception. Exploring all of this unfathomable mystery, forces Hu-man possibilities. You can do anything you desire, have anything you desire, as long as you follow the Principles of the Universal Law and apply the principles of the Kryah. The law is not about judgment, nor is it about confining you in any way. It is about understanding the working of things, great things. *Kryah* tells us how the Great Mystery works, within you and without you.

It is our inability to comprehend these simple truths that has created the demons within the darkness of the unexpanded *Hu*-man Consciousness. We must be cognizant in dealing with this darkness. Darkness was in our creation during the part of the experience where we forgot our Oneness with the Whole. It was born out of the fear of feeling separated. Our demons are the illusions of the unrealized Dreamer. Darkness only exists in the hearts of limited Beings. Fear is its cloak. It has no face, but it does possess many fingers. Darkness has had its dance. We have already experienced that part of our reality. We now understand limited Mind, and it is time to move on.

The conception of the *Hu*-man Drama is our chosen experience in a Grand Experiment, that was conceived of long ago when Angels dared to dream the dream of experiencing Consciousness through the physical expression as the Hu-man species. In other words, our demons can be very real if we believe we are the dream. For *we* have dreamed this dream, and no one else. If we believe we are the dream, and not the Dreamer, then the dream has the power over us.

So, how do we stop the madness? How does one get off the merry-go-round? We begin by simply not turning to the external world for the answers. The external world is the result of our thought forms manifested. It is the Dream, not the Source. We are not talking about nature, we are talking about the world of man. If you want to feel God, if you want to be with nature, then get away from man, go as all Masters do to the wilderness, and you will hear and feel the power of the silence.

Some times Dreams can be filled with incomplete and distorted thought forms. The outer Vision of Consciousness only reflects back to us the incompleteness of itself. The answers to life, lie within the Source, the Dreamer, the Self.....the one who can see the holographic map and follow the highway through the Stars. The Mind alone will too often confuse the holographic map as being the Dream itself. The Mind exists within a yet undeveloped three-dimensional reality. There it is waiting to be given life by you, the Dreamer, the Creator of the Dream.

The whole dream of expressing in physical reality was unknown territory to us. It had never been done before. To enter the structure of physical mass and give it life with supreme purpose, and evolve through that process and make it Divine was unheard of. The Mystery itself was to experience death, to conceive of ourselves as having an ending and existing in limitation. We, as Beings of Light, did not know of endings. We were and are intrinsically eternal. We are the great I AM. Mortality was an experiment in temporal experience.

The dogmatists would have us think through their vehicles called *Organized Religion,* that we are less than God, unworthy of God. Over the years, they have managed manipulating documents and the original teachings of the Great Masters, to convince the collective unconscious, the sleeping Gods, to accept that we are separated from the Source. They have convinced us that we are not worthy of this eternal presence of the God Force. Yet, without that presence in all things, anything, including the dogmatists, could and would not be. It is Universal Law.

It is the dogmatic programming of the masses, generation after generation up to and including us, that we were *not* part of the Creator, that we were *not* eternal Beings and it has taken its toll. Those warrior kings, mighty emperors of Rome, would themselves one day be taken over and replaced by those priests who administered their will. Thus the regressive inheritors of this grand plot managed to keep control over the masses through the manipulation of our fears. They needed control to keep up the veil of the illusion. Thus they had to rule through the illusion of power and with teachings they could not comprehend or exercise, because they were not their predecessors who had the original knowledge.

In looking at the historical flow chart of our neoteric society, it reveals to us a story where priests became politicians and the new kings. Then they themselves would fall prey over time to the money lenders. Today we experience a world where the architecture is not built to affirm our connection to Higher Consciousness and Divine beginnings, but rather to the glorification of the material power of the money lenders, who have become the new lords of mankind. Instead of temples, we now build jails.

The degeneration of our Consciousness had its beginnings in attempts by petty tyrants to keep us from the original knowledge. The knowledge that told of our beginnings..... our origins. If the reality that we were born to was allowed to be remembered, the present system of power would collapse. If the schools of the original teachings were allowed to survive the game plan, and the intent to keep us in ignorance was revealed, the current power system would collapse upon itself.

What would be the ultimate fear they could control us with? "Ahh"..... said one priest, "*Why not let them suffer the fear of losing their immortality. They do not know how to awaken that part of themselves. Only we hold the knowledge to that doorway between worlds......*" And thus the plot to keep mankind in ignorance began. All the teachings of the *Kryah* had to be removed, wiped off the face of the Earth, so that no trace remained.

If you think this is a line from a fairytale, then I suggest you contemplate the source of all your fears. Contemplate what could hurt an eternal Spirit. Would it not be the loss of your immortality? Would it not be, never being able to be close to God again? Think about it.

All fear at its source, stems from our feelings of no longer being eternal....... losing our right to Divinity.....getting stuck in the *murk and mire* of this limited temporal existence..... stuck in third dimensional expression, with no hope of contact with Source for eternity. In other words, HELL! God would not talk to us because of our evil beginnings, only the priests had privy to that kind of conversation, because they held all the cards. Is this not a master plan for perpetuating fear?

Fear of the loss of immortality has been woven through every fabric of our social consciousness. From the time we are young children we are programmed that we have an ending, we are temporal, that we are the Dream, not the Dreamer. Someone else has control. We are without power. We must turn to and worship and serve the one with the power, or the chosen, to whom God speaks.

Why would you need to worship the one in power? It is a combination of Pavlovian conditioning and the lack of our Divine Reasoning that keeps Dogmatic Religions in power. Remember fear only has power as long as it maintains its illusion. Fear must defend itself and color all things that *it* touches to reflect *it-self*. And it can allow no other truth to exist, absolutely none. Reason it out.

Realize that the word **religion** comes from the Latin root *religio-*meaning Political. The word *religion* itself means constrained, or sanctioned practice, or worship of the supernatural. In other words, religion is sanctioned by the political body in power. Are you having trouble with this concept?.......O.K., what happened in Tibet when China invaded it, because the Spirituality of the Tibetans threatened their grand plan for non-religion? Why is it that Jesus, (Yeshua), like the Dali Lama lived like a refugee?

Think again about the word evil itself. The Old English spelling is, *E-VEIL,* meaning the veil of illusion, the illusion of existence without God, or being separate therefrom. We never started out evil, we started out Divine. So ask yourself, when did you become evil? Who declared it so?

From the Divine we come, and to the Divine we return. Evil is the result of improper thinking through the perception of the Image. We are viewing life by viewing the reflection, not from Being the Light. When we bring the Light into our Being, others perceive themselves from the reflection of themselves they see in us. If we are as God is, they see the God in themselves.

These Ancient Schools freely taught the Principle of Universal Laws. They taught that we are the co-creators of everything we experience through the senses, by doctrine of the Universal Law of Freedom of Choice. Our body is likened to a great bio-chemical computer. Its circuitry designed and programmed to project and receive what we allow ourselves to envision within the expanses of the Mind, which in proper per-spective is the software for our Consciousness to determine experience, and translate our intentions into the physical reality of the material world. The stuff we call matter, is only coagulated thought, coagulated light.

Each one of us is a particum of light, a microscopic part of the whole. We are like a single cell within a great cosmic embodiment of Consciousness. The whole can only be identified, as the Great Mystery, for we have no way of comprehending the vastness of the whole. The Awareness of our unique oneness with this presence is beginning to awaken throughout the *Hu*-man family. It is occurring on a Global level, as well as a Galactic one. That Consciousness, by the virtue of the Universal Law, is our own.

As an example, we now know that by taking a single cell from our body, scientists can clone the body as a whole. Each cell of our body contains within its DNA structure the blueprint for the entirety that we are. Thus, scientists are able to inject into our body a single liver cell and it will travel through our blood stream, through our entire body and find its way to our liver. This single cell has that much intelligence, that much Awareness. We are no different than that single cell and in that understanding, we are no less than the Universe itself.

SECRETS OF THE BREATH

There is a wisdom, that is taught in the Mystery Schools, which tells us that Spirit enters the body via the breath. We are taught that the Breath is the carrier of Spirit. It is a known fact that life and our Awareness begins with the taking of the first Breath at the time of birth. Later at the completion of our experience, our Awareness leaves the body via the Breath. So the cycle of our Spirit expressing through the body, is then complete and we return to Source.

The invisible veil that stands between us and our remembrance of actually being a part of this incredible unlimited Divine Sources can be overcome through our Awareness and use of the Sacred breath. All the feelings of being separated, all the fears which we have harbored for thousands of years, even our fear of losing immortality, could all be released just as easily as taking a Breath.

Within each of us, there are seven levels or Great Seals. Once a long time ago, we knew the proper method of breathing and we could allow for Spirit to enter our Being through all seven seals, as do the Dolphins, and Whales........as did some of our ancestors as little as 1,000 years ago. In our present diminished state, we breathe out of balance with the Earth and her creatures. We have therefore diverted the Breath of Life to flow only through the three lower seals.

By adopting this altered method of breathing, the ductless glands which activate these Great Seals within the body, have fallen into a state of atrophy. They have diminished in size as a result of lack of use. This has caused within us the inability to access the higher vibratory octaves of Divine Consciousness that we once enjoyed.

The glands corresponding to our upper four Seals, are: The *Thymus,* which is the 4th, the *Thyroid* is the 5th, the *Pituitary* is the 6th, and the 7th being the *Pineal.* In ordinary human beings, upon reaching about forty years of age, these glands are almost non-functional.   This condition has also has contributed greatly to our being only able to access less than 10% of our actual brain capacity and bio-chemical functionality. The closing down of these glands causes the release of the death hormone within the body. We are shutting down cosmically.   We are a dying race if we continue along the present pathway.

To move beyond this limitation of thought we must expand beyond our present concept of ourselves, and beyond the cultural images of Self. We need new points of reference. Part of the process of purification the Hopi and the Mayan speak of is the *de-structur-ing* of all form during the great purification. Not as a punishment creating the condition of us having to endure a reality of hell, but so that we can take hold of reality and have the opportunity to change the outcome......because we will then understand all, within each of us, that is no longer in balance with valued life.

We have created a world of fractalized reality, by thinking fractalized thoughts. This has contributed to the imprisonment within limited reality, resulting from believing the illusion of limited Mind. The concepts that are the sum result of seeing only fragments of truth come from somewhere in somebody else's past. We are working with partial information, living in the confines of our own past life experiences.

We must expand into the Being we are NOW, the Being within. The eternal Being that has the Awareness of the existence of the "I, that is the All, that is the One," simultaneously. It can be painful to expand our Consciousness beyond the prison of the Mind. It is a birthing process. It is a matter of letting go of our superimposed judgments.

We are as Hu-manity the individualized expressions of the same Being. We are multidimensional. This part of us which we consciously choose to express in the material illusion called matter, is a very small part of what we are. We have become caught in the spell of matter, the spider's web of illusion. Illusion exists in Darkness,

Awareness exists in Light.

There are seven levels of Light in which matter exists. These seven levels of Light which make up what is called the Light spectrum are like seven pages in the *Book of Life*. The material plane is only page three in that *Book of Life*. We have to turn to the next page of our story. We have fallen asleep reading the book. WAKE UP!

STEP EIGHT: The Twelve Rays of Light

The following is an explanation of the first Seven Rays. There are many different parts of the prophecies. They seem to have survived in that manner, so that only the gathering of all the people and the sharing of all their parts, would complete the picture of the Day of Purification. This understanding is part of the Rainbow teaching. It is information that is known in fragments by the Indigenous Peoples of this Land, from the Cherokee, and their use of Crystals, to the Dené and their sand paintings.

Indigenous people also use much chanting and sound from instruments in their ceremony. The tones that result, align them with these Rays, and can bring about the opening to much knowledge. They are tools for awakening the Spirit, by allowing the physical to " Lighten up."

These Rays in the Divine Order of the Creator, form the Rainbow. The Light Spectrum through which all creation in the Heavens has manifested, is called in the higher octaves, the assembly of the Amethystine Order. They are not material in nature. The information presented here has nothing to do with a linear order of the Light Spectrum. It explains the influences upon Consciousness on the Earth Plane of the Seven Rays.

In the time that is coming, these Seven Rays will, and already are, developing into twelve. Eleven have already come into existence. These include the color Aquamarine, and Magenta, which have not previously appeared in our rainbow. These new colors usher into this plane, new octaves of vibration, causing *the Quickening* of our evolutionary process.

This information is given at this time, so that you might awaken your Con sciousness to the existence of the higher octaves and their influences on all life here. This is an n-depth understanding given on the Rays and their relation to the harmonics of the blood. There will be another in depth understandings of these Rays and the Amethystine Order in the upcomingseries of books on the teachings of don Lobos which is the continuation of the Kryah knowledge.

The First Ray-Red, is the ray in which the vibratory essence of this Earth is held. It is the Ray of Leadership. It is the Ray that gives all things the intelligence of the Creator. It is the Ray of authority from the highest order. The Red Earth, The good Red Road.

The Second Ray- Sky Blue, is the Ray of education, and understanding. This is the Ray of knowledge. Here the Knowledge of the Creator and the Wisdom that comes from understanding the Earth Forces come into union. The Sky is reflected in the Ocean. Where they meet is often unseen, only realized.

The Third Ray-Green, is known as the Healing Ray. Also, in the Third Ray is kept the vibration of memory of all events. It is called the Ray of Philosophy, and higher thought patterns which connect us to the Great Spirit......the trees, plants, flowers, and the ocean. It is the color seen given off by those who are in harmony with the Emerald Mother and her Divine Nurturing.

The Fourth Ray-Yellow, is sometimes called the Crystal Ray and is often expressed in man through the Arts. It holds within it the ability to connect to the source of Earth Mother's life giving elements and renewal of Spirit. The Sun gives its Yellow Ray and all life is stimulated to growth. The light is reflected in all Creator's creatures. This is the color often seen in those who possess the ability to be great teachers, it is the color of mind, intelligence.

The Fifth Ray-Cobalt Blue, is the Ray of Scientific understanding.....taking our Awareness and seeing the order, and inter-relationship of all things......the cycles of the Universe and how energies work.....understanding how thought creates all reality.....the color of the night sky......where dreams come from.....where Spirit becomes the physical. It is the quantum Physics of reality, sometimes called Alchemy. This is the color that is given off by those who are of unbending faith.

The Sixth Ray-Rose, is the Ray of Devotion, and Unconditional Love. This is the unique essence that allows us the state of Oneness, and the inter-connection with Creator.....seeing the perfection in all as it is, part of the great plan.....knowing the heart. It is often associated with renewal, as it is abundant in spring skies, and young flora. It is representative of youth, new beginnings.

The Seventh Ray-Violet, is the Ray of Ceremony, and transition of the Physical and the Spirit. This Ray is the passageway for all transition and interaction between that which is known as Spirit and that which manifests as the physical. All that is touched by the Violet Ray is transformed into its highest potential. This is where matter becomes Spirit and takes on Divine Consciousness. It is the Ray of Transformation.

In all there are Twelve Rays that effect our existence as Spirit come alive in the flesh. The realization of this interaction of these Twelve Rays, can only come when one has truly evolved into the union of Spirit and flesh......Christ Consciousness. For here we go beyond language, we are merged with the Divine Source Itself.

The remaining Rays are caused when the Light Rays from the Seven, merge and cause a harmonic. They are realized through emotion.

The Eighth Ray-Turquoise (Aquamarine), is The Ray of Protection. This Ray is born of the union of the Sky Blue of the Father and the Emerald of the Mother. This is traditionally the color used by Native Americans to ward off the evil eye of the sorcerer, and negative energies.

The Ninth Ray-Orange(iridescent pink), is the Ray of Personal Power, and psychic medicine. It is reflected on the wings of the Flicker, the medicine Warrior of the Northwest tribes. It is also the Ray of Discerning Judgment. It is the Ray of focused intent.

The Tenth Ray-Burgundy (Magenta), is the Harmonic of the First and Second Ray. It is of the house of Divine Man, the Spirit attained, undying faith and knowing. It is often related to the power of the heart, or the true Spirit of the soul of man.

The Eleventh Ray-Indigo (Midnight Blue), is the Great Void, the Black Light where all knowledge is. It is the color of the night, where Creator dreams the Divine Law of Creation.....all things potentially, yet no thing materially. This is the realm of

Spirit, where no thing is seen, yet all things are revealed in their true essence.

The Twelfth Ray-White-Rose-Gold, is the Light that can be found within all things that exist, it is the very thought of Creator. It is the color of the Christos... the awakened soul/

Remember these new colors will have both male and female energy aspects. Depending on our own emotional state, which greatly influences our perception, these tones can be different to each individual. The Twelfth Ray colors have never been seen before in the rainbow, and there are no specific terms for them. They will become visible as our Consciousness expands and the pituitary opens. They are the results of harmonics, or new frequencies that are entering our plane at this time.

We are travelers of *Spirit*, traveling upon waves of *Light*. *Light is* the vehicle by which *Thought* travels or expands itself. As the *Light* moves, it experiences through *Emotion*. *Emotion* is related to our Being as *Feelings*. These *Feelings*, which are our *Emotions*, express themselves as *Colors*. The alignment of *Emotion* and *Light,* produces *Sound*. Are you aware that all *Color* has a *Sound* vibration? You can even purchase computer software that can register its intensity, as well as its physical, mental, and emotional effects on the human body.

We exist on both sides of the veil simultaneously. We are therefore the receiver as well as the sender of Thought. The Thought traveling by Light Waves enters the Material Plane and becomes linear by nature of the Universal Law. They slow down to such an extent that coagulation occurs. All Matter is coagulated Thought, no more, no less.

Think of this while holding the thought that you are the Dreamer, not the Dream. You, that which is the I, is the one having the Dream. *Dream Creation* is an art form. It manifests as Light Waves. Your body has been designed to ride upon the crests of these Waves. What keeps you on top of the Wave instead of under it, is Balance. When these Light Waves become linear and begin to coagulate, they experience the sensation of time. You are connected to these Light Waves, they are your projections. You therefore, experience time.

Time and space do not revolve around you. Time is attached to the Dream of material existence. It is in the fabric of material manifestation. It is through the Dream that we can obtain mastery over material experience, for the Awareness of the whole of what we are. This is why the Dream always appears to be changing. It is a process of a constantly expanding Awareness of our experiences. With each experience, our Awareness changes through expansion, and the nature of the Dream is thus altered to accommodate a new frequency resulting from change of our expanded awareness.

Space exists around all things. It is here that the Thought, the God Force that holds all things together exists. It allows individual expression within the whole. There are those who would say this is preposterous, that space is nothingness. I would say to you, "How then does this nothingness hold up the Universe, your Sun, your Solar System, your Earth? How is it then that the whole of this Cosmos is held in Divine Balance? If space is nothingness, how then are there ten billion Universes that know their place in the Cosmos? What is the cosmic glue that holds it all together, that holds you together?" It is called LOVE, Unconditional Love. Use your Divine Reasoning !

Science tells us that ninety eight percent of our Body is water. The rest, a mere two percent, is composed of particums of matter. Around each cell of this mere two percent, which is floating in a sea of one particle of Hydrogen to two particles of Oxygen, is SPACE.......The Void, a no-thing. Within each of the particums, there is SPACE.......the Void, a no-thing. So I ask you to ponder, what is in that space?... *Or is it that we are lost in space?*

CONSCIOUSNESS, the CONSCIOUSNESS of the I AM that I AM. You are in that SPACE. You, as a particum of Light, are simply having a Dream. A Dream....... a Dream ......a Dream......!

STEP NINE: UNDERSTANDING FOREVER

CONSCIOUSNESS AND ENERGY THE EBB AND FLOW OF LIFE

One of the most important wisdom's one can acquire is Self-knowledge and a holistic perspective of reality......meaning your relationship to all of life around you, to the whole process of creation that is occurring simultaneously through all things and all dimensions in the moment. All that there is, *IS* Consciousness in Action, and that understanding is the key to the door of manifestation.

Consciousness is pervasive in all that *IS*. Consciousness exists in the rock, the animal, the microorganism, the tree, the fish, the cloud, the Sun, in the Light, and it is also inter-dimensional. We as Hu-man Beings have the unique quality of being able to connect to the whole of Consciousness. Our bodies were designed with certain Divine cosmic proportions that replicate the sacred geometry of the Universe, in the form of *Epigenetics*.......the Sacred geometry through which all physical mass is expressed.

Then there is *Kryahgenetices* which is the sacred geometry through which all Consciousness connects to matter through the magnetics of subtle energies. There seemingly is no ending to the levels of Consciousness that exist in our Universe. If one were to travel to the ends of human potential, then we would most likely find ourselves within the Consciousness of Source, which has no boundaries.

The Consciousness of Source is the pure cosmic essence of all things potentially, yet no thing materially. When Consciousness become aware of itself, that very action creates an energy and when Consciousness is combined with energy, Creation takes place. Consciousness and energy create thought. Thought creates light, light creates vibration and the energy in the thought moves the light and creates velocity, which creates frequency.

The combination of light and vibration creates sound and color, which can be measured in frequency, which is the rate by which thought vibrates. The faster the vibration, the higher the energy octave, the more intense the sound and color produced. Thus it is a certainty that dimensions can simultaneously exist interwoven within each other.

This is why the ascended Masters can be standing in the same room we are standing in and yet only certain individuals can perceive their presence. They can enter a room or our field of energy, coming from seemingly nowhere and then vanish. These Masters simply have developed the ability to control their vibrational frequencies. They have become a causal force.

We who are still aspiring to achieve mastership for the most part remain stuck in reactionary reality. We have little control over our emotions, let alone our thought focus, and we hardly have enough energy to discern our own thoughts from the thought patterns projected in the grid of social consciousness.   So our lives seem like a constant recycled motion picture of experiences that manifest, and we call it luck.

Eventually the reel of film degenerates from overuse and we see our life falling apart. We suffer the fall, through the various levels of depression, and Self condemnation, eventually bottoming out. We have at that point drained our energy so to speak, and we then wait for the miraculous stimulation from the Divine to give us new direction. Somehow, the miracle will occur for those who still maintain a shred of Self respect, and we once again find ourselves going through the process of recreating our lives, piece by piece from the debris of shattered dreams.

Seldom in this process however, do we ever access new information. Thus we keep reconstructing our lives according to old energy patterns, which are blueprints of the past. This is why we find that each period of reconstruction, perhaps lasts a little longer, but in the end it crumbles and we find ourselves in exactly the same situation. It is beyond any doubt, we are living our reality through *recycled ignorance*. It is the merry-go-round of life and a circle game. We relive the same patterns over and over and over......like drunken sailors sailing aimlessly upon a ship of fools.

THE ART OF **BEING**

We cannot find direction if we do not know Self.   We simply do not know who and what we are. So let us begin anew and take a look at the beauty that you are. Being you means being happy, being happy with the decisions you make, and how you accept yourself. It means literally loving yourself into a state of accepting the truth that your Self offers. Not being in competition with anyone else, is called *the Art of Being*.

You are a multi-faceted individual, you have had many, many lifetimes here upon this plane…...more than you can count. You have had many sojourns on other worlds, and you have expressed in a myriad of other dimensions. Your embodiment is composed of a complexity of Divine proportions, as well as an array of remarkable genetics, that resulted in your creation as the physical expression of God manifest in *HU*-man form.

Do you think God only has one truth….. a set of regulations and laws you might abide by? If that were true then it would effect the whole of you, and everyone would be a duplicate of the other. Everyone would be the same. They would have the same mind, the same voice, the same eyes, and the same body. They would have the same thoughts, like the same movies, wear the same colors…how boring and mundane that reality would be.

You are greatly loved by God, the Source…..loved for you unique energy, your unique beauty, and your unique creative Self. You are loved for you individuality, and your differences…..each one of them being a Divine expression of the living God. The problems in realizing your individuality are that you have developed so many expectations of your Self, even in just this lifetime alone.

These were based upon someone else's expectations of *their* own life, *not yours*. You have done this so many times that you have gotten lost in your journey by pleasing everyone else and forgetting to follow your own Star. Many of you have lost the Divine Connection to who you are, and with that, your connection to All That Is.

You continue to build idols of perfection to which you can mold yourself after. This is fine in concept, however it is usually once again someone else's image that you are trying to fit yourself into and not your own. How many of you are waiting for the coming of the Christos? Waiting, it seems, for centuries, staring off into the Heavens, looking for some ship that will take you up and lift you away from all this muck and mire.

Well get a clue, the Christos has already come! It is living in you, it is you, and it is trying desperately to express through you. It is pushing all your buttons, upsetting all your routines. It is causing holy havoc in your lives…..desperately trying to get you to break the old habits that keep you contained in your prisons of limitation. And it is succeeding. Just look at the world around you. Is there not chaos everywhere?

The Christos is at work creating the situation in each and everyone of your lives, that will force you to break off from old patterns and find new ones, sometimes with only a moment's notice....... *RIGHT*?

As the Christos is being you, it is loving you. It is grasping whatever desire you choose and holding on to it. It is you when you are formulating the brilliance of ideas, and then seeing them manifest before your eyes, and in every experience along your life's journey. It is the voice that is heard from within your Being.

It is you in every action that you engage, and every word that you utter. It *IS* you. So who is God? God is you! And now that you are likened unto God, what shall you be? You are to be yourself. You are to love yourself......and express yourself, as God would.

In recognizing yourself, Consciousness becomes Divine Awareness. And in that Awareness is the reality potential for all that you desire. All the knowledge that you ever need is already alive within you. You are in connection to the omnipresent Isness that flows through all things, therefore you know all things by being their very nature. All That IS exists for your experience, and what is to be in your world, is sanctioned by your Divine decree.

Everything in your life you created for your own experience that you might live and grow, and learn to become. All of it. You drew into your experience every person and every circumstance, every success and every failure. You are the Master of your own destiny, no one else. You did it all. Look at what you have created!

Awesome isn't it. Look around you. Look at the sky, the trees, the streets of the city, the squirrel, the clouds, the flower, and the bum on the street...... everywhere your eye lands....... this is your world. Welcome to virtual reality. Earth is the advanced school for Gods in Training. Only Gods can play. There is one danger that you must consider before participating in the game of virtual reality however, and that is the disease of ALTERED E.G. O. *Edging God Out*

The Disease of Altered Ego
AND IT IS AN ENGINEERED VIRUS WHICH TOOK CENTURIES TO DEVELOP

Altered Ego (A-Ego) is a disease that many Gods in training get while attending this great school. It is a terrible affliction that for some unknown reason scientists cannot come up with a cure for. A-Ego stands for *Always Edging God Out.* When you come down with A-EGO it can be terminal.

The God in you allows you to adopt the twisted perception of mortality...... you being separated from God. Your dreams begin to die, and you suffer from extreme depression, mood swings and limited vision. You develop Alzheimer's, and go around looking for God, forgetting that God lives in you, and that you are God.

Then the next thing you know, you are Creating a God outside yourself...... building boxes and trying to lure God inside, so you can hold God prisoner for the select few that have the ability to keep God contained within the parameters of their specific belief patterns. You then fall victim to the effects of judgment, thinking that your way is the only way, and that everyone else on the planet is lost. All your problems are being placed upon you by them, their curses and evil spells, and it is all because they see the world differently than your God told you to see the world. This is the dance of *US* and *Them.*

You then begin to develop paranoia and think that all others are plotting against you to try and steal your secret information about God........a God which only you have access to. So you create armies to protect your imprisoned God who lives in the building that you created in your Mind. Here you are protected because you know that your God is the only true God.

You know this although you have never seen your God, or talked to your God. Your entire reality relies upon this because someone told this to you when you were young. They also told you that if you believed differently, if you saw things from a different perspective, you would be thrown out of God's graces. They themselves would be forced perhaps to excommunicate you, and you will have to go live with *them*, out there.

You need to be accepted so you adopt their ways, even though inside you feel that you are losing part of you. You grow up and are taken into the fold. You may even be so good that they recruit you to fight for the cause. Suddenly one day there you are, a young leader amongst them, defending the faith. They applaud you as you assemble your armies and proceed to kill off everyone that disagrees with, *"The One Way".......* *"The True Way."*

You take on the whole of the world knowing in the end only you will survive and there will be one God. With one Law, and one way of thinking, What a dream you would actually create, one world where everyone looks and acts the same. Sounds like *"Pleasantville"* to me.....where everything is clear and black and white.

Funny thing is, you can do that, and accomplish that in life. It is always so perfect in "Pleasantville" until we meet someone with a bigger God. Perhaps a rougher God, one who perhaps destroys your God and you become slaves to their God.......Can you see it? We have all done it in one lifetime or another.

Can you remember when you bashed your friends dreams while you were growing up, because they got in your way, or they went out with the one special person you wanted, and you launched your campaign against them? We wonder why God doesn't talk to us anymore. Perhaps it is because this is what God sees, as we play our games of limited vision suffering from the virus known as A-EGO. So, be aware of *Always Edging God Out*. It can have terminal effects on your participation in the game of life.

In order to have love in your life and to experience the love that flows abundantly without ending through the entire Universe, you must become Love itself......otherwise you would draw to you the lack of love. For Love is the only way through what lies before us in these times of change and transformation. All forms of negativity only feed off of and transmute into ever larger and larger forms of negativity. For that is the nature of the purification we are now experiencing. Know that this is not occurring because you are not worthy of receiving love, rather that you are in disharmony with the Love Vibration itself.

In order for Love to flow freely through your Being, and in order to attract that vibration to yourself, one must resist the temptation to give way to the lesser vibratory fields of energy that have for so long been programmed into our cellular structure. This poison has seeped into your Consciousness from centuries of being fed diluted truth, partial truth and arranged truth for the manipulative agenda of the lessor Gods. It keeps you enslaved in third dimensional expression.

For the most part we are caught up in a Consciousness that is very condemning of everything except its own ideal of itself. In its endeavors to enforce that ideal, it would enslave the whole of humanity in a game of virtual reality. One where we are caught up in the endless pursuit of struggling to become the ideal of the illusion it projects. Yet time after time in the moment the ideal is achieved, it changes into yet another aspect of itself, for the ideal is predicated upon the illusion of an image and not tangible reality.

The image is likened to a mirage, and remains forevermore just out of reach. And too often if we do arrive, it dissipates in our hands and returns to the illusionary plasma that leaves us forever unfulfilled. For this artificial Consciousness is designed to leave us feeling unworthy and in a sate of subjective Consciousness, the Consciousness of enslavement.

It becomes very arduous for anyone to keep up with the constant pattern of win and lose, gain and release, reward and punishment. It simply wears you down. Achieve......only to change upon arrival. It is a friction that wears us down energetically. It leaves us with such a low energy level that it is a wonderment that we can even contemplate ordinary thought, never mind super-Consciousness. It is very much like the snake that eats its own tail, and thus leads us further into the cycle of Self-destruction.

We are fast approaching the time of the perfection of the human body and we claim our right to become fully *HU*-man. We are a species in global transformation. We are becoming a new race, and that reality is emerging from within, meeting much resistance from without, where the illusion lives. This is why no matter how hard you struggle to keep in the confinement of the false reality, you keep breaking apart, and falling into a state of confusion.

The state of confusion is actually a blessing, for from that confusion you can recreate yourself anew, and have another chance to become all that you can be. All is possible if we can restructure the ideal to come into harmony with our inner Being.

You are at this time remembering that you are Spiritual Beings first and foremost. The friction you feel is your struggle to listen once again to your inner Being, the *you* that lives within God's Temple, and strives not to please everyone else's requirements for Being. Rather you are endeavoring to fulfill the direction of the inner-Self, learning again to listen to the quiet voice that has been with you since the beginning of time immortal.

Learn to hear your own power in the silence......being who you are and never compromising that essence that burns within, like the eternal flame you truly are. The God that is the God of everything and everyone, will never forsake you, for when you look into the mirror and truly Love the Self reflected, you will see the eyes of the Master that you are.

Divinity is not to be found in a document of Holy and Divine Laws, Codes, Covenants, and Regulations that must be followed. The road to true Divinity was never found by one who was unresponsive to their own flow of free and original thought, or by not possessing the basic creative ability to access new thought.

Without creativity we are but blind monkeys, playing in a desperate game of someone else's perception of what we are........surrendering to the tendency to make ourselves feel, *no matter what the cost to our Spirit*, in the hopes that by some random act of Divine intervention we might feel enough, to desire to wake up.

Enlightenment and Divinity both are reached when balance and understanding are mixed with compassion. Love is then seen in its perfection within us, and is experienced by being near one who lives in accordance with their inner truth, which is the Truth of God.

To desire to become the totality of your Truth, is to desire to become an enlightened Being. This state of reality can only be attained when we surrender Self for the greater picture. In order to change the programming, we must exercise discipline. *Practice makes perfect.......* know the phrase?

Constant affirmation of the Divine Light that moves through you, acknowledges the Life Force that allows for you to think and feel, and to have an opinion, and individual thought. It is learning to walk in Gratitude. To become the total truth of yourself, is to become a holistic Being, acknowledging the wholeness of your entirety, the totality of your essence and not succumbing to Self-doubt or fear.

It is knowing in the core of your Being, that once we ignore the Divine spark that lives within all of us, it leads to the affliction of relying upon A-EGO and then we *Always Edging God Out.* We wind up having to justify to ourselves, and everyone around us every action we take, and relentlessly defend our position, never having the courage, or the energy to just BE.

God is not a singular formulated thought. God is the truth in all thoughts. There are those who would challenge your right to live in the *freedom of Being.* They would try to pull you back into the murk and mire, only to justify their own struggles with owning their self-truth and worth. Daring to have your very own thought makes you different. It makes you in many ways the "Outcast"....... the "Misfit" in our society. In daring to have original thought, to have your own thought, and be in touch with your own God, you oftentimes struggle with experiencing what it is like to be unloved and not the approved version of the ideal, because of how you appear rather than how you are.

Know always that there is a beauty in you that is beyond earthy description, for you are more than flesh and bone. So awesome is your Light and the colors that express from your true essence, that you cannot comprehend while expressing in this form, or have the means to even formulate the magnificence of how you will appear when you once again merge with the Light of the Living God. When you leave this plane you shall take with you the sum total that you are, from every experience you have had, since the dawning, and in a moment...... death will be a no thing, as you come to know the glory that is God

Love all that you are and if you find within your Being even one thing that does not come into harmony with the radiance of your Inner Light, change it. Change it by affirming and acknowledging that which expresses in the inner-Self, in the perfection of your Spirit. Begin to listen to *you*. Listen long and hard for perhaps the first time, to hear your own words. That is when you will find the power to correct any malady that exists in your projection of outward reality. It occurs when you come into the point of Being, when no thought exists, but the Awareness of Being. The change will come instantly and be all encompassing.

Always reaffirm your realizations. Start a constant practice of affirming the connection to the Living God and thusly acknowledging the Divinity that lives in all things. See always the wonderment in the mystery of how it all connects, and how the Light expresses in all its forms. See the wonderment in the interaction and the playing back and forth of energies that swirl in the holographic reality, like Dolphins at play in a vast ocean of Light.

For thought is the most powerful tool of the Alchemist, as though it has within its vibration the ability to sculpt the very nature of all reality. Thought molds reality and shapes it like an artist working with their media. You are what you think, and the exterior world responds to the way you think you are. We did not create the web of life but we are a part of it, an eternal part of Creation. For we are the Suns and Daughters of the Living God. That bond is eternal, and immutable.

The formula for creation is simple to understand. All around you is a field of energy, likened to the layers of the atmosphere. These layers are striated and merge within and without each other. It is like a great force field around you. These energy bands could be simply identified as Thought, Feeling, Emotion and Action. These bands fold within and without you like a swirling extravaganza of light, twisting and whirling like the Aurora Borealis in the northern skies.

These bands are activated by thought arising from the inner-Self, the essence of your Being, simply by placing your Awareness upon their existence. This starts an energy to flow whereby they begin to swirl in opposite directions creating a great field, a causal energy that spews forth from the inner Being, directly from the heart chakra. The energy of the Divine within you, begins to spin the web of life, and create openings in the light fields that surround you.....like the wind disperses the clouds after the storm.

Through this action, your thoughts will actually spin out into the Universe. It is similar to frequency fibers that appear like little threads of lightning. At first they are short pulses, then longer pulses, until they become long threads of light reaching out in the higher octaves. All of these strands of light create an energy field that begins to not only surround you, but feeds the inner-Self with harmonic frequency. You first perceive this as a feeling of bliss, a harmonic convergence of thought and light.

The action that results, is the merging of the aqueous substance that is the light essence of pure potentiality, as you reconnect to All That Is. This fiber optic flaring of energy begins to spin with your thought frequencies and as it comes down the seven layers of light that sustain physical expression upon this plane, the light begins to slow and coagulate. As it does, the manifestation of like attracts like frequency, designed by your thought, comes into an alignment and expresses itself as experience. You then merge with your foreverness.

There are sounds that occur that cannot be perceived by the normal human ear, and light that expresses in twelve colors of the New Rainbow, which also cannot be perceived by the normal eye. However these frequencies can be felt by the emotional body, and transferred to the physical body as sensations like, "Oh I have goose bumps." Or the hair on the back of your neck stands up, resulting from a feeling.

The feeling, which accompanies Creation, is Joy. It is pure orgon energy that creates a state of bliss. Remember, if one sensory element is afflicted, another will compensate for that lack of physical perception. This allows for the participatory functions of the twelve senses, which connect us to Divine Source. (The twelve senses will be explained in detail in the next book of the don Lobos series.)

You are but an extended part of the Creator. The Creator, though separate from you, is also one and the same as you. The Creator gave unto you, Itself, Its Life Force and Its Consciousness. The Creator is the Universal, while you are the singular expression of the same thought. All that the Creator is, was given unto you so that you might be and have all that you desire. Whatever you can conceive of in your contemplative thought, so can it be....if you so choose to *Will* it into existence.

It is Source that is the energy that fulfills your dreams and desires, and it is Source that is the dream maker. And who are you? You are the dreamer, the spinner of what flows through your Consciousness, which is of the Source as It contemplates Its experience through your adventure. So, what are dreams made from? They are made from thought.

The Creator has given you the energy, as it has unto the Earth that derives its Life Force from the Sun. The Source has created the seed that the grasses grow from, and from the grasses the Great Spirit has given you the means to spin the cloth and make the robe that you wear. While in another moment it has given you the grasses from which you harvest the seed and make the bread that you subsist upon. It is a dance, and you are the choreographer designing each step and the tempo of the experience, as you express in the moment.

It is your Divine right to take from the gifts Creator has bestowed upon you and create anything that you wish, be it great or be it vile, be it ugly or be it beautiful, be it happy or be it sad, be it abundance, be it lack...... it is your right to create anything you so desire. The Source of All That Is, sees all things as splendid beauty and an emanation of Its Life Force..... for all things of themselves are ultimately pure. Source, the Father/Mother principle of all that expresses Itself in material form, judges not Its Creations, nor does Source discern one better than the other...... for all is life, and life itself is Sacred.

THE WISDOM OF THE LION

That which flows through the Lion flows through you, and you are closer in relationship than you might consider. For you are both of the flesh, and you both share the dream of temporal existence, but there is a difference between the Lion and yourself. The Lion knows that in its essence it is eternal, it knows its world, and who it is. The lion is free from asking itself, "Who am I?" "Why am I?"

The Lion knows its place and sees the perfection in its kingdom, while we struggle beyond hope to justify our Beingness, carrying the yoke of guilt, and shame, and drowning in thoughts of our unworthiness. The Lion knows that it is king of its kingdom, and would not annihilate another species for the sake of its own pleasure. Nor would the Lion condemn itself or its Creator.

The Lion walks with the joy and freedom of Spirit, expressing what it is in every action, celebrating what it is, and loving what it is in a full experience. How many of us can say that about ourselves? How many of us are content to live in the glory of the Light of God, and give not a thought as to what tomorrow will bring, for we know that the God of All, is there for us and within us, and we will be provided for?

How many of us can live and run free from fear......feeling only the Joy of living, and feeling the power of our Being expressing, every moment in the majesty of our Beingness? We have much to learn from the Lion, and little to teach.

The Lion can teach us what it is like to know that we are always perfect in the Eyes of God. When we became separate parts of God, our bodies were wondrous vessels of Light synthesis.....wonderful and in full balance, and loving our expression, knowing our immortal nature, and expressing only the purity of the Source from which we came. We did not have the feeling that we were incomplete, that we had a missing part, that we were imperfect, or that we were less than the perfect expression of God.

How much of your day do you spend in the glory of yourself, contemplating Divine thought? How much is spent in the senseless labyrinths of Self Doubt, and Self Criticism, and Self Denial? How much of your day is spent in thoughts of your connectedness to the Divine Source? How much of your day is spent in thoughts of the mundane? If all we do is dwell within the world of the mundane then what are we to experience, what are we to dream?

A difference between you and the Lion is that you have the ability to dream.....to contemplate growth and expansion of Consciousness. The Lion lives within the confines of its world and is king. But we are the dreamers, and through the gift of dreaming can create reality with each thought. We decree the conditions of our reality with each word and action. The Lion simply IS.

The Creator's Love for us is unending. It has no limitation. We may do whatever we choose, and It does not judge us, for no thing can take us from It. Only our own judgments and decrees create our conditions of experience. For we have built around us a wall of FEAR. And living so long in that fear, we are now caught in an endless struggle to perpetuate its existence..... for we have forgotten there is another way. We express fears existence, which in our blindness has become the only measure by which we can evaluate our existence.

This is a Spell which must be broken. For we have *never* sinned. God has *never* judged us. We have only created our own situations based upon the laws of cause and effect. We are a species that condemns itself, and abuses our own Divinity because we allow reckless thinking to create before us a picture of abandonment, and judgment. We are trying to fit all of reality into the ideal of the one law, one expression, and one outcome. And that is a law, which does not exist. Fear is an illusion that is born from belief that we are separate from God. And nothing has ever been farther from the truth.

... AND SPEAKING OF DEATH

So what is it we must take care of, in order to break the Spell and begin to live as we were meant to live? The unseen essence called Thought. Collectively your Thoughts make up your attitude. You are afraid of death because you have been fed the concept that death is an ending.... it is the loss of All That Is. Yet in the same moment, you crave for seers to tell you of your past and future lives.

Again the Consciousness that believes in separation from God the Source, has caused a paradox within your own reality. Most, when they die, will fall into the abyss of emptiness, only because they have allowed themselves to believe that this is so. Yet I tell you now, it is not so, for when you leave your body you will still be. You will be more yourself than you are now. You will be the totality of yourself, all feeling, all knowing, and all Being.

Yes, you will be in another world. A world of pure Thought, where what you think will be in the moment. But there is sadness on the other side of the veil for so many have surrendered their right to think and agreed to accept someone else's thought. With no sense of themselves, they reach Divinity only to return because they cannot sustain their own thoughts. They cannot sustain the Awareness of their own

Being, because they have never been that Being.   They are strangers unto themselves. They have lived their entire experience here on this side of the veil.

When you die, you will know instantly the connection to All That Is.   You will know the wonderment of energy and frequency, and how the web of life contains within it all things. You will know how our existence is dependent upon another essence, and how what you do effects the whole of life.

Our challenge here is to awaken the memory of our immortality and realize that connectedness here and now, expressing upon the physical plane of limited reality. Once the veil of separation has been removed, we will see with our true eye........The Eye of the Shaman.

Love is the answer...

If we could only allow ourselves to live our path, always striving to follow the pure direction of the inner-Soul-Being...... if we could only allow ourselves to be the wholeness of what we are.... *we would transform in a moment.* But we are afraid to let go of our identity aren't we? We hold on to this identity with everything that we have. And yet in the end the ultimate experience of living this life, is in the surrendering of the identity......the Image which imprisons us.

We resist change with all the energy that we can summon with our physical bodies, and yet the only way to make it through this Virtual Reality game is to allow ourselves the freedom to transmute, to let go. For the more ridged we are, the more vulnerable we are to the Life Force Itself. For the Life Force is always changing, It is never constant. The only constant It has, is that It is always changing. We are in many ways like kites trying not to fly in the wind.

We have been created as the ultimate biological computer in the Universe. We are creatures of change, Living Light Beings experimenting with physical form. Love is the premise of life. Love is allowing, and permits life to BE. Love is the virtue that creates all other virtues. Allow, allow, and allow......just allow it all to be.

When you tire of fighting it all, when the adrenaline rush of aggression and war no longer thrill you, when you tire of all the games of materialism, and no longer desire to be **A**lways **E**dging **G**od **O**ut......you will let go of the A-EGO, and lose all sense of the separateness. You will come back to the essence of Love.

If you refuse to let go and live your life as a fixed ridged expression of God, committed to living within the experience of limited reality, you will have done just that. You will know the fullest extent of limited reality, and you will still, upon surrendering your final holding, the embodiment itself, come to Love. For Love, is what gave you expression to be, in the first place!

It is your nature to Love. To Love is automatic, the struggle, our feeling of agony, is in our trying to shut it down or in keeping it turned off. *"Love is you, you are love, love is giving, giving love."* John Lennon was right.   It is the nature of all Beings to have Love. It is the nature of all Beings to try to express Love. What you have suffered in your many lifetimes is your separation from Love. You have suffered in your denial of Love. For the pain you feel is equal to the Love you withhold.

If you want to know Love, then you must become Love. Love is the permissive God Nature within all of us that allows life to express unbounded, in the full expression of the living God.

FREEDOM

Is freedom just an illusive fantasy that we place somewhere out before us, so that we have an imaginary yet unattainable goal to achieve? Is it just an illusionary condition that does not exist in this reality? NO, it really does exist!

Where we began to lose our freedom was when we began to compromise our dreams for the sake of pleasing someone else. That is when we began to shut down. Eventually we let the pattern go too far and we then could no longer reach out nor could we receive. We became somehow isolated, feeling like we were alone. We no longer were players in the game. We were observers, merely wall flowers.

Being alone is not being isolated. Being *isolated*, is being separated from. On the outside looking in. Being alone is a natural part of the growth of our Being. When we out grow one belief pattern we must learn to allow the new belief pattern to emerge, and for the most part this is always a solitary journey. Freedom is not found in the state of denial. Denial is simply resistance. It is refusing to participate. It is a non-action.

If we resist that emergence, we often slip into a state of confusion, and non-directional experience. That experience although temporal will leave us lost in the wilderness, where we remain long after our time to change the scene has come due. It is called getting *stuck*. It is not a curse, it is a situation that can be changed.

The result is, everything around you pulls back, because you are no longer getting the Life Force from your experience in that situation. Our experience of the amount of time it takes us to realize the energy reality of the situation, and our agreeing to listen to our inner Spirit that is telling us it is time to move on, is up to us. The longer we stay *stuck*, the more painful that experience can be. Again, the ability to change circumstance is in our hands, not another's.

The reason you get *stuck,* is because you lost the signal to yourself. You can no longer hear your own inner voice. You have disconnected from the inner Being. This is the primary reason for many personal manifestations not materializing, or if they do, they are somehow twisted and seem to work out almost contrary to the original intent of our desire. When we become disconnected with our signature frequency, we lose our ability to track our energy resources to the main power supply.

True power lies in the silence, the great expanse of unlimited potential of the Void. This power is inexhaustible, and ceaseless in its flow. If we are walking in balance and truly attuned to our inner-Self, it is instantly accessible to us, all of us. When we are connected to the Universal Source, our thoughts, attitudes, emotions, intentions, words, and actions activate this power we call the God Force. This understanding is one of the Keys to our personal utilization of the applied science of *Kryahgenetics.*

All that exists outside of your personal inner frequency, is for good or for bad, illusionary. All that lies within your personal frequency range, is what effects your ability to perform as you desire in the game of Virtual Reality. Everything is energy. All material perceptions are the result of a frequency, which has projected thought into the universal field. The universal field then picks up that frequency thought, and sends the transmission back to us as a thought form.

What makes the external illusionary, is that in the greater degree it is not born from our inner frequency. It exists outside of our field of cause and effect, or it is someone else's frequency we are subjugating our perceptions to. No matter how hard we try to hold on to that which comes from outside our personal frequency range, it will ultimately disintegrate, and dissipate back to the source from which it was conceived.

Whatever the life situation one chooses to experience, it must come from within, in order to be held in substance. It must be born from heart. If born of the heart, then all that you manifest must and will come back to you without interference, or obligation to an external source. The pathway is clear, all things must return to their creator, all thoughts like migratory birds will return to their creator. This is part of the Universal Law of Attraction, amplified by the Universal Laws of Love, and an integral part of the creation process.

Freedom is the inherent ability to create and exercise free *Will* in the circum- stances of your own reality, and to experience that reality without the presence of fear. The balance and harmony of co-existing with others around you who are also equally endowed, is that you never infringe your *Will* knowingly upon them, without their consent. You never manipulate the reality to such an extent that it will impose vibratory shifting that is not in the natural order of their own ability to create.

One of the most powerful elements of manifesting our desired reality, is our intent. By developing our Awareness of True-Self, we strengthen our connection to Source. By affirming our gratitude, Awareness, and reconnection to Source, we then act with the intent of Source. This God Force is very, very powerful. The God Force that emanates from Source then becomes the empowerment of our desire, which motivates our intent. Intent in hand becomes the trigger for transformation.

There are three main components for transformation. One is desire. Desire is the fire that triggers you into taking action. The key to guiding your desire is your intention. Your intent creates the nature of your projected thoughts, and gives them quality. With quality we create substance and tenacity. These two elements create emotion, or passion within ourselves, our path, and to the delivery of the manifested thought responding to the Universal Laws of Attraction.

Then there is our Awareness, for our Awareness tells us where to place our attention, and what level of our attention to activate. When we create with Awareness we are in control of our thoughts, the nature of our thoughts, and the quality of our thoughts. We can change them and choose the thoughts. We can direct the thoughts we choose, rather than just stumble through our life experience, taking what comes by gift of accident.

Our thoughts are carried by our intent. This creates a mode of action, a vibration. The higher the vibration, the more intense the creation or experience. Our thoughts are given a vitality through our experience of them, realized through our emotions. The Laws of LOVE govern this action. Remember, all that is born from thought, and all that we experience, is thought in action. It is living thought. In order to create any positive outcome, we must develop constructive purpose. The purpose is realized through our intent.

Your intention focuses your Awareness, which dictates where, and how to place your attention upon a specific result. You, in your Awareness then begin to interact with the elements. You interact with the elements on a multi-dimensional level, Spiritually through Consciousness, Emotion, as well as with Body and Mind. The elements, then in turn become aware of your attention, determining your intention, also on a multi-dimensional level.

This is *Kryahgenetics* in its simplest form. If both are harmonically merged then the signal that is perceived equals that which is manifest whether it be experience, matter, or intellectual understanding of a greater concept than that which created the intent to discover.

The elemental world is in perpetual connection to Source. They are receptive to the pure intent of this God Force. One need not climb a mountain, or even cross the ocean for the world to come to them, if they are in harmony. For if they are in harmony with the inner-Self, then the world will come to them and unfold at their feet, willingly and in a state of ecstatic Joy.

THE CHRIST CONSCIOUSNESS PRINCIPLE

EXPERIMENT 1

A simple example of how *Kryahgenetics* relates to the Christ Consciousness can be experienced and easily understood through the following meditative experiment. Go into a meditative state by whatever process you are comfortable with. Allow yourself the simple pleasure of lying down......... *most likely the first few times you try this you will fall asleep.* That is all right. It takes a little time to be able to go beyond the Alpha State and stay awake so you can drive the vehicle through the deeper states of meditation.

Eventually, you will be able to stay awake. It might even be better to do this when you are not tired, perhaps in the early morning, and early evening when you are naturally awake and your energy level is up.

You will only need to do this for about 20 minutes. You can progress with the practice, to a point where you do it twice a day, allowing 15 minutes for each period. You will enter a magical journey into reconnecting to Self, plus understand how your particular process of *Kryahgenetics* works best for you.

Once in the silence, picture yourself, your Body, Mind and Spirit in absolute perfection. This is your canvas so you can paint any picture you desire. You can redesign the picture of yourself, as you would like to see yourself. If you have not developed a picture of yourself, then try to relate to how you would like to feel. It is the feeling that carries the intent, anyway.

Picture yourself without pain, without energy deficiencies, possessing total mental clarity, as if you were already in the Christos. Being there is very important. Be there and the reality will follow, remember again that the elemental energies will always realign to come into harmony with the thought of God. It's only because we have fallen out of harmony with God's vision, that we are in conflict with the natural forces that pour out through the Mother's embodiment, as endlessly as the trees breathe, and the tide ebbs and flows.

The renewal of the embodiment is simply a matter of reconnecting with the boundless energy that is already there, that has always been there, and will be there into forever. Affirm your connection to that foreverness. Allow yourself to review your day, and life direction. Let the voices go on, and on, keep steering yourself to go beyond the voices, to the silence. Allow the heaviness of your life situation to fall away, and off you. Become the pure essence of your Being….the essence that has no name, no identity other than your feeling, your knowing…. your connection to the God Force.

The endless energy of the God Force will assist you, and you will go into a place of non-Being. There you will find the place of IS. Non-Being is an art form. It is a very important place for all initiates to arrive at. For here, away from the persona, you are removed from the reactionary existence of social consciousness, where we slip over and over into reactionary living.

This is where you can feel *you,* and the Source of all that is flowing through you. Here is where you can re-program Self. You can use the free energy of this endless God Force to literally re-design the package to come into alignment with the thought process of inner-Self. Remember inner-Self is not bound by the rules of social con- sciousness, so it expresses as True Being, expressing your true desires, your true feelings. You will hear your own song, and come to understand your true thoughts, through those feelings.

Exercise non-judgment and just allow the energy to flow through you. Remem- ber this is Source, the God energy that sustains all life throughout the Universe. You will not fall into a wasteland, and that energy will sustain you, it *always* has and it *always* will. Constantly and subtlety reaffirm your connection to the God Force, and allow yourself to be. As you get to a place of feeling the energy flowing through you, and the ecstasy of life throughout your embodiment, the journey begins.

You can actually direct this energy and it will follow your *Will.* Now remain firm with these simple but necessary instructions for the journey to Self-rejuvenation 101.

Remember, everything is done slowly at first. Do not force anything, move slowly with grace and poise.

EXERCISE...*after you use this a a preliminary guide create your own*

1. Move the energy from your feet up to the top of your head, becoming aware of every part of you along the journey. Once you arrive at the top of the head, allow the energy to pass through to the Source. Then bring in that energy down through your crown chakra and down through your feet. Visualize it like a silver thread connecting to the very center of the Earth. Try this a few times, there now you've got it. You've made the connection.

2. See your body surrounded by light, liquid light moving and swirling all around you. Bathe in the wonderment of it. Concentrate on the Light and not the physical aspects. Allow that light to give you a picture of your nervous system by simply becoming aware of a part of your body. Let's try your forefinger first.

3. Become aware of the command, and the reaction of the body to the command, actually see the connection in the light. Don't resist the picture or try to manipulate it, just allow it to come to you in its own way. You may have to resist the tendency to argue with the simplicity of this exercise. Simple......yes, but it will show you the keys to the highway of changing the entire paradigm of your reality.

In phase one, we are looking at how intent triggers movement in the body. We are understanding how in the holographic reality, we move through the light rather than the physical mass. In this state, the embodiment is seen as an endless spinning of light, like a fiber optic nebula, spinning what is perceived as physical mass in normal awareness. This state of mind is called our Second attention.

From the Second attention we can learn to move rather easily into Third, Fourth and beyond, as we journey to the very place that is known as the Eye of the Shaman. There we move through an intensely bright white light, almost as if we were moving into a cool star. As a matter of fact it is oftentimes referred to as the Shaman's Star. There are twelve levels of attention, which we learn to navigate and utilize along the pathway to mastership of our physical expression in the Earth plane.

As we develop our techniques, we can and will, by simple participatory action, cause transformation, and shift the paradigm that presently keeps us bound in mediocrity. If we can change our concepts of ourselves, our perception will alter accordingly. We have the ability as children of the Living Light of the God Force, to totally reconstruct ourselves in the corrected Image.

We can do that, by reconnecting to God, and becoming an extension of that essence Itself, as we express that essence upon this plane. Essentially the destination point is the wisdom of Yeshua's (Jesus) teachings, realized.

APPLYING THE PRINCIPLES OF KRYAH

We suffer mostly from lazy attitude, we are thus subjected to unconscious habits born of a lazy atrophic thinking processes, which we have inherited genetically from generations of being asleep. We can, through the exercise of our *Will* overcome these detriments to our God-Consciousness.

To overcome this dilemma does not mean that we must suffer through arduous, painful and dangerous disciplines, that only create further confusion so that we find ourselves focusing on the experience of denial rather than achievement and Self-growth. Denying one's Self is a ridiculous and erroneous concept. The focus we are trying to achieve is actually based on allowing ourselves to receive. It is a matter of changing our perceptions, adjusting our belief patterns. Remember always that the body does not communicate in words, it communicates through feelings.

Source is not empty. It is full. The great Void is not a place of nothingness. It is the place of totality, Being in Consciousness with full potentiality. It is all things. Source does not operate out of lack, Source operates out of abundance. Source is always in service to us, likewise when we change our perception of I, ME, MY, we become in service to Source, as well as to others. By being in service to others, we open up the river of abundance to flow back to us.

When you look at your garment, or the food upon your table, think of all the hands, and the enormous amount of human effort it took to bring it there. Think of all the energies and people working in cohesiveness to enable you to enjoy it. That thought process will cause something inside of you to begin to shift. Write it down if it helps you to realize that we can do very little on our own. Sovereignty can be an indulgence we unwittingly participate in.

We are not as independent as we like to think we are. Someone even made the tool that you need to build your house in the wilderness from sticks and stones. And from nature you took the results of all the elements that participated in the preparing of those commodities for your use. When you activate your Awareness to this factual reality, you will begin to develop a strong attitude of gratitude.

The more we are in service, the more we give, the more the reality around us will respond in service to us, and the more we will receive. It is the law of the Give-away. In acting with Awareness in this manner we become a channel for the Divine God-Force to flow through us, and we become conduits of God's *Will.* Like attracts like.

By the simple changing of our perception we can turn lemons into lemonade. We create consciously by changing the energy in which we express our actions. This gives the God Force an open channel to fulfill all that It touches, and we as recipients of that energy, create the ideal of ourselves rather than the Image. We empower all we touch with this inexhaustible God Force in humble joyful service.

Desire is the motivating force behind our *Will,* so do not be in denial of desire..... embrace it and direct it for good purpose. Desire is the gravity of creation. When we join desire with the God Force we pull into our energy field all that is of like vibration. By controlling our thoughts we can navigate away from fear, judgment, and self-condemnation. We can instead choose to walk in a state of grace and poise. We can dictate by Divine decree the nature of our state of mind. It is called Conscious Living.

How then do we change our perception? We simply refuse to allow anything that is not in harmony with our God Self to express through us. How do we know what the God Self desires? We listen to the silence. What are the results? We walk through life as causal Beings, realizing that all is God in motion. We exist in a plane of action, not contemplation. We exist as conduits for God to realize the Divine Order of Life. We are givers of life, and by living, we are in a perpetual state of realizing ourselves. It takes work, and we cannot find it in a box of Cracker Jacks, but we will quickly realize that the results are the rewards of our applied efforts. By taking action, you will alter your perception from mundane, into God Consciousness, and that is a forever change. It is all a matter of perception and relative truth.

Once you change your perception, the entire phenomenon we call reality changes. We possess through reconnecting to this God Force energy, the ability to create miracles and change the paradigm of limited consciousness. God becomes our teacher, and the Earth our schoolroom. All the mathematical codes to sacred geometry can be observed in nature. The whole encoding of creation has been before us for the extent of our eternity, if we could only develop the eyes to see. By understanding the process of *Kryahgenetics,* we are given the gift of coming home, on our own terms.......fully awake, and conscious of our evolutionary process.

You create the reality you desire by consciously choosing what you think, and how you respond to experience. You get out of reactionary behavior and move into thinking behavior. You choose to no longer be a leaf at the mercy of the wind, and become God In Action. All things will gravitate to you, ass you use your new found energy that is fueled by the God Force.

All of this is strengthened by constant affirmations of your connection to the Source that flows through you effortlessly. You develop new thinking patterns, and open up new neuronal pathways for new thought to emerge into your Consciousness. Simply desire to get out of your own way and allow the God Force to direct your thinking, your words, and your actions.

Take control of your thoughts. The most important thoughts you have, are the thoughts you have with yourself. The most important words that you speak, are the words you speak to yourself when you are alone. So make the effort to stop the merry-go-round. The power is in the silence, not in the noise in your head. Pay attention and listen, observe what kind of game you are playing with yourself and find out why.

Utilize the basic principles of fifth dimension Mastery....... Discernment, Discretion, Detachment, Desire and Discipline. Learn to *BE* first, then become the action, dare to do, and then give yourself permission to receive. Allow your Self to experience JOY.

Then consider this, if you can cause a reaction in the physical mass you call your body, which is perhaps the biggest block to your being able to move as free as the Angels, why then can't you change aspects about yourself and how you perceive the embodiment? Why can't you change your state of ordinary consciousness to a state of Super-Consciousness? It is only a thought that is preventing you from doing so, is it not? If you can command the physical mass then why not the light itself that creates the pattern by which the body reacts? You see the body cannot move of its own accord. It is reactionary, it must respond to the thought impulse. You are the architect of the thought impulse, you and only the True you has the magical ability of connecting to the God Force. You are the Master.

Remember, the God Force is incapable of creating imperfection. The God Force that flows through you is the same God Force that created the whole of the Universe. You, your embodiment, and your Consciousness are already programmed for the God program. It has been so since your conception as a Spirit. The only thing that went wrong along the journey, is that you in your growing and education were turned away from your True knowingness. You have the ability to redirect your attention to Source, and that power is inexhaustible in its Source. It can never run out. But our connection to or non-connection to Source is all a matter of choice.

Our embodiment is held together by a holographic network of information and energy. What keeps the whole network together and allows us to perceive ourselves in third dimensional expression, or any expression for that matter, is the Cosmic Glue….. LOVE. The principles that apply to our embodiment also apply to the whole of the Universe. "Know thyself and you will know God," was not actually a metaphor, it was a map. All that makes up the embodiment is composed of Universal Mind. We can call upon that authority at any moment to come into expression, and it will respond. All is Light expressing as matter. All that you perceive is in constant motion, and the *Isness*, is ever changing. Anything that ceases to abide by the Universal Laws of change, ceases to BE.

Our embodiment is the outpouring so to speak of our belief system. The embodiment is a thought projection. All our attitudes, our emotions, our jubilation as well as our fears and sorrow can be read in that holographic field, and are continuously expressed in our body language. The true nature of one's Self is always being broadcast if we have the eyes to see, and stand out of our own way to allow our own very natural abilities to shine through the fog of our not remembering who we are. We are so worried we will make a mistake. Mistakes are OK. Once we teach ourselves the new patterns, then only the God Force will come through, and all along the pathway God has and continues to be, our guide and teacher. The transmission of the God Force never shuts down, only we can turn it off. That is because we have free *Will*.

What has this got to do with paradigm shifting? Everything. The external world is but the reactionary response, the summation of our thought patterns, what makes up our belief system. All that exists in the external experience which is outside of us, is in a constant process of creation and dis-creation. We are transmitting the God energy constantly, and by doing so we are dictating the very nature of our reality. We are calling in our experiences. If they are uncalculated experiences, then we are calling in that state of mind as well, we are allowing random experience to occur.

Our embodiment is little more than the transformation of our experiences into physical expression. Our environment, our life situation responds to us in the same manner. Our very physical body reacts to our needs and has the potentiality to produce any chemical that is required to respond to life's experience upon demand. For example, if you are stressed, your body will actually start to produce valium. If you are excited, and in Joy, your body will begin to produce interleukins and interferons. These chemicals by the way, have very, very powerful effects upon cancer and aging. They can stop cancer and reverse the aging process. These chemicals are artificially manufactured by major drug companies and are available only to a very affluent few, for treatment of cancer, and anti-aging at very exclusive health facilities.

When we allow ourselves to exist in a state of Harmony and Joy, we have the natural ability to create what is necessary for our health and peak performance within our own Divinely designed embodiment. Our bodies are constantly converting our experiences into molecules. The physical body is in a constant process of creation and dis-creation. Actually it was never the intent for our bodies to be temporal, rather they were designed for an eternal Self adjusting existence to facilitate our Spirits. However, the proper programming or improper programming of Mind controls all that. The concept of temporal existence is something born of limitation. It is a reality adopted by Gods suffering from amnesia.

There are those who ask why I insert such a constant flow of humor into my lectures. It is amazing how many people have a difficult time dealing with humor. I often will stop and make the effort to explain to those who think that Spiritual stuff is supposed to be solemn and pious......that in fact nothing can be farther from the truth. When we laugh, we open a doorway and it allows our God to come into us. In that moment of Joy we are in direct contact with the God Force. It is a moment of eternity. This is why we perceive it as a blissful experience. And by the way, laughter is very healing to the body. Rolling thunder upon the Mountain tops, could be thought of as the sound of God laughing while immersed in a complete state of Joy over the Creation.

We must remember that we can change our perception of our experiences at any given moment. One man's ceiling is another man's floor. It is all in our attitude, which directly dictates the conditions of our perception. We can be in any situation and command that we see this experience through the eye of our Godhead, and it is so, in that moment. We can change the charging of any situation in a moment, if we can learn to get out of our own way, and let our God come through.

To some, this concept of immortality may sound ridiculous and there are those that say I am really stepping out there. Well, I would ask you to consider this. The physical embodiment is the end line product of the summation of our thoughts. Illness does not begin in the body, it ends up as a physical expression of the Consciousness. The principle that thought creates the nature of reality is an absolute.

So it is a scientific fact that the embodiment is a result of our thoughts and our experiences. It is literally shaped and molded by our thoughts of acceptance, and rejection, Joy and depression. The physical expression is dictated by our attitude, and our ability or lack of ability to direct thought. It is a product of intelligence, and intelligence is an unseen factor. It is a force, an energy, an aspect of thought, in the process of experiencing. For without movement, without action, intelligence does not exist.

Our embodiment has a field of energy around it. Remember the liquid light that surrounds you? This field of energy is a field of interpretation, a field of thought. Remember the formula for how we affect the 3-*D reality*...Thought-Feeling-Action? When you change the perception of your reality, you change your experience of yourself, and that process can only be done by Spirit. When you reconnect to your Spiritual reality, and the God Force, the body expresses that emanation, it transmits that reality, and it becomes your truth.

Therefore, the body becomes the living expression of our belief system. It becomes the transmitter of the God Force. When you draw the God Force into everything you do, think and say, you are drawing in the eternalness of that God Force. When you trigger transformation, and affirm that conformation by applied practices of discipline, you shift the paradigm. Therefore, you transform the conditions of your reality. You now live under a new set of laws dictated by your belief patterns. You create the new paradigm.

By drawing in the infusion of the God Force energy into you, you create a body that resonates to that energy, that octave of thought. The embodiment then becomes as eternal as the thought that is creating it, moment by moment in a constant flow of creation. In other words you can have immortality here.......now....... not in some distant place, some piece of real-estate in a foreign land called Heaven. You can have it here, now, in this moment, if you command it to be the nature of your experience.

Our ideas, our thoughts, are the architects of our experienced reality. You are the dreamer who directs and allows or disallows those thoughts to be or not to be. You are the Master having the Dream. This is why it is so important to live our lives with passion, to have dreams, and the reason need only to be for Joy. For in the energy of Joy, is the secret chemical formula that opens the doorway to eternity for the physical embodiment. Joy, is the key to the Life Force. It is an orgon experience that always leaves us in a state of blissful ecstasy.

We are here experiencing this plane of reality to discover the True nature of who and what we are. We are here to learn to assist and have compassion for each other, and to discover the God within us all. This is realized by our remembering who we are beyond identity, beyond the character we play in this movie. We need to constantly affirm that Divineness within us through our unique actions, and talents. When we do this we naturally step out of the time space continuum.

Try it. Do the exercise in experiment one and direct your intention to thoughts of Joy, things that make you happy. Put your intention on your assets and not you deficits. Feel it move. Put your attention, your Awareness there and direct that energy into the whole of your embodiment. Do it twice a day for seven consecutive days. Think from abundance not from lack, dream you have it, dream the emotion of it......then stand back out of your own way and watch life affirm your decrees. The Divine will follow.

Dare to do something you truly enjoy, get into it one hundred and fifty percent, get into the Zen of it, and see if you can keep track of time. You can't, it is impossible. You will disconnect, you lose track of time, you are not connected to time, you are free of the paradigm. You are in Joy, and Joy is immortal. Joy and Sorrow can not live in the same house (your body) and all the while you are in the state of Joy you become immortal.

Impossible, says the part of you that is still caught in the Image, the illusion of being what you have been told you are. Illusion, because most people have never made the space to have the opportunity to find out what and who they were. They are again living someone else's ideal......not their own. How do you know that you are here only to die? Is that the purpose of life? Well some of us, like myself, and my friend Dannion Brinkley, can tell you from experience that death does not exist..... at least not in the perception that was handed down to us by neoteric religions. Death is a state of mind, Death is part of the *IT,* and the *IT* does not exist. Only the thought of death exists as an experiential reality. Even in its deepest sense, Death is the thing that is temporal, life is eternally yours to enjoy. For when you find yourself on the other side you are still there in all your glorious radiance.

If you constantly walk around thinking that you are running out of time, then that will become your reality. If you think I am this, so shall you be. However, if you know that you are part of forever, if you own that as your own thought, then the dominating thought that you hold will create that as the pattern of your experienced reality. There is an internal part of you that is not subject to temporal existence. It is the silent witness that has been there for each of your life experiences, observing from behind the scenes. It is your Spirit. You are that Spirit Being, and that reality is much more stable than this projection into the hologram of third dimensional experience.

Your Spirit is as real as anything here. It is as real as gravity, and has more substance than time. Your Spirit is unlimited and as incomprehensible as the God Force Itself, for they are one and the same. Spirit is mysterious and without form, it is eternal, without beginnings and without end. It is more powerful than time or space and can exist in multidimensional realities simultaneously.

When you can, get in touch with that part of yourself that exists in an eternal moment of forever. You are the foreverness that creates each moment, so that you can be aware of your existence. You are an essence of eternity, expressing through an embodiment that you yourself designed as the architect of your reality, with every moment that you experience. Your embodiment is constantly being affected by your thoughts, your words, your attitudes, your emotions, and your deeds.

We are experiencing our mortality as a quantified expression of our immortality. We keep changing, and recreating ourselves along the pathway so that we can constantly remind ourselves of our immortality. Every time one of our dreams fails, we are forced as it were to return to our immortal Self to recreate reality. We are forced to go home and return to Source for a recharge of our eternal Self. When you see this in yourself and view it against the back drop of who the character is, and what the scenery is, when you are in contact with who you really are, the anxiety that causes friction in your daily life ceases to exist.

You will cease to be influenced by the trivial things of daily existence. And you will cease to worry about where the next moment is coming from. Remember the lilies of the field? You leave your troubles of the mundane existence behind. You see the fruitless pursuit in having enemies, being angry and in falling into judgment. So existence, living in interaction with other human beings is a condition of the Universal Reality. The art of living with other human beings, is in living your life with compassion. Develop compassion for yourself and for those around you.

Life, when you are in contact with Self, when you are in contact with the God

Force, becomes much more joyful, and you understand the present moment is exactly as it should be. And that the conditions of those around you are Self created and they do not necessarily effect your pathway, unless you elect to allow them to do so. All that exists around you is a culmination of all other moments of experience, and where you are in this moment is the center point of your eternity.

You begin to pay attention to every moment, and what is occurring in that moment. Your life is full, and your perception becomes unlimited, because you are in your knowing, and free of judgment. Knowing that you are eternal removes the FEAR of dying, FEAR of your ending. You realize that every moment is the experience of the God Force, and that the God Force is in everything, and the Force behind every experience. By embracing that factual understanding of the nature of reality, it becomes the place of your Awareness, because that is where your attention is. Then all of your intentions are born from that place of existence. You are creating from abundance rather than creating from lack. You are using the Life Force Itself to empower your thoughts, and what you think then becomes the *Will* of the God Force.

You have only to consciously embrace the God Force in your Awareness and that becomes the motivating force behind your Consciousness. You then have a true picture of reality, and the knowingness that all reality is eternal and forever. If you desire to embrace forever, then you must create reality from a place of foreverness.

However, the Monkey Mind says we are physical Beings, and everything physical breaks down, degenerates and exists for a temporal amount of time. This is good in concept but it is impractical in applied physics. "O.K. Monkey Mind consider this. If we look at the body or anything physical for that matter, we will find that at the quantum level, it is non-physical. This is scientific fact, and not metaphorical hypothesizing."

Matter is composed of atoms and subatomic particles that scurry around at speeds faster than light around empty space. The physical embodiment gives off constant fluctuations of light, energy and frequencies. These atoms are transferring information constantly in what appears to be little explosions of pulsing light, transmitting and receiving from some point in a huge void of potentiality.

Now, when we apply this to our physical bodies, we easily see that our embodiments are essentially made up of the same stuff as intergalactic space. We are light particums surrounding proportions of the great void. We are essentially made up from nothing. And what is even more perplexing is, that nothing seems to be the Source of intelligent information and eternal energy.

Now looking at ourselves from a quantum understanding of physics, we are essentially little more than printouts from some ambiguous ever-changing computer that has its origins in nothingness. We are children of the void, composed of thought projections that again originate from an unseen and unidentifiable Source. The conditions of our existence, or the software program that runs the computer and is creating the nature of our form, is mutable and not fixed. If it's possible to get in touch with the program designer of the software, we can expect that we can reproduce the program at any time, provided we are acceptable to the idea that the program operates in a predictable random pattern. This pattern creates frequency pulses which work on recognizable rhythms of calculated mathematical equations, and although they make no sense whatsoever, they are totally possible and in fact do exist......because we are here, and I am your other self in all reality......because all the program can do is replicate itself for infinity.

Simply put, we are God, existing in a process of eternal procreation. We are addicted to procreating ourselves. We are eternal Beings born from our own concept of ourselves. We are thought, we are little more than a Dream.

"BE HERE NOW," has become an icon. Ram Dass' little hippie bible of the 70's seemingly projects a life force of its own. Yet the wisdom in that understanding leads us to foreverness. Every moment is the essence of forever, and like the essential oil that contains the essence of the Lavender flower it contains the eternal nature of all Lavender, it is the memory, the sense, the character, and the intelligence of the whole. We are the essence of the God Force, and respectfully represent the whole of creation that is eternal by our very nature.

Every moment of time contains the flavor of eternity, and one can come to know eternity simply by living in that moment. Most do not see the fragile quality of our reality, and choose not to experience the subtle omnipotent effects in the silence of the moment, being aware of everything that is occurring in that moment of Divine creative expression. They are caught up with the necessity of all the important things they have to do which take their attention away from that moment, when in all reality that moment is all they ever really have.

Most people either live in the past or the future neither of which is reality. For the past is no more and the future is not yet here. So basically they are nowhere. It is also by the very nature of this existence, impossible for the physical body to metabolize any experience of eternity. So the cellular structure creates the temporal existence for lack of proper information.

This kind of existence teaches us only to rob the essence from someone else, because we are always in a state of lack. Therefore, we wind up creating a consciousness of Psycho-Phantia...where we are but phantoms of our True Selves, necromancers lost in the creation of death cult religions, that keep us enslaved in a cycle of mortality. This is enforced by an artificial state of reality that causes us to keep employing a cyclical behavior pattern of Self-destruction. We are constantly trying to break out of the illusion and return to God and our eternal nature.

Our response to the thought of time exists, because we choose it to be so. *Time* does not exist, especially the current perception that has been given to us. Our calendars, our clocks, are in direct opposition to the natural order of the Universe. They are imposed artificial realities that were created during the time of the Roman Empire, strictly for the purposes of manipulating the reality of the masses. All this, for the end means of creating a work force to perpetuate the Empire of the Caesars. It was not the Caesars' concept of being a god that was in error, it was in thinking that they were gods *above* the people, and god above God that eventually brought about their own demise. **For all are God's children.**

Who are you? You are the thinker behind the thought...... the Dreamer having the Dream. You are the one having the experience and not the experience itself. This is a recreational Universe, created for those who desire to share God's passion for beauty and experience. We are meant in the natural order of life, to live in a perpetual state of Joy, ever exploring the potentiality of our Being in a participatory Universe. We are born to a Divine heritage.

Where are you? You are the where your Consciousness comes from, that is where the real you is to be found. You live in an eternal flow of Awareness that exists in a boundless ocean of Consciousness. You are forever, and all that you are composed of is at your command….. if you are in humble harmony with the reality of All That Is. For you are as connected to Source as the thought itself.

How far are we from God?…….. We are but a thought away.

How vast is the abyss that separates us from God?….
 We are but a thought away.

What is that thought?……. It is the thought of God.

When you own this on an experiential level, you spontaneously realize that you have choices, that you have the right and the ability to exercise those choices, and the power of focused thought is instantaneous. The Awareness of your right and capability to choose your life circumstance, through the conscious application of Thought, Emotion, Intent and Desire, literally creates the nature of reality.

Reality is experienced in life, and life, is Consciousness and energy in action. When you own this, when you are aware of your connection to Source, you then become the Master of your own Destiny. The energy of the God Force is inexhaustible and is always there for you to draw upon for your creation……

It is the understanding of this that allows us to be co-creators of reality throughout the universe Be not afraid of being one with Mother Father God, rather be aware of your turning away from the essence of Source…For then you will surley loose your direction and purpose in life.

The Shaman has spoken...Go and be the light to the World.
Blessed BE

Printed in the United States
By Bookmasters